DOUGLASS AND MELVILLE

DOUGLASS AND MELVILLE

Anchored Together In Neighborly Style

[handwritten annotation]

Elizabeth

p 40-41 Melville, when/living in NYC would eat dinner w/his wife at 4 then have a "cozy chat" with her for about 1 hour, then walk to the library for and read for 1 to 2 hrs. Esp English + Am. journals

— Melville lived in New York from ~~1847~~ 1847-50 + wrote Mardi ('48), Redburn + White-Jacket ('49) + began Moby Dick ('50)

Robert K. Wallace

To the Melville Society Cultural Project Team &
Our New Bedford Friends and Affiliates

Front cover photographs:
  Frederick Douglass, albumen print, 1870s. National Archives.
  Herman Melville, carte-de-visite, 1861. Rodney Dewey photograph, Berkshire Athenaeum.
  New Bedford waterfront, 1880s. Spinner Collection.

Frontispiece:
  Frederick Douglass, etching from of My Bondage and My Freedom, *1855.* New Bedford Historical Society.
  Herman Melville, oil on canvas, painted in 1870 by J. O. Eaton. Houghton Library, Harvard University.

Cover design: Jay Avila

© Spinner Publications, Inc.
New Bedford, Massachusetts 02740
Printed in the United States of America

Library of Congress Cataloging-in-Publication Data

Wallace, Robert K.
  Douglass & Melville : anchored together in neighborly style / by Robert K. Wallace.
      p. cm.
  Includes bibliographical references and index.
  ISBN 0-932027-91-1 (pbk.)
  1. Melville, Herman, 1819-1891--Political and social views. 2. Literature and
  society--United States--History--19th century. 3. Douglass, Frederick, 1818-1895--
  Contemporaries. 4. Douglass, Frederick, 1818-1895--Influence. 5. African American
  abolitionists--Biography. 6. Abolitionists--United States--Biography. 7. Race relations
  in literature. 8. Race in literature. I. Title.

PS2388.P6W35 2005
813'.3--dc22   2005012300

Contents

Preface vi

A Douglass and Melville Chronology x

Introduction
Bringing Douglass and Melville Together 3
    Converging and Diverging Lives (1818–1895) 4
    Diverging and Converging Afterlives (1895–2005) 8
    "Anchored together in neighborly style" 11

Part I
Did Douglass and Melville Meet in Person? 12

Chapter One
In the Whaling City 15

Chapter Two
In the Hudson River Valley 23

Chapter Three
Up and Down Broadway 35

Part II
Did Douglass and Melville Know Each Other's Work? 52

Chapter Four
Melville in the *North Star* and *Frederick Douglass' Paper* 55

Chapter Five
Traces of Douglass in Melville's Writing 65
    Typee 66
    Omoo 69
    Mardi 73
    Redburn 78
    White-Jacket 85
    Moby-Dick 94
    Benito Cereno 109

American Epilogue 119
    What Is a Representative American? 124
    How Separate are Black and White America? 125
    What Are the Boundaries of the Color Line? 127
    How Should We Classify Douglass and Melville? 128

Notes 134

Works Cited 140

Aknowledgments 142

Index 144

About the Author 148

PREFACE

I first began to think about bringing Frederick Douglass and Herman Melville together in July 2001. I was a guest professor at an NEH Seminar on "Melville and Multiculturalism" in New Bedford. I greatly enjoyed my interaction with high school teachers from across the nation. I began to think specifically about Douglass and Melville in conversation with Sam Otter, another of the guest professors. Discussing the multicultural insights of these two authors in the city that was so important in the early lives of each made us both begin to think that a conference devoted to their lives and works, located in New Bedford, might be a worthwhile idea. When the Executive Committee of the Melville Society approved my proposal for such a conference later that year, I began to think about Douglass and Melville in a more active way.

The next stage in my own thinking about the two men came in September 2002, when Joan Beaubian of the New Bedford Historical Society organized a panel on "Douglass and Melville: New Bedford and Beyond" as a way of stimulating local interest in the future conference. I prepared a short talk in which I began to plot out for the first time some of the ways in which the two men's lives diverged and converged during their almost identical lifespans. The quality of the other presentations that evening, and the keen interest of the large crowd that had gathered under a large tent outside the Rotch-Jones-Duff house, helped me to feel that the subject of Douglass and Melville could appeal to a wide and diverse audience.

In March 2003 I attended a conference at the University of Rochester about the public life of Frederick Douglass so that I could begin to learn about his life and legacy in a more comprehensive way. Here I was able to try out an expanded version of my New Bedford presentation, as well as to recruit Douglass scholars for the conference to be held in New Bedford in 2005. Among the Douglass scholars I met in Rochester was John Stauffer, whose new book, *The Black Hearts of Men* (2002), had turned up absolutely new information about the presence of *Moby-Dick* in *Frederick Douglass' Paper*. I was assisted in recruiting Douglass scholars by Robert Levine, who with Sam Otter had recently been named program chair for the New Bedford conference.

In September 2003 I attended a conference on Frederick Douglass at Howard University in Washington, D. C. In addition to hearing a number of papers about his private life, I saw an exhibition of Douglass artifacts organized by Donna Wells of the Moorland-Springarn Research Center. I also visited Douglass's house at Cedar Hill for the first time. Seeing the books and art that he had collected in the home in which he lived brought me closer to the man than I had previously been. I was beginning to know Douglass in the way that I had come to know Melville at Arrowhead, his home in Pittsfield, Massachusetts, and in the Melville Memorial Room of the nearby Berkshire Athenaeum.

When my research began to reveal that the two men's parallel lives may have intersected in Albany, New York, in 1845, I arranged to attend a conference on the Underground Railroad in New York's Capitol Region in February 2004. In addition to meeting Albany historians who have assisted with my subsequent research, I was able to do archival work at the New York State Library, assisted by Catherine Reynolds from Arrowhead. There I found new information about Melville's slaveholding ancestors in Albany. I also discovered that Frederick Douglass was a major presence in Thurlow Weed's Albany *Evening Journal* during the years in which Melville was writing *Typee* and *Omoo* in nearby Lansingburgh.

By the time of the trip to Albany, I knew that I wanted to write a book about the two men—but what kind? The ideal, for me, would be a comprehensive examination of the two men's lives from their births in 1818/1819 to their deaths in 1895/1891 in the context of their fluctuating reputations since. Such a book would obviously have been impossible to write by the time of the 2005 conference, yet I wanted to share what I had been learning in a way that would be useful to everyone attending the conference, to teachers and students who will be studying Douglass and Melville for decades to come, and to general readers interested in Douglass and Melville either separately or together.

I therefore designed this book to focus on the two men's lives and works from 1845 to 1855, the one decade in which they were jointly popular in their lifetime. This is also the decade in which they are likely to have meant the most to each other. From the time of Douglass's visit to Albany while Melville was writing *Typee* in 1845 until the publication of Douglass's *My Bondage and My Freedom* a few months before Melville's *Benito Cereno* in 1855, the worlds of these two major American writers and thinkers turned out to be much closer than I had originally imagined. Like the 2005 conference in New Bedford, this book is a sesquicentennial celebration of the men who created *My Bondage and My Freedom* and *Benito Cereno* in 1855.

My work on this book throughout the year 2004 increasingly benefited from my work as a guest curator of the exhibition "Our Bondage / Our Freedom: Frederick Douglass and Herman Melville," scheduled by the New Bedford Whaling Museum for the summer of 2005. As the themes and materials of the exhibition came into focus, I realized that this book could also be a unique supplement to the exhibition itself. Visitors to the exhibition would recognize many of its visual images and paired quotations in these pages. Here they would find the biographical background and literary analysis for interrelations that could only be suggested in brief on the walls of a museum.

Although this book has a special meaning in relation to the 2005 conference and exhibition, its primary goal is to introduce a compelling American story in a way that provides a secure foundation for future research and discussion. In writing it I have kept in mind both the general public in that tent in New Bedford and the diverse community audience at the conference in Albany, as well as the more academic audience for research of this kind. I have structured my scholarly discoveries in response to two questions that people invariably ask me: Did Douglass and Melville meet? Did they know each other's work? The answers to these seemingly simple questions have become increasingly rich and complex in the process of researching and writing this book. My research has turned into a detective story of sorts. Pursuing these primary questions has led to secondary questions of equal interest.

Having taught, researched, and written about Melville for more than thirty years, I have found intense pleasure and inspiration while immersing myself in the life and writings of Frederick Douglass. His brilliance as a thinker and writer, his courage as an orator and editor, and his fearless and cogent way of confronting issue after issue in America's national life without flinching or giving an inch are rare qualities to find united in one person. I am amazed that, during the single decade that is the primary focus of this study, a young man in his mid-twenties to mid-thirties could write two autobiographies and edit two consecutive weekly newspapers while also giving sometimes more than a hundred speeches a year in widely spaced cities in America or Great Britain. The quality of his mind, the forthrightness of his heart, the stamina of his travels, the cogency of his words, and the charm of his person astounded me afresh as I have descended into the minutia of his life during the decade of it that I now know best.

As I came to appreciate the fearless public persona of Douglass, I began to admire him even more than I do Melville. Although

Melville wrote nine amazing volumes of fiction between 1845 and 1855, he was not on the front lines of public conflict as visibly as Douglass was. Yet, slowly, as I began to learn in some depth about Douglass's travels, speeches, and writings, I began to see the ease, depth, and sophistication with which Melville incorporated traces of Douglass, his environs, his language, and his pressing national concerns into one work after another during the entire decade of the two men's joint popularity. The degree to which Melville seamlessly assimilates elements of Douglass and of African American life into his own fiction was itself a remarkable achievement for a young writer who has generally been thought of as writing with a white American consciousness for a white American audience.

I began this book with the intuition that these two men's lives and careers were compatible in significant ways. In the process of researching and writing, that initial intuition has deepened and expanded in multiple directions that I hope will stimulate thought and discussion for some time to come.

A Note on Sources and Findings

Because this book is the first extended comparison of the lives, writings, and legacies of Douglass and Melville, it depends more on primary than on secondary sources. Primary sources directly relating their lives to each other's have been relatively scarce.

Neither author is known to have kept any personal record of his daily activities or thoughts that would provide direct evidence of their precise degree of physical or mental proximity during the periods of interest. In Melville's case this lack has been to some degree compensated by *The Melville Log* (1969), Jay Leyda's day-by-day compilation of documents relating to Melville's life from 1819 through 1891. No comparable resource exists for Douglass's life; however, beginning in December 1847, Douglass did publish intermittent glimpses into selected areas of his personal activities in the editorial correspondence of his

weekly newspaper, the *North Star*, later known as *Frederick Douglass' Paper*.

No surviving, published letter from either man appears to mention the other's name or show an awareness of the other's work. Douglass and his works are absent from the Northwestern-Newberry edition of Melville's *Correspondence* (1993), which provides complete, annotated transcriptions of every known, extant letter (plus entries for every additional letter not currently extant that Melville is known or thought to have written). Sadly, no such edition of Douglass's correspondence yet exists, although the first volume of the *Correspondence* series of his papers (1841–1852) is currently in development. Herman Melville is not among the correspondents currently listed for inclusion in this volume, but without access to the letters themselves there is no way of knowing whether he or his works may be directly or indirectly included.

No book by Douglass or Melville is listed among the contents of the library of the other as currently known. Douglass's writings do not appear in *Melville's Reading* (1988), Merton Sealts's inventory of nearly 600 books known to have been owned or borrowed by Melville. Nor do Melville's writings appear among the two thousand titles in the *Bibliography of the Frederick Douglass Library at Cedar Hill* compiled by William L. Petrie and Douglass E. Stover in 1995. Still, neither compilation provides a full record of the books that either author owned. Many of the books that Douglass acquired in the 1840s and 1850s, when Melville's novels were published, were destroyed by the fire in his Rochester house in 1872 that also consumed his only complete runs of the *North Star* and *Frederick Douglass' Paper*. Sealts estimates that about half of Melville's library was disposed of by his widow Elizabeth in a way that has left those lost contents unknown.

Given these gaps and uncertainties in direct evidence from the documented lives of either figure, the words that they published provide the best current evidence of their mutual awareness. In the case of Douglass, that evidence is relatively sparse but extremely explicit. In 1848 Douglass published an extract on "Tattooing" from Melville's *Typee* in the *North Star*. In 1851, 1854, and 1856, he printed references to Melville's *Moby-Dick* in *Frederick Douglass' Paper*, which also contained references to installments of Melville's "Israel Potter" in 1854 and 1855.

In Melville's fiction, possible references to Douglass are more numerous but less direct. Potential traces of the man and his works are found all the way from *Typee* in 1846 through *Benito Cereno* in 1855. Some of these suggest that Douglass may have had a profound influence on Melville's artistry and social vision; others may instead be the product of two writers who addressed similar subjects in "neighborly style" within a single community of discourse. The examination of seven Melville novels in relation to Douglass's life and writings in Chapter 5 is designed to engage the reader's own intuition and judgment in such matters.

Given the paucity of direct evidence from either author about the degree to which they may have been in personal contact as their professional awareness of each other increased, I began to explore other kinds of primary sources that turned out to be revealing in ways not anticipated. Consulting daily newspapers from Albany to see if Melville was likely to have been aware of the lectures that Douglass gave in June and July 1845, while Melville was writing *Typee* in nearby Lansingburgh, led to the discovery that Douglass, his writings, and his subsequent travels in England were given celebrity status in Thurlow Weed's Albany *Evening Journal* from June 1845 until July 1846, when Weed was bestowing comparable status on Melville himself as author of *Typee*.

The reception of these two young, talented Americans by the culture at large has turned out to be as interesting as whether they met in person. Culturally influential Americans who were concerned with both Douglass and Melville during their young professional lives include figures as diverse as Weed in Albany; Charles Briggs, Isaiah Rynders, and James McCune Smith in New York City; and Edmund Quincy, Elizur Wright, and Richard Henry Dana, Jr., in Boston.

Investigating possible interrelations between Douglass and Melville in New York City from 1847 through 1850 has led to broader insights about life there at a time of intense local—as well as national—conflict. Douglass and Melville were each highly praised and reviewed in some of the same papers for similar reasons; they were each active in the same neighborhoods, and responded to some of the same social issues at the same time; and they were each vilified by some of the same newspapers and some of the same social forces, either for very similar or for very different reasons. Whatever personal involvement, if any, they had in each other's lives, the degree to which they addressed central issues in American life from separate social positions within the same city is itself revealing.

Because some of the peripheral sources consulted in the hope of answering the book's two primary questions became more central in its findings, this book is as much about American discourse on race and identity in the mid-nineteenth-century as it is about Douglass and Melville themselves. Plot-level curiosity about when the two men might have met and the degree to which they were aware of each other's work has resulted in a view of American culture, through two complementary lenses, at a crucial time in the nation's history. Through those lenses can be seen two remarkable young Americans, each fearless in his own way, responding to enduring conditions in our national life.

One of Douglass's favorite turns of phrase, which also has a place in Melville's writing, is "from centre to circumference." That phrase aptly describes the way in which the search for somewhat scarce primary sources has led to a wealth of circumferential findings that point back to primary questions in intriguing ways.

Highland Heights, Kentucky, March 1, 2005.

A Douglass and Melville Chronology

1818   Frederick Augustus Washington Bailey born in Talbot County on the Eastern Shore of Maryland, son of Harriet Bailey, a slave, and unknown white father; raised by grandmother Betsey Bailey on Holme Hill farm owned by master Aaron Anthony

1819   Herman Melvill born in New York City, the son of Allan and Maria (Gansevoort) Melvill

1824   FD taken to live at the Lloyd plantation on the Wye River

1825   Harriet Bailey visits FD, dies
HM enters New York Male High School

1826   FD sent to Baltimore, where he lives with Hugh and Sophia Auld

1827   FD is taught to read by Sophia Auld until lessons stopped by husband Hugh; he returns to Baltimore after the "division" of the Anthony slaves

1828   Allan Melvill borrows against expected inheritance to sustain business ventures

1829   FD works at Auld's shipyard as errand boy, copies the shapes of letters made by carpenters

1830   Allan Melvill moves family to Albany after losing business in New York City

1831   FD surreptitiously studies the Bible and *The Columbian Orator*

1832   Allan Melvill dies; HM removed from Albany Academy to work as clerk in bank; family name changes to Melville

1833   FD returns to his master Thomas Auld on the Eastern Shore; begins to organize and teach reading in a Sunday school for blacks

1834   FD is hired out for the year to Edward Covey, resists being 'broken'

1835   FD is hired out to William Freeland, again teaches slaves to read on Sundays
HM clerks at brother Gansevoort's store and enters Albany Classical Academy

1836   FD makes unsuccessful in attempt to escape slavery; returns to Baltimore to learn the caulking trade

1837   FD joins the East Baltimore Mental Improvement Society debating club
HM revives the Philo Logos Society debating club in Albany; takes a teaching job in Pittsfield, Massachusetts

1838   FD escapes slavery from Baltimore, dressed as a sailor; marries Anna Murray in New York City; establishes home in New Bedford; takes name of Frederick Douglass
Maria Melville moves with children to Lansingburgh to escape creditors in Albany

1839   FD works as a laborer in New Bedford, licensed to preach at Zion Church on Second Street
HM sails from New York to Liverpool on merchant ship *St. Lawrence*

1840   HM teaches in Greenbush, N. Y. without being paid; after a visit to Illinois, arrives in New Bedford in search of work

1841   HM sails for the South Seas on whaleship *Acushnet*
FD speaks before William Lloyd Garrison at Nantucket, hired by Massachusetts Anti-Slavery Society

1842   FD supports fugitive slave George Latimer against Chief Justice Lemuel Shaw (Melville's future father-in-law); moves family to Lynn, Massachusetts
HM deserts the *Acushnet* at Nukuheva Bay; is imprisoned at Tahiti for refusing duty on whaleship *Lucy Ann*

1843   FD lectures throughout western states, is beaten by Indiana mob
HM completes last whaling cruise; sails from Honolulu on U. S. *United States*

1844   FD joins Garrison in condemning Constitution and calling for disunion
HM discharged from *United States* after landing at Boston, returns to Lansingburgh

1845   FD publishes *Narrative of Frederick Douglass*; lectures in Albany and Troy as fugitive slave; sails for England on the *Cambria*
HM writes *Typee* in Lansingburgh, sends manuscript to brother Gansevoort, who sells it to John Murray in London

1846 FD continues successful lecture tour throughout Great Britain, where supporters purchase his freedom
HM publishes *Typee* in London and New York, writes *Omoo*

1847 FD returns from England on the *Cambria*, moves to Rochester as editor of the *North Star*
HM marries Elizabeth Shaw in Boston, they move to New York City with his extended family
FD and HM praised highly by "B" in same issue of *National Anti-Slavery Standard*

1848 FD establishes family in Rochester, publishes "Tattooing" from *Typee* in *The North Star*
HM writes *Mardi* in New York

1849 FD delivers "Slumbering Volcano" speech at Shiloh Presbyterian Church and publishes "Colorphobia in New York!"
HM writes *Redburn* and *White-Jacket* and sails for England

1850 FD confronts Isaiah Rynders at Broadway Tabernacle, is targeted by mob at New York Society Library, is attacked when walking near the Battery with Julia and Elizabeth Griffiths
HM returns from England, begins *Moby-Dick*, moves family to Pittsfield, MA

1851 FD breaks with Garrison over anti-slavery strategy, begins *Frederick Douglass' Paper* with support from Gerrit Smith
HM completes and publishes *Moby-Dick*

1852 FD delivers "What to the Slave is the Fourth of July?" in Rochester
HM publishes *Pierre*; Austin Bearse launches yacht *Moby Dick* in Boston harbor

1853 FD publishes *The Heroic Slave*
HM fails to get consular appointment in Pierce administration, publishes "Bartleby, the Scrivener" in *Putnam's Monthly* magazine

1854 FD addresses "The Claims of the Negro Ethnologically Considered" in Ohio
HM begins serial publication of *Israel Potter* in *Putnam's*; *Frederick Douglass' Paper* prints story "Moby Dick Captured" and praises installment of "Israel Potter"

1855 FD publishes *My Bondage and My Freedom* with introduction by James McCune Smith
HM publishes *Benito Cereno* in three installments in *Putnam's*
November *Putnam's* includes highly appreciative review of *My Bondage and My Freedom*

1856 James McCune Smith cites *Moby-Dick* in discussion of presidential election in *Frederick Douglass' Paper*
Benito Cereno appears in book form in *The Piazza Tales*; HM sails on Mediterranean voyage financed by Chief Justice Shaw

1857 FD publishes speeches on the Dred Scott decision and West Indian Emancipation
HM publishes *The Confidence Man*, returns from Europe, lectures on "The Statues in Rome"

1858 FD begins to publish *Douglass' Monthly* as a supplement to *Frederick Douglass' Paper*
Melville continues lecturing in northeastern and midwestern states

1859 FD begins giving lecture on "Self-Made Men," advises John Brown against Harper's Ferry raid, sails to England to avoid arrest after Brown captured
HM lectures on "The South Seas" and "Traveling" but gets fewer and fewer engagements

1860 FD returns from England, supports Lincoln's nomination by Republican Party, and Gerrit Smith's by Radical Abolition Party
HM sails for San Francisco, returns to New York, where publishers have rejected his first book of poetry

1861 FD welcomes outbreak of Civil War, calling for the arming of slaves and free blacks
HM fails in attempt for consular appointment; father-in-law Lemuel Shaw dies in Boston

1862 FD alternately praises and condemns policies of Abraham Lincoln
HM suffers from rheumatism, is seriously injured in road accident

1863 FD welcomes Emancipation Proclamation, writes "Men of Color to Arms!"; becomes recruiting agent for 54th Massachusetts Infantry regiment, in which sons Charles and Lewis enlist
HM moves family from Pittsfield to 104 East 26th Street in New York City

1864 FD works for Lincoln's reelection and meets with the President
HM visits the camp of the Union army in Vienna, Virginia

1865 FD attends President Lincoln's second inauguration and White House reception
HM is sworn in as Inspector of Customs at the Port of New York

1866 FD attacks Reconstruction policies of President Andrew Johnson and begins career as a lyceum lecturer
HM publishes *Battle-Pieces*, a book of poems in response to the Civil War

1867 FD declines offer from Johnson administration to become commissioner of the Freedman's Bureau
HM finds son Malcolm dead of self-inflicted gunshot

Son suicide →

1868 FD is criticized by Women's Rights advocates for giving higher priority to black suffrage
HM is invited by editor Charles Briggs to contribute to new *Putnam's Magazine*

1869 FD is active in meetings of the National Convention of Colored Citizens and the American Equal Rights Association
HM has a Rembrandt mezzotint framed in New York

1870 FD moves to Washington, D. C., to become editor of the *New National Era*
HM sits for portrait by J. O. Eaton in New York City

1871 FD is appointed by President Ulysses Grant to commission considering the annexation of the Dominican Republic
HM acquires books on poetry, landscape, art, and engraving

1872 FD endorses President Grant's reelection and loses important archival materials when house in Rochester burns
HM's brother Allan dies

1874 FD named president of Freedmen's Savings and Trust Company, which fails; loses personal investment when the *New National Era* ceases publication

1876 FD delivers address at dedication of Freedman's Monument to Lincoln in Washington, D. C.
HM publishes *Clarel: A Poem and Pilgrimage of the Holy Land*

1877 FD appointed U. S. Marshal for District of Columbia by President Rutherford B. Hayes
HM sends brother-in-law his poem "The Age of the Antonines"

1878 FD moves to Cedar Hill estate in Anacostia, District of Columbia

1879 FD criticized for not supporting migration of Exodusters to Kansas from the South
HM's *Typee* published in Swedish in Stockholm

1881 FD appointed Recorder of Deeds for the District of Columbia by President James A. Garfield, publishes *Life and Times of Frederick Douglass*

1882 FD's wife Anna Murray Douglass dies
HM's first grandchild, Eleanor Melville Thomas, is born

1884 FD marries Helen Pitts and is criticized for interracial marriage
Elizabeth Shaw Melville receives legacy from which she gives HM $25 a month to spend on books and prints

1885 HM resigns post as Inspector of Customs in New York

1886 FD resigns office of Recorder of Deeds and leaves on tour of Europe with his wife Helen
HM's son Stanwix dies in San Francisco

1887 FD and Helen travel in Europe and Egypt

1888 FD campaigns for Republican presidential nominee Benjamin Harrison
HM sails to Bermuda, publishes *John Marr and Other Sailors*

1889 FD is appointed Minister and Consul General to Haiti by President Harrison
HM acquires new membership in New York Society Library

1891 FD resigns as Minister to Haiti
HM completes work on *Billy Budd*, publishes *Timoleon*, dies in New York City, and is buried in Woodlawn Cemetery

1892 FD publishes expanded edition of *Life and Times of Frederick Douglass*; writes "Lynch Law in the South" for *North American Review*

1893 FD writes introduction to *The Reason Why the Colored American is Not in the World Columbian Exposition*

1894 FD publishes *The Lesson of the Hour*, a denunciation of lynching; delivers an address in New Bedford, Massachusetts

1895 FD dies at Cedar Hill after addressing the National Council of Women and is buried in Rochester's Mount Hope Cemetery

A whale-ship was my Yale College and my Harvard.
— Herman Melville, Moby-Dick, 1851

The ship-yard was . . . our school-house.
— Frederick Douglass, New National Era, 1871

The slaveholders are sleeping on slumbering
volcanoes, if they did but know it.
— Douglass, "The Slumbering Volcano," 1849

Might not the San Dominick, like a slumbering
volcano, suddenly let loose energies now hid?
— Melville, Benito Cereno, 1855

The fiend-like skill we display in the invention of all
manner of death-dealing engines, the vindictiveness
with which we carry on our wars, and the misery and
desolation that follow in their train, are enough of
themselves to distinguish the white civilized man as
the most ferocious animal on the face of the earth.
— Melville, Typee, 1846

Go where you may, search where you will,
roam through all the monarchies and despotisms of
the old world, travel through South America,
search out every abuse, and when you have found
the last, lay your facts by the side of the every day
practices of this nation, and you will say with me,
that, for revolting barbarity and shameless hypocrisy,
America reigns without a rival.
— Douglass, "What to the Slave is the Fourth of July?" 1852

AT THE WHARF IN NEWPORT.

Frederick Douglass and his bride Anna Murray being invited to ride in a New Bedford-bound stagecoach. From Life and Times of Frederick Douglass, *1881.* New Bedford Historical Society.

Bringing Douglass and Melville Together

Frederick Douglass (1818–1895) and Herman Melville (1819–1891) were exact contemporaries. They were great nineteenth-century Americans of equal magnitude who addressed issues of identity, race, freedom, and nationhood in ways that are increasingly compelling in the early twenty-first century. Yet their lives and legacies still tend to be seen separately rather than together. This study shows the value of seeing their lives and achievements in relation to each other—during their own lifetimes as well as our own.

Humans can come together in both body and mind. Douglass and Melville moved in physical proximity between 1840 and 1850 and in mutual awareness between 1847 and 1855. Following these two young Americans during the middle of the nineteenth century provides a better sense of the nation's shared heritage—and squandered legacy—in the early twenty-first century.

The two men first came into physical proximity in New Bedford, Massachusetts, in December 1840. Douglass, twenty-two years old and still a fugitive from slavery, had been working along the wharves of the city for two years. Melville, twenty-one years old and unemployed, came to find a job on a whaleship. From January 3, 1841, when Melville sailed from New Bedford for the South Seas, the two men's lives diverged and converged in significant ways for fifteen years. During the last four decades of each man's life, Melville dropped increasingly into cultural obscurity as Douglass remained a prominent national figure.

The posthumous reputations of Douglass and Melville followed different trajectories during the twentieth century. Melville was the first to emerge from cultural obscurity in the 1920s, but, even after Douglass followed him in the second half of the century, the two men's professional resurrections have tended to be celebrated by separate congregations. During the 1990s Douglass and Melville began to appear together in important critical studies. By 2005 they had become the joint subjects of an international conference.

A quick overview of the two men's lives and afterlives in this introduction will set the stage for a more detailed exploration of their physical proximity and mutual awareness between 1840 and 1855.

Converging and Diverging Lives (1818–1895)

The young men whose lives converged in New Bedford in 1840 came from worlds apart. Frederick Douglass was a fugitive from slavery in Maryland. He had barely known his mother, Harriet Bailey, he never knew which white man had fathered him, and he never knew the year or day on which he was born. Enslaved to a series of masters who intended to subdue his body and mind to perpetual servitude, he taught himself to read, think, and act in self-defense and self-assertion. On an August day in 1834, inspired by the white sails of ships gliding by on Chesapeake Bay, he defended himself by fighting back against Edward Covey, the farmer to whom he was hired out, in "the turning-point in my career as a slave."

On September 3, 1838, Douglass committed the ultimate act of self-actualization by escaping to the North. After traveling to New York by train and boat, and by boat to Rhode Island, he rode a stage into New Bedford. He was accompanied by his wife, Anna Murray, whom he had married in New York according to the plan they had devised in Baltimore. Nathan and Polly Johnson invited the newlyweds into their New Bedford home, where Frederick Bailey took on the name Douglass at Nathan Johnson's suggestion.

Whereas young Douglass came to New Bedford to escape a life of enslavement, young Melville was seeking freedom from economic impoverishment and societal expectations. Herman Melvill (the "e" was added later) was born into a prosperous family in New York City on August 1, 1819. His father, Allan Melvill, was the son of Major Thomas Melvill of Boston, a Revolutionary War hero known for his exploits in the Tea Party of 1773. His mother, Maria Gansevoort, was the daughter of General Peter Gansevoort of Albany, known as a hero for his defense of Fort Stanwix in 1777.

Melville's prosperous childhood ended with his father's bankruptcy in 1830 and death in 1832. Pulled out of school to help support the family at the age of twelve, he eventually became a sailor because he had no financial prospects. In 1839 he sailed from New York to Liverpool and back on a merchant ship. By December 1840 he had decided to sail from New Bedford as a whaleman. That decision was ultimately as liberating as the one that Douglass made to flee *to* that city, but Melville could hardly have seen it as such at the time.

For each young man New Bedford offered a window into the future as well as an escape from the past. Each saw a vision of economic opportunity and human community such as he had never known. Douglass had worked as a caulker in Baltimore, but there he was enslaved to Hugh Auld, who received his wages. In New Bedford he was paid for his labor. He lived among free blacks and fugitive slaves in an anti-slavery city in which William Lloyd Garrison's *Liberator* "took its place with me next to the bible."

On the whaleship Melville not only got a personal reprieve from the economic despair that had gripped his family since the death of his father in 1832, he shipped out with a multicultural and multinational crew whose human diversity had much to do with his declaration in *Moby-Dick* that "a whale-ship was my Yale College and my Harvard." Douglass was similarly indebted to the ship-yards of Baltimore in which he had learned the caulking trade. "The ship-yard . . . was our school-house," he wrote in 1871, after returning to the wharves of his youth.

Douglass lived in New Bedford for four years, from 1838 to 1842, whereas Melville was there for less than two weeks in 1840 and 1841. Yet the city was to remain a touchstone for each man in later life. In July 1851 Douglass reverted to memories of New Bedford when his Rochester newspaper was under savage attack by his former Garrisonian friends. He reassured his readers that "he who . . . has caulked ships in the shipyards of Baltimore . . . [and] who has rolled oil casks, stowed ships, sawed wood, swept chimneys, and labored at the bellows in New Bedford for a living, until he has hands like horns, has . . . no dread of returning to manual labor" should his newspaper career be destroyed.

Melville in 1851 was recalling the New Bedford waterfront in the manuscript of *Moby-Dick*, published in October of that year. From Ishmael's arrival in New Bedford in Chapter 2 ("The Carpet-Bag") until his departure in Chapter 13 ("Wheelbarrow"), Melville brilliantly recreates the city he had visited ten years earlier.

In 1851 each young man was already a figure of national importance. Douglass,

who had been "discovered" by William Lloyd Garrison on Nantucket in 1841, became a national figure with the publication of the *Narrative of Frederick Douglass* in May 1845. After two dangerous months in which he lectured in New York and Massachusetts as a self-identified fugitive slave who had named his master in the South, he sailed to Great Britain in August for an extremely successful lecture tour from which he returned in 1847. By the end of that year, he had moved from Lynn, Massachusetts, to Rochester, New York, where he began his *North Star* newspaper in December.

From 1847 until 1851, when he changed the name of his newspaper to *Frederick Douglass' Paper*, Douglass was an ardent and articulate abolitionist as an orator, author, and editor. Some of his most visible and volatile lectures during this period were at the annual

New Bedford dock workers maneuver casks of whale oil on the waterfront, circa 1910. Spinner Collection.

meetings of the American Anti-Slavery Society at the Broadway Tabernacle in New York City in May 1847, 1848, 1849, and 1850. He gave each of these talks in close physical and intellectual proximity to Herman Melville.

Melville deserted the whaleship *Acushnet* in Nukuheva Bay in July 1842. After landing in Boston as a sailor on the U. S. frigate *United States* in October 1844, he rejoined his mother and siblings in Lansingburgh, New York. There he was already writing his first novel, *Typee,* when the celebrated fugitive author Frederick Douglass was lecturing in nearby Albany and Troy in June and July 1845. Melville himself became a literary celebrity upon the publication of *Typee* in 1846. This book was followed by *Omoo* in 1847, *Mardi* and *Redburn* in 1849, *White-Jacket* in 1850, and *Moby-Dick* in 1851.

Melville had moved from Lansingburgh to New York City in September 1847 after marrying Elizabeth Shaw of Boston. He was therefore writing *Mardi, Redburn, White-Jacket*, and *Moby-Dick* in New York during Douglass's increasingly volatile visits there in May 1848, 1849, and 1850. A major surprise in writing this book has been to discover the degree to which Melville and Douglass were aware of each other during this crucial period in their young professional lives. Douglass's highly contested presence in New York City in May 1850 was to leave traces in both *Moby-Dick* and *Benito Cereno.*

Douglass was thirty-three years old in 1851 when he broke with Garrison, changed the name of the *North Star* to *Frederick Douglass' Paper,* and told his readers he would gladly go back to the wharves of New Bedford if his enemies managed to destroy his paper. He remained extremely productive and effective during the next five years. In addition to editing his newspaper, he delivered his lecture "What to the Slave is the Fourth of

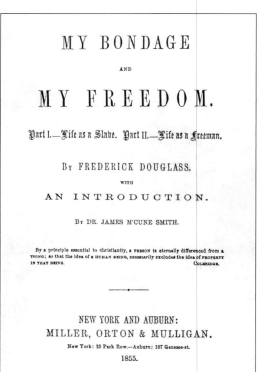

Title page, first edition. New Bedford Historical Society.

July?" in 1852, published the *The Heroic Slave* in 1853, delivered "The Claims of the Negro Ethnologically Considered" in 1854, and published *My Bondage and My Freedom,* his second autobiography, in 1855.

In *My Bondage and My Freedom* Douglass thoroughly revised the 1845 *Narrative* while also depicting his subsequent ten years in the North. The new autobiography sold more than four thousand copies in its first year, received favorable reviews, and increased Douglass's stature as a leading abolitionist and a representative American. The image of Douglass reproduced as the frontispiece of the book enhanced his status as a commanding public figure.

Melville's productivity remained strong after *Moby-Dick,* but his reputation and visibility fell into sudden decline. The great whaling novel received at least mixed reviews, but *Pierre,* published in 1852, was an out-and-out failure, both critically and financially.

"Benito Cereno" in Putnam's Monthly *magazine, October 1855.*

With a growing family to feed, Melville began writing stories for magazines, which paid by the page. This generated a steadier, but much smaller income, than he had once hoped to produce with his novels.

The stories that Melville published in *Harper's* and *Putnam's* between 1853 and 1856 include such now-classic texts as "Bartleby, the Scrivener," "The Tartarus of Maids," and the serialization of *Benito Cereno*. However, some of his readers would not have known he was the author because his contributions to both magazines were published anonymously. Nor would most readers of *Putnam's* have known Melville visually. In May 1854 he refused to submit an image of himself to be engraved for the magazine's "series of portraits." In 1851 he had refused a similar request from *Holden's Magazine*, declaring, "I respectfully decline being *oblivionated* by a Daguerretype (what a devel of an unspellable word!)."

Although the public profiles of Douglass and Melville were diverging sharply in 1855, the insights they were offering to their readers were surprisingly similar. *My Bondage and My Freedom* and *Benito Cereno* express each artist's most cogent critique of racism in the North and enslavement in the South. Douglass offers his critique in his own authorial voice—factually precise, imaginatively generous, intellectually fearless, and rhetorically bold. In addition to expanding and deepening the earlier account of his "bondage" in the South, Douglass now provides an ironic and sometimes shocking account of his "freedom" in the North. He reveals the extent to which some of the abolitionists who had seemingly encouraged him were in fact attempting to suppress his thought and speech. Only after being treated with true equality in Great Britain does he now feel the full force of the racism that pervaded Massachusetts, where he was routinely told, "*We don't allow niggers in here!*"

Whereas the bondage and the freedom in Douglass's text are relatively explicit and overt, Melville offers his critique through crafty impersonation and ironic indirection. He adapts the story line and the authorial voice of an episode in Captain Amasa Delano's 1817 *Narrative of Voyages and Travels* to reveal unconscious racism and moral obtuseness from the inside out. An imaginative and empathetic reader must read against the grain of the story to see Babo, the African slave, as its hero. Babo has led a successful mutiny that he hides from the oblivious Delano by wearing the mask of the humble servant. Through that mask he choreographs the charade by which the ship and its living cargo appear to be under the control of Benito Cereno, the Spanish captain, who himself endures a physical and spiritual torture to which Delano remains oblivious. In Melville's text the deeper realities of bondage and freedom remain implicit and covert until the dramatic moment in which the mask is ripped off, a moment in which "past, present, and future seemed one."

Douglass, after the success of *My Bondage and My Freedom*, continued as a leading abolitionist editor and orator in advance of the Civil War. During the war, he advised President Lincoln on the Emacipation Proclamation and recruited black troops for the 54th Massachusetts Regiment. From the end of the war until his death thirty years later, he remained in the public eye as editor, orator, and author and was appointed by Presidents Grant, Hayes, Garfield, and Harrison to a succession of federal positions. Douglass moved from Rochester to Washington in 1870 and established his home at Cedar Hill in 1878. His death there in 1895 was a national event, as was his subsequent burial at Mount Hope Cemetery in Rochester.

By the time *Benito Cereno* was reprinted as part of his *Piazza Tales* in 1856, Melville had exhausted his audience and himself as a fiction writer. After publishing nine books of fiction in ten years, he took a nine-month voyage to the Mediterranean and the Near East for rest and recuperation. Although he tried for three years to earn a living as a lecturer after his return to the United States, he was essentially unemployed during the early years of the Civil War. In 1863 he moved his family from Pittsfield, Massachusetts, back to New York City, where he was hired as a customs inspector in 1865. After publishing *Battle-Pieces*, a book of Civil War poetry, in 1866, Melville worked in cultural obscurity in the customs house until his retirement in 1885.

During the six years remaining before his death in 1891, Melville enjoyed the private pleasures of writing poetry, composing the unpublished manuscript of "Billy Budd," and building an art collection of more than four hundred prints and engravings. At his death in 1891, one New York newspaper was surprised he had still been alive. The tombstone he chose for his grave in New York's Woodlawn Cemetery features a scroll whose surface is blank.

Diverging and Converging Afterlives (1895–2005)

The afterlife of a writer, when it occurs, is a somewhat miraculous phenomenon. Words on a page that may have been unread for decades while the author was alive suddenly begin to speak to a new generation or even a new century. Later generations find the words of a writer long dead more valuable than did the living writer's own contemporaries. This has certainly been the case with Melville. A revival of interest in his work in the early twentieth century reached a strong crest in mid-century from which it has only continued to rise at the beginning of the twenty-first.

Douglass was more important to his own contemporaries for a much longer time than was Melville. Even so, the renewed interest in his life and work that has intensified during the last quarter-century is giving him an afterlife that is beginning to rival the life he lived. When my students are reading and discussing Douglass and Melville during an entire semes-

Ambrotype of Herman Melville, 1860.
Berkshire Athenaeum.

Ambrotype of Frederick Douglass, 1856.
National Portrait Gallery, Smithsonian Institution.

ter at Northern Kentucky University, these two long-dead men are as alive to their hearts and minds as are many of the people they know in their everyday lives. Their separate value to readers today is more than doubled when they are considered in relation to each other.

After being essentially lost to American culture since the mid-1850s, Melville's works enjoyed their first signs of revival in the 1920s when *Billy Budd* was published posthumously, when the Constable edition of his works was published, when Howard Mumford published a popular biography, and when Rockwell Kent drew the illustrations that were published in his celebrated edition of *Moby-Dick* in 1930. By the 1940s F. O. Matthiessen had positioned Melville at the heart of the *American Renaissance* a century earlier, the ambitious Hendricks House edition of Melville's works was under way, and Jackson Pollock was painting such Melville-inspired works as *Pasiphaë* and *(Blue (Moby-Dick))*.

By the time I reached graduate school at Columbia University in 1966, Melville had

become one of *Eight American Authors* in the leading reference book in the field (none of the eight were female or African-American). Unfortunately, Frederick Douglass made no appearance in my graduate studies in American Literature at Columbia University from 1966 to 1972.

Douglass's popularity as an author had begun to decline immediately before his death, as shown by the extremely small sales of the expanded edition of his *Life and Times of Frederick Douglass* published in 1892. As the Melville revival was building up steam in the first half of the twentieth century, Douglass's life and writing were slipping into relative obscurity (at least within those academic circles whose pronouncements are often taken as a guide to a writer's worth to the larger culture).

A key development in the rehabilitation of Douglass's academic reputation was the publication of four volumes of Philip S. Foner's *The Life and Writings of Frederick Douglass* between 1950 and 1955. In 1968 *My Bondage*

1966 College

and *My Freedom* returned to print after being out of circulation for nearly a century. Then, with the publication of the first volume of *The Frederick Douglass Papers* edited by John W. Blassingame (*Speeches, Debates, Interviews, 1841–46*) in 1979, Douglass finally began to be treated as an essential American figure by the academy.

Starting in the mid-1960s, Douglass and Melville have each become increasingly important to America's cultural legacy and national future. As the Civil Rights and Black Power movements moved from public life through the universities and into the schools, Douglass again become a necessary figure in our understanding of African American life, writing, and history. His speeches, essays, and autobiographies are regaining the kind of wide circulation they enjoyed in his lifetime.

Melville's canonical status continued to expand during the same four decades. Not only *Moby-Dick* but many of his novels, short stories, and poems are now appreciated for their multicultural and postcolonial insights. Melville is valued for addressing many of the same contemporary issues that have brought new attention to the writings of Douglass. The evolution in our culture's understanding of each of these authors can be seen in the growing appreciation being shown for both *Benito Cereno* and *My Bondage and My Freedom*.

Benito Cereno received very little commentary in Melville's lifetime. Its complex ironies were relatively slow to be appreciated during the Melville revival in the twentieth century. Not until the 1980s did Carolyn Karcher (1980) and Sterling Stuckey (1982) begin to elevate *Benito Cereno* to a major place among Melville's writings. William L. Andrews was the first Douglass scholar to make a similar case for *My Bondage and My Freedom*, arguing in 1987 that this autobiography was fully equal to the *Narrative of Frederick Douglass*.

In 1993 Eric J. Sundquist became the first scholar to place both *My Bondage and My Freedom* and *Benito Cereno* at the very center of an understanding of nineteenth-century American literature and culture. In *To Wake the Nations: Race in the Making of American Literature*, he argued that these two 1855 books are pivotal in our understanding of race relations in the North as well as the South (and in the late twentieth century as well as the mid-nineteenth).

Although Douglass and Melville have now regained much of the national importance they each had during the one decade of joint popularity in their lifetimes, their comparable achievements still tend to be seen separately rather than together. Melville is often treated as a "white" American figure and Douglass as a "black" African American figure—even though the life and writings of each man take us beyond the color line in ways the culture needs to appreciate and understand. Academic disciplines tend to confine Melville to the literary curriculum, whereas Douglass can be found in history and political science as well as literature. Yet the works of both men cross disciplinary boundaries with a holistic vision now needed in American life more than ever.

The words that Douglass and Melville wrote and spoke still provide powerful insight into the issues of race, slavery, and freedom in the nineteenth century. Sundquist rightly declared, without having space to elaborate, that "Melville, along with Douglass, is probably the foremost analyst of American slavery in the nineteenth century—and not simply from a 'white' perspective." The primary goal of this book is to see what the words of these two men have to say to each other and to society—in their own time as well as the present. To know them both is to know oneself—past, present, and future.

"Anchored together in neighborly style"

The November 1855 installment of *Benito Cereno* in *Putnam's Monthly* magazine ends with the "two vessels" of the story "anchored together . . . in neighborly style." Melville's phrasing suggests both proximity and a degree of separation. The relative disposition of his two vessels resembles the relation between Douglass and Melville to be revealed in this book.

Active, seaworthy vessels tend to be "anchored together" only occasionally and temporarily. Douglass's and Melville's young, buoyant lives brought them into proximity in New Bedford in 1840, in Albany in 1845, and in New York City in 1847, 1848, 1849, and 1850. Although their two lives were closer in these times and places than one might have previously thought, they were also separate enough that no evidence of their having met on any of these occasions has as yet surfaced.

A "neighborly style" between two vessels suggests proximity with a difference. Neighbors are physically close to each other but occupy their own spaces. Neighborly styles are compatible but not identical. So it is with Douglass's and Melville's styles during the period examined here. These gifted young men expressed their shared American experience in compatible verbal styles from neighboring social spaces. They did so in conscious awareness of each other as the one wrote fiction and the other gave speeches, wrote essays, and edited newspapers.

Douglass was a committed abolitionist orator and editor who addressed pressing national concerns week after week in no uncertain terms. Melville was a writer of fiction who addressed similar concerns year after year in novels that were often sympathetic to abolition but seldom explicitly so. Together, their lives and writings express a search for a national consensus about the necessity of human equality.

Part I of this book examines the proximity of Douglass and Melville in New Bedford, Albany, and New York City in the 1840s. Part II explores the "neighborly style" in which the writings of both men addressed similar subjects between 1845 and 1855, sometimes in conscious awareness of each other, sometimes with coincidentally powerful mutual force. The Epilogue looks beyond the lives of Douglass and Melville in the nineteenth century to consider their mutual importance for American life today.

Wall mural in downtown New Bedford celebrates the city's labor history. Painted by Dan Devenny and commissioned by the Labor Education Center at UMass Dartmouth in 2001, the full mural measures about 45 feet in length. Spinner Collection.

Part I

Did Douglass and Melville
Meet in Person?

*Winter on Seventh Street in New Bedford, circa 1880, showing the
Nathan and Polly Johnson house (far right) in which Frederick and Anna Douglass
first found refuge in 1838.* Kingman Family Collection.

*T*he writing of this book began with no expectation that Douglass and Melville had ever met in person or been particularly conscious of each other's work. However, it soon became clear that their individual lives did converge in time and space as well as heart and mind.

In Part I Douglass and Melville move through three American cities in which they might have met. Although current evidence does not document any actual meeting in New Bedford in 1840, Albany in 1845, or New York in the later 1840s, the possibilities for such a meeting increased as the two men's mutual awareness—and cultural importance—grew.

Part II follows the two men's hearts and minds through their spoken and written words. Successive chapters examine the presence of Melville in Douglass's publications, and traces of Douglass in those of Melville, during a period in which each writer was addressing American issues of race and identity in different genres.

The motions through space and time in Part I are not entirely separable from those of heart and mind in Part II. Such motions were related in Douglass's and Melville's lives, as they are in any life, so the story will unfold in a way that does justice to the interrelatedness of its two-part structure.

Because this study explores a multiplicity of connections of varying degrees of certainty, Melville's discourse on "Fast-Fish and Loose-Fish" in *Moby-Dick* offers a helpful point of reference. A "loose fish" in the whaling industry is a whale that is swimming free. A whale is "technically fast…when it is connected with an occupied ship or boat, by any medium at all controllable by the occupant or occupants." As for the kind of medium, "a mast, an oar, a nine-inch cable, a telegraph wire, or a strand of cobweb, it is all the same."

The medium for connections between Douglass and Melville is consciousness. It begins with whatever consciousness either man had of the other, extends to that of contemporaries who were conscious of them both, embraces each man's conscious response to the challenges of American life, and culminates in a contemporary consciousness of their joint value to society today. Connections in each of these categories range from Melville's "strand of cobweb" back to the mast.

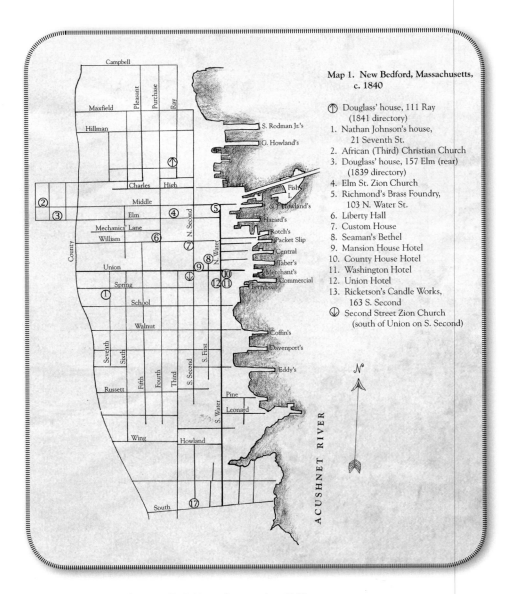

Map 1. New Bedford, Massachusetts, c. 1840

- Douglass' house, 111 Ray (1841 directory)
1. Nathan Johnson's house, 21 Seventh St.
2. African (Third) Christian Church
3. Douglass' house, 157 Elm (rear) (1839 directory)
4. Elm St. Zion Church
5. Richmond's Brass Foundry, 103 N. Water St.
6. Liberty Hall
7. Custom House
8. Seaman's Bethel
9. Mansion House Hotel
10. County House Hotel
11. Washington Hotel
12. Union Hotel
13. Ricketson's Candle Works, 163 S. Second
- Second Street Zion Church (south of Union on S. Second)

Map of New Bedford, Massachusetts, circa 1840. Drawing by Kathleen Piercefield.

CHAPTER ONE

IN THE WHALING CITY
New Bedford, December 1840 – January 1841

*H*erman Melville had arrived in New Bedford by Christmas Day, 1840. That was the day he signed up for a voyage on the whaleship *Acushnet*, berthed at Old South Wharf across the river in Fairhaven. On December 26 he signed his Seaman's Protection Paper at the Custom House in New Bedford, and four days later his name appeared on the *Acushnet's* multi-ethnic crew list along with twenty-four shipmates. He is one of eleven whose complexion is listed as "dark"; two are "black," one "mulatto," and eleven "light." On January 3 Melville sailed out of New Bedford Harbor and into the Atlantic Ocean.

During the nine days and nights between the signing and the sailing, Melville had plenty of time to explore the city that Ishmael was to depict in *Moby-Dick*. This was the same city in which Frederick Douglass had been living and working since his arrival on September 17, 1838. At first Douglass and his wife Anna lived with Nathan and Polly Johnson at 21 Seventh Street. By the time their daughter Rosetta was born in June 1839, they were living at the rear of 157 Elm Street, west of County Street. In the City Directory for 1841, they are listed at 111 Ray Street.

Much of Douglass's work during these years was along the wharves that lined the Acushnet River. In *My Bondage and My Freedom*, he recalled that he "rolled oil casks on the wharves—helped to load and unload vessels—worked in Ricketson's candleworks—in Richmond's brass foundry, and elsewhere." During 1839, at George Howland's Wharf at the upper end of North Water Street, Douglass helped prepare two whaling vessels, the *Java* and *Golconda*, for voyages. At Richmond's brass foundry, also on North Water Street, he worked the bellows. Having "little time for mental improvement," he later recalled, "I often nailed a newspaper to the post near my bellows, and read while I was performing the up and down motion of the heavy beam by which the bellows was inflated and discharged." Ricketson's candleworks was at the other end of the waterfront, on the corner of South and South Second, where Douglass's main job was to move large oil casks from one place to another.

William McFeely, in his 1991 biography of Douglass, speculates that Douglass might have met Melville in the week before Melville sailed.

It is intriguing to imagine the meeting that could so easily have taken place with that other prowler of New Bedford, Herman Melville. The novelist came to know the streets and wharves that he evoked so splendidly in the opening pages of Moby-Dick in the same months that Douglass was walking them. . . .It is pure conjecture, but not implausible, to imagine two of the nineteenth-century's most striking men catching sight of each other one clear day in New Bedford.

This could have happened anywhere along Water Street, from the wharves that Melville would have been exploring as he waited to sail, to the shops that clustered at the intersection with Union.

Soon after Melville's arrival a dramatic event captured the attention of both towns-

View of New Bedford from Mill and Summer streets, looking east, circa 1868. Douglass's Ray Street (now Acushnet Avenue) residence in 1841 was near lower Mill Street, just beyond the left edge of this view. The Old South Wharf that Melville sailed from in January 1841 is directly across the harbor in Fairhaven. Spinner Collection.

people and visitors. On December 26 the whaleship *Charles* arrived in the harbor from a three-year voyage to the South Seas but could not dock, because of heavy cargo, at Rodman's Wharf, immediately north of George Howland's Wharf. Her owner, Samuel Rodman, recorded in his diary that "she lacked one large whale of being full," and therefore had to be lightened of her oil before she could ride high enough to reach the wharf. The ship's navigational problems were further complicated by ice on the river and work on a nearby bridge. On December 28 Rodman was still "occupied in clearing the dock of ice and the wharf of snow to admit the *Charles* when lightened so she could pass . . . the obstruction made to navigation by the bridge company."

Was Douglass among the local laborers employed to lighten the ship of oil by moving loaded casks out of the hold and conveying them to shore? Did he help in clearing the dock and the wharf of ice and snow? Or was he among the watergazers who from time to time would have been monitoring this nautical drama from the shore—as one can easily imagine Melville doing?

Whether Douglass and Melville saw each other along the streets and wharves of New Bedford in the closing days of 1840, they were to recall those environs in similar ways ten years later. To Douglass's 1851 Rochester recollection of having "rolled oil casks, stowed ships, sawed wood, swept chimneys, and labored at the bellows in New Bedford," compare Ishmael's view of the city as he and Queequeg sail for Nantucket in the "Wheelbarrow" chapter of *Moby-Dick*: "Huge hills and mountains of casks on casks were piled upon her wharves, and side by side the world-wandering whale ships lay silent and safely moored at last; while from others came a sound of carpenters and coopers, with blended noises of fires and forges to melt the pitch, all betokening that new cruises were on the start." Ishmael's "mountains of casks" compare with those that Douglass rolled. His "moored ships" compare with those

that Douglass stowed, and his "fires and forges" compare with Douglass's labor at the bellows. Ishmael's phrase about "the world-wandering whale ships . . . safely moored at last" probably refers to the three-day drama of getting the *Charles* to the wharf. Melville evokes the wharves on which Douglass worked whether or not he saw him working there.

That Douglass and Melville might also have glimpsed each other indoors and at night can be imagined given the scene in which Ishmael arrives in New Bedford and has nowhere to stay. After passing two inns he cannot possibly afford, "I now by instinct followed the streets that took me waterward, for there, doubtless, were the cheapest, if not the cheeriest inns." Walking through "blocks of blackness" on a dark December night,

presently I came to a smoky light proceeding from a low, wide building, the door of

Winter wharf scene in New Bedford, 1890s. William R. Hegarty Collection.

which stood invitingly open. . . . Entering, the first thing I did was to stumble over an ash-box in the porch . . . The flying particles almost choked me. . . . However, I picked myself up and hearing a loud voice within, pushed on and opened a second, interior door. It seemed the great Black Parliament sitting in Tophet. A hundred black faces turned round in their rows to peer; and beyond, a black Angel of Doom was beating a book in a pulpit. It was a negro church; and the preacher's text was about the blackness of darkness.

Uncomfortable, Ishmael quickly retreats from the negro church and its "wretched entertainment." Moving on, he sees the sign of the Spouter-Inn, where he takes a room even though he will have to share it with a harpooner who is out on Saturday night trying to "sell his head." His roommate, Queequeg, turns out to be a tattooed "savage" whose face is "dark, purplish, yellow." When he enters the room—and then the bed—Ishmael's multi-racial and multi-cultural education begins. The two spend only one more day and night in New Bedford, but they are already "bosom friends" by the time they sail past the wharves to Nantucket. Ishmael notes that certain "green" white sailors stare at him and Queequeg for simply being companionable. This happens first on the streets of New Bedford and then on the boat to Nantucket, where one such taunting greenhorn is swept overboard and saved only by Queequeg's good grace.

The "negro church" that Ishmael enters is a fictional counterpart to the Zion Methodist church on Second Street, where Douglass was already preaching by the time Melville arrived in the city. Douglass had intended to join the Methodist church on Elm Street but left when its minister served holy communion to white members before allowing colored

With casks of oil piled upon the wharf, bark Josephine sets her sails to dry, circa 1900. William R. Hegarty Collection.

members to come forward. After trying "all other churches in New Bedford with the same result, [I] attached myself to a small body of colored Methodists, known as the Zion Methodists. . . . I was soon made a class-leader and a local preacher." In this capacity, he enjoyed "speaking to my colored friends, in the little school-house on Second street, New Bedford, where we worshipped."

Douglass's "colored Methodists" met in the only negro church that Ishmael could have reached by following "the streets . . . waterward." Second Street runs north and south near the waterfront, and the other negro church in New Bedford at the time, African (Third) Christian, was far from the wharves, on Middle Street west of County. The 1841 City Directory locates Zion Church on South Second but does not provide a number. South Second begins at Union Street in the area of the city that is also the most likely location for a real-life counterpart of the Spouter-Inn. Walking waterward from the more expensive Mansion House at the corner of North Second and Union, a visitor in search of a room would find only three other options, according to the City Directory for 1839: the County House, the Washington Hotel, and the Union Hotel. All were on South Water Street near its intersection with Union.

When Rev. Thomas James became pastor of Zion Methodist in 1840, Frederick Douglass "had already been given authority to act as an exhorter." James soon thereafter "licensed him to preach." In the 1841 City Directory, Douglass is listed not as a laborer but as a preacher: "Douglas, Frederick, Rev. house 111 Ray." If Melville, like Ishmael, actually entered Douglass's church in December 1840, and heard a loud voice from a "black Angel of Doom" who was preaching about "the blackness of darkness," the voice could have been that of Thomas James, Frederick Douglass, or someone else James had licensed. If Douglass was not the preacher in the pulpit, his face may have been among the hundred that turned around to peer at the visitor.

Douglass's fond memories of "speaking to my colored friends, in the little school-house on Second street," persisted long after his 1855

View south on First Street from Union Street, circa 1870, in the old neighborhood where Douglass preached (on South Second Street) and Melville walked in 1840. Kingman Family Collection.

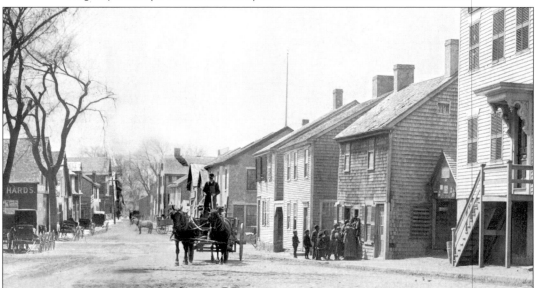

Zion Methodist Church on Elm Street, circa 1890, the parish to which Douglass belonged in 1840 on Second Street. New Bedford Historical Society.

recollection in *My Bondage and My Freedom.* In a letter he wrote to a church historian in 1894, a year before his death, he recalled "the days I spent in little Zion, New Bedford, in the several capacities of sexton, steward, class leader, clerk, and local preacher, as among the happiest days of my life."

The more famous New Bedford church scene in *Moby-Dick* is Ishmael's visit to the Seaman's Bethel to hear Father Mapple's sermon. Biographers have always assumed that Melville made a real-life visit to the Seaman's Bethel, near Union and North Water Street, because of Ishmael's fictional declaration that he did not "fail to make a Sunday visit to the spot." But Ishmael also makes a Saturday night visit to the negro church. Whether or not Melville himself made such a visit, Ishmael's inadvertent visit adds a new dimension to the novel. It brings readers of *Moby-Dick* as close to Douglass's spiritual life as the view of the wharves does to his laboring life.

Unlike Ishmael, who was in New Bedford for only two nights before sailing for Nantucket, Melville was in town for at least

nine nights before the *Acushnet* sailed on January 3. If he did enter Douglass's church and hear him speak, even by accident, he may have been one of the first white men to do so. Reverend James recalled that when he arrived at Zion Church "Douglass had already begun to talk in public, though not before white people." By August 1841 one white person who had heard Douglass speak in "the little school-house on Second street" was William C. Coffin, the man who urged him to address the meeting in Nantucket that launched his career as an anti-slavery orator.

If Melville did see Douglass briefly in the Zion Church in December 1840—either in the pulpit or the congregation—then Douglass would have seen him, too. The key to Melville's fictional scene is its reciprocity. As Ishmael gazes in at the worshippers, they "peer" back at him. What they would have seen is a white man covered with ash from the ash-box he had accidentally stumbled over when entering the outer door on a dark night.

The specificity with which Melville depicts Ishmael's accidental incursion into the negro church suggests that Melville may well have entered Douglass's church, but even then he would not necessarily have known who Douglass was. Still, the thought of these two young men meeting in New Bedford is sufficiently tantalizing that biographers and poets will continue to speculate as to what might have happened if they had.

At the time Melville published *Moby-Dick* in 1851, he *did* know who Douglass was. By that time he might also have acquired considerable information about where Douglass had been working, praying, and preaching during Melville's brief time in the city ten years earlier. We are therefore left with two questions. What, if anything, did Melville know of Douglass? When did he know it—either in 1840 or by 1851?

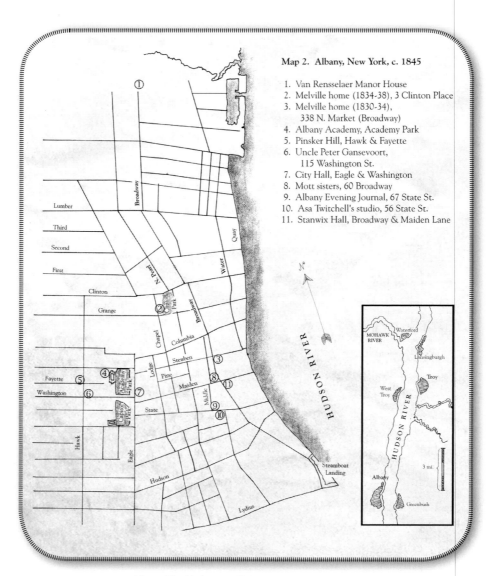

Map 2. Albany, New York, c. 1845

1. Van Rensselaer Manor House
2. Melville home (1834-38), 3 Clinton Place
3. Melville home (1830-34),
   338 N. Market (Broadway)
4. Albany Academy, Academy Park
5. Pinsker Hill, Hawk & Fayette
6. Uncle Peter Gansevoort,
   115 Washington St.
7. City Hall, Eagle & Washington
8. Mott sisters, 60 Broadway
9. Albany Evening Journal, 67 State St.
10. Asa Twitchell's studio, 56 State St.
11. Stanwix Hall, Broadway & Maiden Lane

Albany, New York, circa 1845. Drawn by Kathleen Piercefield.

CHAPTER TWO

IN THE HUDSON RIVER VALLEY
Albany and Troy, June and July 1845

*I*n May 1845, less than four years after he was "discovered" by Garrison on Nantucket, Douglass published his *Narrative of the Life of Frederick Douglass, An American Slave, Written by Himself*. It was an immediate sensation, selling out its first printing of five thousand copies in four months. One reason Douglass wrote the book is that many who heard him speak doubted he was ever a slave, so brilliant was his mind and eloquent his diction. Yet in proving that he was, Douglass put his own life in jeopardy. Revealing his former name as Frederick Bailey, and naming the successive men who had owned him in Tuckahoe, Wye, St. Michaels, and Baltimore, Maryland, suddenly made Douglass much more liable to capture under the Fugitive Slave Law of 1793.

Douglass was now living in Lynn, Massachusetts, where he had moved from New Bedford in 1842. His associates in the Massachusetts Anti-Slavery Society would not easily have let him be recaptured, but even so, Wendell Phillips prefaced the 1845 *Narrative* by declaring that if he were in the author's place, he "should throw the MS. into the fire." As a fugitive slave, Phillips wrote Douglass, "the whole armory of Northern Law has no shield for you." This had been made clear in the fugitive slave case of George Latimer in 1842, decided by Massachusetts Chief Justice Lemuel Shaw, Melville's future father-in-law. Frederick Douglass's first published piece of writing was a letter to the editor of the *Liberator* on November 18, 1842, supporting George Latimer against Judge Shaw's decision.

In spite of the heightened danger Douglass faced as a fugitive, he lectured extensively from late May until mid-August 1845. During the month of July alone he gave 23 lectures in 24 days in 19 cities, beginning in Worcester, Massachusetts, and ending in Rochester, New York. His entire July itinerary was announced each week in the *Liberator* beginning in June. Slave catchers as well as well-wishers would have known exactly where to find him. The lectures on July 12 and 13 were in Albany and Troy, New York, only a few miles from the Lansingburgh home in which Herman Melville was then writing the manuscript of his first novel, *Typee*.

Left: George Latimer, circa 1845. *Lithograph by Benjamin Thayer & Co., National Archives.*

Right: Judge Lemuel Shaw, carte de visite, 1850s. *Berkshire Athenaeum.*

In 1842 Frederick Douglass campaigned passionately for the freedom of George Latimer, a fugitive slave whose habeas corpus petition was denied by Chief Justice Shaw, Melville's future father-in-law.

Melville had returned from his voyage to the South Seas in October 1844. He rejoined his mother and siblings in their Lansingburgh house on the Hudson River adjacent to Troy. He found that family and friends were absolutely enchanted by his stories about "life among the cannibals," depicting his exotic, risky adventures after deserting his whaleship in Nukuheva Bay. When Douglass spoke in Albany and Troy on July 12 and 13, Melville had already written much of *Typee*. By the end of the month he was able to send a substantial manuscript to England with his brother Gansevoort, who had just been appointed Secretary to the American Legation in London. During the fall and winter, as Melville sent him more chapters, Gansevoort was able to negotiate a contract with the John Murray publishing house.

The above chronology raises the possibility that Melville took time from writing *Typee* on July 12 or 13 to hear Douglass lecture in Albany or Troy. He also had an opportunity to hear Douglass speak a month earlier, on June 9, in a public lecture in Albany's City Hall. Two days before the lecture, this notice appeared in the Albany *Evening Atlas*: "A

Discourse on Human Freedom will be delivered at the County Court Room, in the City Hall, on Monday Evening, at 7 ½ o'clock by Frederick Douglass, F. S. of Boston. . . . Seats reserved for the ladies." The initials "F. S." presumably stood for Fugitive Slave.

On the evening of the June 9 lecture, a similar notice in the Albany *Evening Journal* was accompanied by "Life of a Fugitive Slave," an extended, and highly favorable review of Douglass's newly-published *Narrative*. After extracting numerous passages from the book, the Albany reviewer concluded by stressing that "This Frederick Douglass is to speak this evening at the County Court Room, City Hall." An editorial note in the *Evening Journal* on June 10 reported that "Frederick Douglass, the Fugitive Slave whose Book we noticed yesterday, delivered a Lecture here last evening, which is spoken of as very eloquent and effective. He evinces extraordinary mental powers, the development of which, in defiance of all obstacles, is still more extraordinary. Should he speak here again, we hope our citizens will not fail to hear him."

Did Melville hear Douglass lecture on June 9, July 12, or July 13? One imagines that

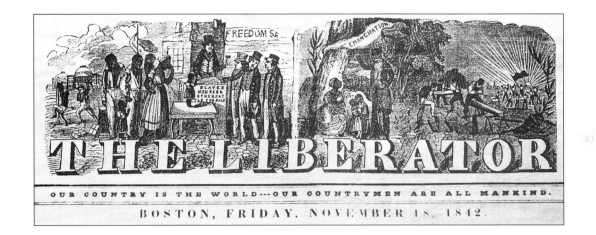

THE LIBERATOR

OUR COUNTRY IS THE WORLD---OUR COUNTRYMEN ARE ALL MANKIND.

BOSTON, FRIDAY, NOVEMBER 18, 1842.

the young American writing about his escape from the "cannibals" of Nukuheva would have been interested in Douglass's account of his escape from his Maryland enslavers. Melville's own interest in human rights and cultural difference would have made him curious about the striking author and orator whom Weed was introducing to readers of the *Evening Journal.* At the least, he would have learned a great deal about Douglass simply by reading the local papers.

The highly favorable coverage in the *Evening Journal* in June continued into the next month with an announcement on July 11 of the next day's lecture: "Frederick Douglass, a Fugitive Slave, who, after obtaining his Liberty, has acquired a good Education and the respect of all who knew him . . . is to speak for the Slaves at the Court Room in the City Hall, tomorrow evening, at 8 o'clock. He is able and eloquent. We hope to see a large audience." The same issue of the *Evening Journal*

Albany City Hall, 1832-1880, from the Albany Chronicles, *1906.* Public Library of Cincinnati and Hamilton County.

printed two announcements of Gansevoort Melville's appointment as Secretary to the Legation in London. Opinion was sharply divided, as Gansevoort had been a polarizing figure as a Democratic orator in support of President Polk and expansion in Texas. The *Evening Journal* supported the appointment even though it was a Whig paper, defending a local boy who had made good.

Weed's embrace of Frederick Douglass was even more dramatic than his defense of Gansevoort Melville. His lead editorial on June 12 cited commentary from the Livingston *Whig* objecting that the *Evening Journal* had "startled the Whig party" by suddenly supporting emancipation in the way an anti-slavery paper might do. Weed answered by arguing that slavery had gone too far in grasping for Texas, seizing more than its pound of flesh. In the same issue Weed continued his advocacy of Douglass by printing a very favorable review of the *Narrative* from Horace Greeley's New York *Tribune*. He also announced that copies of the *Narrative* "are left for sale with Miss [Abigail] Mott" at "No. 60 Broadway." In addition to supporting Douglass in reviews, news stories, and editorials throughout June and July, Weed also ran numerous stories about the horrors of slavery, both domestic and foreign.

All of this activity and information relating to Frederick Douglass in June and July of 1845 occurred in a part of Albany that was loaded with emotion for Herman Melville, beginning when his family arrived from New York in 1830. The monumental Albany City Hall at which Douglass spoke on June 9 and July 12 was across Eagle Street from the Albany Academy at which eleven-year-old Herman had studied. It had been under construction from 1829 to 1832, so Herman would have seen it being built as a schoolboy. On August 4, 1831, three days after his twelfth

Albany Academy, from Albany Chronicles, *1906.*
Public Library of Cincinnati and Hamilton County.

birthday, Herman and his classmates gathered at the new building as part of a ceremonial day in which Herman received the "first best prize in his class . . . for ciphering books."

After the death of their father in January of the next year, Herman and his older brother Gansevoort were withdrawn from the Academy on Eagle Street in order to support their mother's large family. Gansevoort took over their father's fur and cap shop on South Market Street, while Herman became a clerk at the New York State Bank on State Street. Maria Gansevoort Melville and her seven children had suddenly become the poor relatives of her brother Peter Gansevoort—as well as of her Van Rensselaer relatives in the Mansion House at the north end of the city. As Melville was to write in *Redburn*, "Talk not of the bitterness of middle-age and after life; a boy can feel all that, and much more, when upon his soul the mildew has fallen; and the fruit, which to others is only blasted after ripeness, with him is nipped in the first blossom and bud."

The immediate vicinity of City Hall and the Albany Academy had one very specific historical association for Herman Melville as a direct descendent of his mother's slaveholding Gansevoort ancestors in Albany. Maria

Gansevoort and her brother Peter had both grown up with slaves in the family home until the death of their father, General Peter Gansevoort of Revolutionary War fame, in 1812. In 1794 three slaves of other families in Albany, a man named Pomp and two teenage girls, had been hanged on Pinsker Hill for having set fire to the stable of Leonard Gansevoort, Maria's uncle. Because the stable was between State Street and Maiden Lane in the block immediately above Market Street (later Broadway), the resulting "Conflagration of 1793" destroyed much of the center of the city. Pinsker Hill, where the slaves were executed, "was a few rods west of the Academy, or about on the corner of Fayette and Hawk streets."

Bet, one of the girls who was hanged, was a favored slave of the Van Rensselaer family, to which the Gansevoorts were related. The other young girl, Dinah, was enslaved to Volkert Douw. Melville gives the Douw family name to one the three "stable slaves" in *Pierre*, the 1852 novel in which he addresses his Albany family's slaveholding history. Pierre's grandfather General Pierre Glendinning in the novel is modeled on Melville's grandfather General Peter Gansevoort; each man, like Peter's brother Leonard Gansevoort, owned house slaves as well as stable slaves (whose names in the novel are "Crantz, Kit, and Douw"). All of this local history relating to Melville's ancestors made the Court Room of City Hall, near Pinsker Hill on which Pomp, Bet, and Dinah had been hanged by order of the city fathers, a most appropriate place for Frederick Douglass to be "speaking for the Slaves" in June and July 1845.

For the Melville family in 1845, another important landmark in that immediate neighborhood was the fashionable house of Peter Gansevoort, Herman's uncle, at 115 Washington Street, only steps away from Pinsker Hill, City Hall, and Albany Academy. Gansevoort was now the proprietor of Stanwix Hall, down the hill toward the river at the intersection of Maiden Lane and Broadway, a grand entrepreneurial complex built on land held by the family's Gansevoort

Stanwix Hall, from Albany Chronicles, *1906. Public Library of Cincinnati and Hamilton County.*

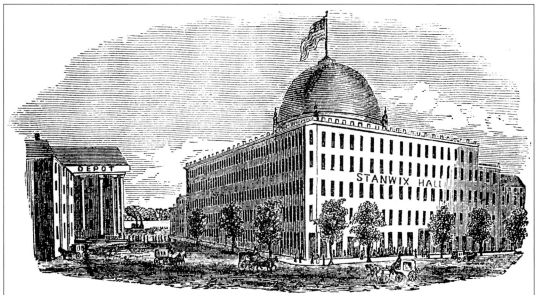

ancestors since 1677. "Built of Quincy granite and surmounted by a large dome," it ranked with City Hall, Albany Academy, and the State House as one of the city's most distinguished buildings in *Wilson's Illustrated Guide to the Hudson River* in 1849.

Diagonally across from Stanwix Hall at the intersection of Broadway and Maiden Lane was 60 Broadway, the address of the "Miss Mott" to whom Weed had referred readers for copies of Frederick Douglass's brand-new *Narrative*. There the abolitionist sisters Lydia and Abigail Mott lived and ran a men's clothing store. Abigail had already published an appreciation of the *Narrative* in the June 6 issue of the *Liberator* in Boston under the initials "A. M."

The office of Thurlow Weed at the Albany *Evening Journal* was in easy walking distance of all of these sites. Its address at 67 State Street was immediately adjacent to the New York State Bank at No. 69, where Herman Melville had worked as a clerk after being withdrawn from the Academy in 1832. Back in 1793 this block of State Street had been the site of the Leonard Gansevoort house that was destroyed in the stable fire.

What might Douglass's visits to Albany—and the conspicuous attention that Weed had given to both his lectures and his *Narrative* in the *Evening Journal*—have meant to Melville as he was writing the manuscript of *Typee* in 1845? Part of the answer can wait until Part II. Here will be addressed the degree to which Melville's knowledge of Douglass as an orator might have influenced his depiction of Marnoo, the Nukuhevan orator who makes such a striking appearance in Chapter 18 of *Typee.*

At this point in the story, Tommo, Melville's narrator, is living in the valley of the Typee, separated by a high ridge from the valley of the Happar, the Typee's

tribal enemies. In addition to his oratorical skills, Marnoo is *taboo*, which means that he is able to travel freely between the feuding Nukuhevan tribes. He is also proficient enough in European languages to bring the latest news from the English, American, and French whalers or frigates that visited the bay. For all of these reasons, in addition to his striking physical beauty, his visits are always highly anticipated.

At the approach of the visitor in Chapter 18, *"Marnoo!—Marnoo!" was shouted by every tongue. . . . The stranger could not have been more than twenty-five years of age, and was a little above the ordinary height; had he been a single hair's breadth taller, the matchless symmetry of his form would have been destroyed. His unclad limbs were beautifully formed; whilst the elegant outline of his figure, together with his beardless cheeks, might have entitled him to the distinction of standing for the statue of the Polynesian Apollo; and indeed the oval of his countenance and the regularity of every feature reminded me of an antique bust. But the marble repose of art was supplied by a warmth and liveliness of expression only to be seen in the South Sea Islander under the most favorable developments of nature.*

Like Marnoo, Douglass and Melville were each in their mid-twenties when Melville wrote this passage. Marnoo's Apollonian beauty combines Grecian and Polynesian attributes much as Douglass's commanding presence combined African and American attributes. Socially and politically Marnoo's *taboo* status resembled the role Douglass was increasingly playing in American life by conveying his experiences in the North and the South to both blacks and whites.

Tommo, after describing Marnoo's tattooing, finally shows him in action as an orator.

Never, certainly, had I beheld so power-ful an exhibition of natural eloquence as Marnoo displayed during the course of his oration. The grace of the attitudes into which he threw his flexible figure . . . and above all, the fire which shot from his brilliant eyes, imparted an effect to the continually changing accents of his voice, of which the most accomplished orator might have been proud. At one moment reclining sideways upon the mat, and leaning calmly upon his bended arm, he related circumstantially the aggressions of the French—their hostile visits to the surrounding bays, enumerating each one in succession.

After this, "with clenched hands and a counte-nance distorted with passion, he poured out a tide of invectives. Falling back into an attitude of lofty command, he exhorted the Typees to resist these encroachments." Then, "with a scornful stance he sketched in ironical terms the wondrous intrepidity of the French, who, with five war-canoes and hundreds of men, had not dared to assail the naked warriors of their valley."

Marnoo's oratorical powers have been compared by some to those of Gansevoort Melville, Herman's brother. But his physical presence, striking gestures, fiery eyes, pas-sionate invective, and ironical scorn—not to mention his *taboo* status and his cross-cultural beauty—resemble contemporary descriptions of Douglass much more closely. Each of these characteristics is vividly con-veyed in the contemporary accounts of Douglass's speaking style in Blassingame's introduction to *Speeches, Debates, and Interviews, 1841-1846.*

Throughout Marnoo's speech,
the effect he produced upon his audi-ence was electric; one and all they stood regarding him with sparkling eyes and

Daguerreotype of Frederick Douglass, 1847.
National Portrait Gallery, Smithsonian Institution, Washington.

trembling limbs, as though they were lis-tening to the inspired voice of a prophet. But it soon appeared that Marnoo's powers were as versatile as they were extraordinary. As soon as he had finished this vehement harangue, he threw himself again upon the mats, and, singling out individuals in the crowd, addressed them by name, in a sort of bantering style, the humor of which, though hidden from me, filled the whole assembly with uproari-ous delight. He had a word for everybody; and, turning rapidly from one to another, gave utterance to some hasty witticism, which was sure to be followed by peals of laughter. To the females as well as the men, he addressed his discourse. Heaven only knows what he said to them, but he caused smiles and blushes to mantle their ingenuous faces. I am, indeed, very much inclined to believe that Marnoo, with his handsome person and captivating manners, was a sad deceiver among the simple maidens of the island.

Whaleships and French men-of-war at anchor in Nuku Hiva harbor, Typee Bay, Marquesas Islands, 1842. The French were taking possession of the islands when Melville and "Toby" Greene jumped ship in July. The two men may have been on the island when the sketch for this painting was made in 1845. From Russell and Purrington's, "A Whaling Voyage Round the World," New Bedford Whaling Museum.

This infectious style of bantering humor was also characteristic of Douglass from his earliest days as an orator. So was his incomparable gift of relating to the whole gamut of personalities in a room, females included. As early as 1842 Douglass had displayed the full range of Marnoo's oratorical assets at a "Latimer Meeting" in Salem, Massachusetts. "His remarks and manner created the most indescribable sensations." He was "fluent, graceful, eloquent, shrewd, sarcastic," and yet he also showed "great powers of humor." He "seemed to move the audience at his will, and they at times would hang upon his lips with staring eyes and open mouths."

It may be that at Nukuheva, Melville met a real-life Polynesian who had all of Marnoo's qualities. Even if that were true, Douglass's Albany oratory during the months in which Melville was writing the book is likely to have left its own marks on Marnoo. If Melville attended either of the Albany lectures, or the one in Troy, hearing Douglass speak and seeing him work the crowd (including the ladies for whom seats had been reserved), would have been an unforgettable experience.

If Melville's depiction of Marnoo did incorporate elements of what he had seen, heard, or read about Douglass in Albany, such elements are likely to have been appreciated by Thurlow Weed and others who had heard Douglass speak. A thorough examination of Weed's career as editor of the *Evening Journal* (1831–1863), and of his letters and other archival materials in various collections, may turn up additional insights about this crucial period in Douglass's and Melville's early careers.

In February 1846 John Murray published *Typee* in London as *Narrative of a Four Months' Residence among the Natives of a Valley of the Marquesas*. A month later Wiley and Putnam published the American edition as *Typee: A Peep at Polynesian Life*. On March 23 Weed embraced Melville's new book as warmly as he had Douglass's *Narrative* a year before, publishing three long extracts from the opening chapters in his welcoming review. One of the extracts, after revealing the charms of the "flotilla of Marquesan mermaids" who greet the whaleship in Nukuheva Bay, includes the passage in which "humanity weeps over the ruin thus remorselessly inflicted" upon them through "contaminating contact with the white man."

Weed's interest in *Typee* became even stronger on July 3, when a headline in

Left: Thurlow Weed, circa 1855, painted by Asa W. Twitchell.
Fenimore Art Museum.

Right: Herman Melville, 1846, painted by Asa W. Twitchell.
Berkshire Athenaeum.

his *Evening Journal* announced "Toby Identified!" According to a story in the Buffalo *Commercial Advertiser*, Toby, the bosom friend of Melville's Tommo, had turned up in the form of Richard Tobias Greene, "a sign Painter at Buffalo!" Weed had been one of several reviewers to doubt the literal truth of Melville's fictional adventures, so he was eager to hear about Richard Greene directly from Melville himself. They met in Albany on July 4, and July 6 Weed was able to announce that

> *Mr. Melville, the Author of "Typee," who was in town on Saturday, says that he has no doubt but that the Buffalo Sign Painter is his veritable Ship-Mate and Companion "Toby." If this be so, it furnishes a strong exemplification of the seeming contradiction that "Truth is Stranger than Fiction."*

On July 13 Weed reprinted "Toby's Own Story" from the *Commercial Advertiser*, and August 4 he announced that Melville's version of Toby's story would appear as a sequel to *Typee* in a revised edition soon to be published by Wiley and Putnam in New York. On August 15 Melville brought a copy of the new edition to Weed's office at 67 State Street. As Weed

was not in, he wrote a note indicating that he "takes great pleasure in presenting to Mr. Weed the accompanying copy of *Typee*—and much regrets not seeing him this morning."

During the time in which Melville was writing additional chapters of *Typee* for Gansevoort in 1845 and enjoying the success of the published book in 1846, he would have been able to stay well informed about Douglass's travels in Great Britain simply by reading Weed's *Evening Journal*. On October 17, 1845, Weed reprinted from the *Liberator* the remarkable September 1 letter that Douglass wrote to Garrison as soon as the *Cambria* had landed in Liverpool, describing "AN AMERICAN MOB ON BOARD A BRITISH STEAM PACKET." The mob was led by three slaveholders who not only tried to prevent Douglass from speaking to his fellow passengers on the ship; they actually threatened to throw him overboard. The scene became so riotous that Captain Judkins of the *Cambria* had to threaten to put the "mobocrats . . . in irons" to get them to desist. Douglass's letter included this ironic flourish: "it is enough to make a slave ashamed of the country that had enslaved him."

Wooden paddle-steamer Hibernia, *sister ship of the* Cambria, *built in 1843 for the Cunard Line by Steele's of Greenock, Scotland. The* Cambria *was built in 1845, so Douglass would have sailed on one of its first voyages.* National Archives.

Two weeks before reprinting the letter from Douglass to the *Liberator*, Weed had reprinted another account of the same incident from the Lynn *Pioneer*. This account was provided by the Hutchinson Family Singers, young abolitionists who had accompanied their "intimate friend" Douglass on the same voyage to Liverpool (and who later became friends with Melville's brother Gansevoort in London). Their letter confirmed Douglass's account of the actions of the slaveholders and the intervention of the captain, but it was not quite so circumspect in style. In their account, "all that the cool heads could do was hardly sufficient to prevent a scene of bloodshed." Even after Douglass left the upper deck, some of the slaveholders threatened to "Throw the d—d nigger overboard." Finally the captain issued the order, "*Have the irons ready for them!*"

On December 23 Weed published a long letter in which Douglass thanked him directly for "your noble and timely defense of my conduct on board the British steamership *Cambria.*" In addition to publishing the Hutchinson and Douglass letters on October 2 and 17, Weed had written editorials on October 21 and 29 defending Douglass against editorials in the Utica *Daily Gazette* that had denounced him for having "publicly insulted" the slaveholders on board by speaking against slavery.

This celebrity treatment for Douglass continued throughout the new year as Melville began writing *Omoo*, the sequel to *Typee*, in Lansingburgh. On January 31 the Albany *Evening Journal* printed a long letter that Douglass had written Garrison from Belfast. The February 2 issue announced that the *Narrative of Frederick Douglass* was already entering its fourth edition. A February 21 account of "Frederick Douglass at Belfast" was followed on March 4 by a long letter Douglass had written to the *Liberator* responding to charges made by A. C. C. Thompson in defense of the individuals who had enslaved Douglass in Maryland. On June 1 the *Evening Journal* printed part of a speech Douglass had given in Glasgow. This was followed on June 13 by a letter that Douglass had written to "a Friend" in Albany about his visit to the birthplace of Robert Burns in Scotland.

Douglass's friend was Abigail Mott, who, with her sister Lydia, was currently educating Frederick's daughter Rosetta in Albany while his wife Anna was caring for their young sons in Lynn, Massachusetts. His letter shows keen appreciation for Burns as a poet and a person and includes an interview with three of the poet's living relatives. Weed introduced it with these words: "The writer, be it remembered, is a 'Runaway Slave,' who, during his eight years of stolen Freedom, in defiance of all the disadvantages under which his class labor, has qualified himself to think and write thus."

On June 4, nine days before printing Douglass's letter about Robert Burns, Thurlow Weed had the unhappy task of informing his readers of the death of Gansevoort Melville, who had died in London in May while serving as Secretary to the American Legation. The remains of "this estimable and prominent American citizen" were "now being conveyed to his family by the packet ship Prince Albert." After the body had crossed the Atlantic, Herman accompanied it from New York City to Albany on the *Hendrick Hudson*. On June 27 the *Evening Journal* announced that "the funeral of the deceased" would take place the next day "from the residence of his uncle," General Peter Gansevoort of Washington

Street. On June 29 Weed's paper declared that "there are few young men whose death could be so emphatically regarded as a public loss." On July 6 Weed reported his meeting with the author of *Typee* two days before.

Gansevoort's younger brother Herman was now suddenly the family's best hope for financial success and public acclaim. On December 18, 1846, he signed a contract with Harper and Brothers of New York for the publication of *Omoo*. At about this time he visited the portrait studio of Asa W. Twitchell at 56 State Street, whom Weed had welcomed a year earlier as "an artist of great merit and promise." Twitchell's portrait of the author of *Typee* near the end of 1846 is the first image of Melville as a public figure and a fine companion to Twitchell's portrait of Weed. Each man's attire resembles that of Douglass in the 1847 daguerreotype by an unknown artist.

One can imagine Weed walking across State Street to chat with Melville while Twitchell was painting his portrait. For Thurlow Weed in Albany in December 1846, Frederick Douglass and Herman Melville were each young celebrities of exceptional ability and promise.

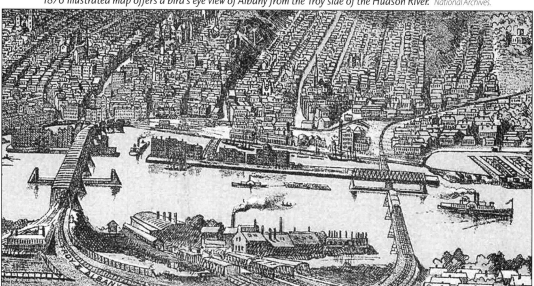

1876 illustrated map offers a bird's eye view of Albany from the Troy side of the Hudson River. National Archives.

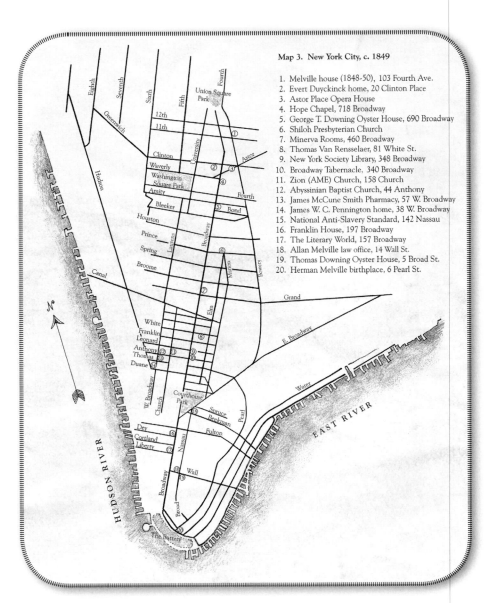

Map 3. New York City, c. 1849

1. Melville house (1848-50), 103 Fourth Ave.
2. Evert Duyckinck home, 20 Clinton Place
3. Astor Place Opera House
4. Hope Chapel, 718 Broadway
5. George T. Downing Oyster House, 690 Broadway
6. Shiloh Presbyterian Church
7. Minerva Rooms, 460 Broadway
8. Thomas Van Rensselaer, 81 White St.
9. New York Society Library, 348 Broadway
10. Broadway Tabernacle, 340 Broadway
11. Zion (AME) Church, 158 Church
12. Abyssinian Baptist Church, 44 Anthony
13. James McCune Smith Pharmacy, 57 W. Broadway
14. James W. C. Pennington home, 38 W. Broadway
15. National Anti-Slavery Standard, 142 Nassau
16. Franklin House, 197 Broadway
17. The Literary World, 157 Broadway
18. Allan Melville law office, 14 Wall St.
19. Thomas Downing Oyster House, 5 Broad St.
20. Herman Melville birthplace, 6 Pearl St.

New York City, circa 1849. Drawn by Kathleen Piercefield.

CHAPTER THREE

UP AND DOWN BROADWAY
New York City, May 1847 – May 1850

When Douglass returned from Great Britain in 1847, he quickly became as visible in New York City as he had been in Albany two years earlier. Two weeks after landing in Boston on the *Cambria*, he visited New York to address the opening session of the annual meeting of the American Anti-Slavery Society, traditionally held in the Broadway Tabernacle, a massive circular hall seating twenty-five hundred persons. The audience that filled the hall on May 11, 1847, was so impatient to hear him that they chanted "Douglass, Douglass" as William Lloyd Garrison tried to introduce him. Garrison, embarrassed, was forced to cut his remarks short.

Douglass began his homecoming address by saying that he was "very glad to be here." He was "pleased to mingle my voice with the voices of my friends on this platform." Yet he was not entirely happy to be back in the country from whose shores he had fled in order to "preserve my liberty." Contrasting conditions in America with those in England, he was compelled to say, "I have no love for America, as such; I have no patriotism. I have no country. What country have I? The institutions of this country do not know me, do not recognize me as a man."

Douglass drew hisses as well as cheers when he declared his wish to see this slaveholding country "overthrown as speedily as possible, and its Constitution shivered in a thousand fragments, rather than this foul curse should continue to remain as now." In response to the hisses, he declared that "I am anxious to irritate the American people on this question. I would *blister it all over, from centre to circumference*, until it gives signs of a purer and better life than it is now manifesting to the world."

According to the *National Anti-Slavery Standard*, which printed the entire speech on May 20, "Mr. Douglass took his seat in the midst of the most enthusiastic and over-whelming applause" from "the whole of the vast assembly." However, the response from the daily press was more mixed. A week after-ward, the *Standard* reprinted commentaries from eight different New York newspapers. The *Tribune* emphasized that Douglass "held the audience in breathless attention," and the *Observer*, the *Inquirer*, and the *Evangelist* all acknowledged that he was "the lion of the occasion." But the *Courier and Enquirer* and the *Sun* both protested harshly "against the unmitigated abuse heaped upon our country by the colored man Douglass."

Douglass's criticism of America in his homecoming speech made him both a marked and a celebrated man in New York. When he returned to the Broadway Tabernacle in May 1848, 1849, and 1850, his presence was increasingly visible and volatile until a show-down in 1850 shut down free speech in New York City. When Douglass had lectured in Albany in 1845, he had had to fear being taken back to the South as a fugitive slave. This was no longer a danger in 1847, as his freedom had been purchased by friends in England while he was overseas. Now in New York, after his blistering remarks at the Tabernacle, he had more to fear from nativist newspaper editors and their northern supporters.

The eight commentaries in the *Standard* on May 27 showed how widely the Tabernacle talk was covered in the daily as well as the anti-slavery press. The *Standard* also printed the *Tribune*'s account of the "Reception of Frederick Douglass by the Coloured People" at the Zion Church on nearby Leonard Street on the same evening. Douglass recounted his experiences in Great Britain to a tumultuous crowd, which also gave a warm greeting to Garrison when he entered the building in the course of Douglass's speech. "The meeting continued to midnight, and notwithstand-

Lithographic print of the interior of the Broadway Tabernacle, 1846, by Francis D'Avignon. The Metropolitan Museum of Art.

DISTRIBUTION OF THE AMERICAN ART-UNION PRIZES,

Left: William Lloyd Garrison of the Liberator and president of the American Anti-Slavery Society.

Right: Captain Judkins of the steamship Cambria of the Cunard Line.

Two staunch supporters of Frederick Douglass between 1845 and 1847.

ing the lateness of the hour, the audience manifested no wish to retire, such was the absorbing interest taken in the subject, his address, and the power of manly eloquence with which it was presented." Melville is quite certain to have read these and other comments about Douglass in the May 27 issue of the *Standard* because the same issue contained a remarkable review of *Typee* and *Omoo*.

The reviewer, identified only as "B," declared that *Typee* had "opened to the reading world views of a new existence, more novel and startling than any of the revelations of Swedenborg," the transcendental philospher. *Typee* had resolved "the great problem of the age" by proving that "happiness was not only possible without the aid of pastry cooks, lawyers, tailors, and clergymen, but that men could be happier without these excrescences of civilization than with them." Furthermore, *Typee* inspired "B" to realize that cannibalism, as feared by sailors in the South Seas, compares favorably to slavery, as actually practiced in the South:

> *It is true that the Typees eat their enemies, but then they do not eat them alive; they have the humanity to wait until their victims are dead before they begin to feast upon them. Here, we reverse the rule, and feed on each other while living. One dead enemy was sufficient to feast a whole tribe of Typees; but with us a hundred slaves hardly suffice to furnish food for one Southern family. The Typee craunches the tendons and muscles of his dead enemy between his molars, but inflicts no pain upon him; but with us, the Calhouns, Clays, and Polks feed daily upon the sweat, the tears, the groans, and the anguished hearts and despairing sighs, of living men and women; they do not eat the insensible flesh of their dead slaves, but they lacerate it when alive with whips, and cauterize it with hot branding-irons.*

The May 27 issue of the *National Anti-Slavery Standard* is a milestone in the joint reception of Douglass and Melville because the accomplishments of each are such a prominent feature in it. Just as Melville is likely to have read the response of the New York press to the Broadway Tabernacle speech, so is Douglass likely to have seen

Charles F. Briggs, engraved for the Knickerbocker Gallery, 1855. Public Library of Cincinnati and Hamilton County.

the response of "B" to *Typee* and *Omoo*. This possibility is even more likely because "B" also wrote a striking column in defense of Douglass in the same four-page issue. His occasion for doing so was a new incident involving the *Cambria*. Upon reaching the ship in Liverpool, Douglass was denied access because of his race to the first-class cabin he had purchased in London. Before sailing Douglass wrote a letter of protest to the London *Times* that eventually resulted in an apology from the president of the Cunard line. On the voyage itself Douglass was again befriended by Captain Judkins, who had rescued him from the "mobocrats" in 1845 and now resolved the new crisis in 1847 by installing Douglass in his own stateroom.

The New York *Courier and Enquirer* responded to this episode by printing a letter from a London correspondent who called Douglass a "negro imposter" and accused him of provoking the whole affair by intentionally booking his cabin from a London office boy who was "literally ignorant of the 'difference between black and white.'" "B" responded in

the *Standard* by attacking the *Courier and Enquirer* for its "base and scurrilous remarks upon the gross injustice done to Frederick Douglass, by the Liverpool agent of the Cunard steamers." In response to a prediction from the *Courier and Enquirer* that Douglass would quickly pass into "obscurity" after his return to America, "B" grandly declared that "Frederick Douglass has already gained a name by his rare talents and most singular history which will save him from obscurity. When the name of Toussaint L'Overture becomes obscure, and suffering and violence have been banished from the world by universal justice, then the name of Frederick Douglass may subside into obscurity."

"B" has never been identified by Melville scholars, among whom his fine review of *Typee* became widely available in 1995 and again in 2002. But he *was* identified in an unpublished May 11, 1847, diary entry by Edmund Quincy, Douglass's long-time colleague in the American (and Massachusetts) Anti-Slavery Society. Quincy wrote that "Mr. Briggs is the 'B' of the Standard," that is, Charles F. Briggs, widely known at the time as a writer for the New York *Daily Mirror*. Later Briggs would be important to both Douglass and Melville as editor of *Holden's Magazine* (1848–51) and *Putnam's Monthly* magazine (1853–55). His keen appreciation of both men in May 1847 raises the possibility that he might have met one or both by that time. That he had met Douglass seems quite likely, since Quincy's diary entry indicates that Briggs had joined Quincy and his companions for lunch on May 11, immediately after Douglass had concluded the opening meeting at the Broadway Tabernacle with his "blistering" speech.

Although Melville's home was still in Lansingburgh in May 1847, he was in New York City from May 4 to 14 as a frequent visitor at the home of Evert Duyckinck at 20 Clinton Place. Duyckinck was then Melville's mentor and guide to New York's publishing scene, having edited *Typee* for Wiley and Putnam. As editor of *The Literary World*, he had promoted Melville's books and solicited reviews from him. Duyckinck was very well acquainted with Briggs, who had satirized him in the March 6 issue of *The Trippings of Tom Pepper,* a novel Briggs was serializing in the New York *Weekly Mirror.* The offices of *The Literary World* on lower Broadway were not far from those of the *National Anti-Slavery Standard* along publisher's row on Nassau Street.

While Melville was in New York in early May 1847, did he meet Douglass, or Briggs, or both? Did the author who had depicted "Marnoo!—Marnoo!" delivering a "tide of invectives" in *Typee* witness "Douglass, Douglass" delivering his own blistering invectives in the Tabernacle? Whether they met in person or not, the two young men's professional lives were strongly converging within a month of Douglass's return from Great Britain. They had each been given the highest possible praise in the *Standard* in a way almost certain to have been visible to the other. Charles Briggs, "the 'B' of the Standard," had now joined Thurlow Weed in expressing prominent, articulate admiration for both Douglass and Melville. Back in Albany Weed was warmly welcoming *Omoo* in the May 1,3, and 12 issues of the *Evening Journal.*

With two of Melville's books now in print, his writing had new opportunities to enter Douglass's consciousness. The first undeniable evidence of that phenomenon was to come on June 2, 1848, when Douglass reprinted a passage from *Typee* in his *North Star* newspaper (an event to be addressed in Chapter 4). When "B's" exceptional review of

Typee appeared in the *National Anti-Slavery Standard* on May 27, 1847, Melville would have become conscious of a specifically anti-slavery component of his reading audience.

The *Standard's* interest in Melville's novels extended to his personal life on August 19, when it announced the marriage in Boston on August 4 of "Mr. Herman Melville (Typee,) of New-York, to Miss Elizabeth Shaw, daughter of Chief Justice Shaw, of Boston." This information was probably provided by Edmund Quincy, who was the Boston correspondent for the *Standard.* Like Charles Briggs, he had both Douglass and Melville on his mind in 1847, as seen in a July 2 letter he wrote to his friend Caroline Weston, then living in New Bedford.

This eight-page handwritten letter, now at the Boston Public Library, contains separate paragraphs on Douglass and Melville. Quincy begins the one about Douglass by calling him an "unconscionable nigger"—a shocking phrase in view of the degree to which they had worked side by side in the anti-slavery cause since 1841, probably written because Quincy was irritated over the fee Douglass had proposed for a series of essays he had been asked to write for the *Standard.*

Quincy's paragraph about the man he calls "'Typee' Melville" was prompted by Herman's upcoming marriage to the daughter of Chief Justice Shaw. He writes Miss Weston quite expansively about Judge Shaw's having himself led "two blushing brides" to the altar—even though he and Shaw had differed bitterly over the issue of fugitive slaves ever since the George Latimer case of 1842. Quincy ends the Melville part of the letter by indicating that the newlyweds "are to live with his mother in Albany or Schenectady" (Lansingburgh). Melville was entering the margins of Quincy's world while Douglass was being estranged within it.

Herman Melville and his wife Elizabeth did return to Lansingburgh after their honeymoon trip from the Saco Valley to Lake Champlain via Montreal, but only for a few weeks. By the end of September 1847, the newlyweds, along with Melville's mother and several of his siblings, had moved downriver to New York City, where they joined Herman's younger brother Allan and his new wife Sophia in a house at 103 Fourth Avenue, largely paid for with a loan from Chief Justice Shaw.

Herman and Elizabeth were to live at this address until September 1850, when they moved to Pittsfield, Massachusetts, again with financial support from Elizabeth's father. Herman was very prolific at 103 Fourth Avenue, writing *Mardi* in 1848 and *Redburn* and *White-Jacket* in 1849 and beginning *Moby-Dick* in 1850. He was becoming very much a New Yorker during Douglass's increasingly visible visits in 1848, 1849, and 1850.

A glance at a few of the spatial coordinates on the map of New York City will show how Douglass and Melville were coming into increasing physical, as well as intellectual, proximity. Melville's house at 103 Fourth Avenue was between Eleventh and Twelfth Streets, a block east of Broadway. This location was close to Evert Duyckinck's house at 20 Clinton Place, west of Broadway near Washington Square. On January 17, 1848, upon Duyckinck's recommendation, Melville became a member of the New York Society Library at 348 Broadway, downtown at Leonard Street. This address was nearly adjacent to the Broadway Tabernacle at 340 Broadway. On May 4, five days before the opening of the 1848 Anti-Slavery Society meeting at the Tabernacle, Melville renewed his membership in the library. One of its main attractions for him was the reading room, "a large and well proportioned apartment" whose "four commodious tables" were filled with newspapers from New York and other American cities, along with American and English periodicals.

The second building of the New York Society Library (1840–1853) was located on Broadway between Leonard Street and Catherine Lane. Courtesy of New York Society Library.

Even before he officially joined the New York Society Library in January, Melville was in the habit of walking downtown to its reading room every evening. We know this from a December 23 letter in which his wife Elizabeth describes their daily routine. "At four we dine, and after dinner is over, Herman and I come up to our room, and enjoy a cosy chat for an hour or so. . . . Then he goes down town for a walk, looks at the papers in the reading room &c, and returns about half past seven or eight." Conveniently for Herman in the winter months, the reading room was well lit at night.

The New York Society Library owned a large collection of books from which Melville promptly withdrew four volumes on the day he became a member. It also provided two small apartments to be used "as studies for those authors who desire to pursue their investigations with their authorities around them." One can imagine Melville taking advantage of this latter convenience, as he was a notorious borrower from a multitude of "authorities," not always acknowledged in his books, and he must have felt crowded at times by the extended family on Fourth Avenue.

His daily walk down Broadway to the New York Society Library brought Melville into the physical environs of Douglass's annual visit as well as into the reading room whose daily newspapers provided detailed coverage of those visits. Beginning in May 1848, Douglass's annual speech at the Broadway Tabernacle was virtually next door to Melville's library. In 1850, as we shall see, the opening session at the Tabernacle was followed by two meetings scheduled for the lecture hall of the library itself.

Melville was writing *Mardi* when Douglass returned to New York in May 1848. Both men were being influenced by the revolutions that were sweeping Europe early that year— Melville in the allegorical chapters in the last

third of this 600-page book, Douglass in the talk he gave at the Broadway Tabernacle on May 9. Douglass had become an editor as well as an orator, having founded the *North Star* in Rochester in December 1847. He was now able to write his own commentary about each year's meeting of the American Anti-Slavery Society. This year's commentary, beginning in the May 19 issue of the *North Star*, was triumphant, with Douglass writing of the "thrilling grandeur" of the opening session in "the vast hall of the Broadway Tabernacle." He was honored to be scheduled in the opening ceremonies after three exceptional speakers: Theodore Parker, Lucretia Mott, and Wendell Phillips. Because the hour was late by the time he was to speak, he curtailed his prepared address and spoke in a more improvisational manner, leaving the final word to the Hutchinson Family Singers, "who poured upon the audience from the gallery, one of their soul-stirring songs."

Judson, John, Asa, and Abby Hutchinson were the young singers who had supported Douglass against the "mobocrats" on the *Cambria* during the voyage to Liverpool in 1845. In the early months of 1846 they had spent considerable time with Gansevoort Melville in London—as had Jesse Hutchinson, their brother and business manager. The

The Hutchinson Family Singers. National Archives.

Hutchinsons were among the last people who had known Gansevoort in good health before his sudden death, and one expects that Herman would have been very interested in meeting them after they returned home. After Douglass and the Hutchinsons closed the opening session at the Broadway Tabernacle on May 9, Douglass remained very active in the subsequent meetings of the 1848 Anniversary Week, most of which took place in the Minerva Rooms at 460 Broadway.

Douglass's impromptu comments at the Tabernacle did not polarize the New York press as much as had the "blistering" homecoming speech of the year before, but they did provide both listeners and readers with food for thought. The *National Anti-Slavery Standard* published a transcript of his remarks in its May 18 issue, which Melville is likely to have read when it was reprinted in the June 2 issue of the *North Star*, the issue in which Douglass also reprinted "Tattooing" from *Typee*. Douglass's remarks might have been particularly interesting for Melville because they addressed issues of international affairs and colonial expansion in addition to his customary subject of slavery in the southern states. Douglass also touched on recent events, including the revolution in France, speeches by Calhoun and Clay, and the arrest of fugitive slaves on the schooner *Pearl* in Washington, D. C. Still, the primary purpose of his talk was to make his audience see the United States as the peoples of other nations did. His most striking way of doing this was to offer his commentary on a cartoon about America that appeared in *Punch*, in London, in December 1847.

Douglass began this section of his remarks by citing Robert Burns: "O wad some power the giftie gie us, / To see oursels as others see us." He then described the "excellent pictorial description of America" that appeared in *Punch*. The figure in the foreground was

a long, lean, gaunt, shrivelled looking creature, stretched out on two chairs, and his legs resting on the prostrate bust of Washington; projecting from behind was a cat o'nine tails knotted at the ends; around his person he wore a belt, in which were stuck those truly American implements, a bowie-knife, dirk, and revolving pistol; behind him was a whipping-post, with a naked woman tied to it, and a strong-armed American citizen in the act of scourging her livid flesh with a cowskin.

Douglass pointed to another group next to this figure:

a sale going on of human cattle, and around the auctioneer's table were gathered the respectability—the religion represented in the person of the clergy—of America, buying them for export to the goodly city of New Orleans. Little further on, there was a scene of branding—a small group of slaves tied hand and foot, while their patriotic and philanthropic masters were burning their name into their quivering flesh. Further on, there was a drove of slaves, driven before the lash to a ship moored out in the stream, bound for New Orleans. Above these and several other scenes illustrative of the character of our institutions, waved the star-spangled banner.

Beyond those other scenes, "still further back in the distance," Douglass called attention to

the picture of the achievements of our gallant army in Mexico, shooting, stabbing, hanging, destroying property, and massacreing the innocent with the innocent, not with the guilty. . . . Over all this was a picture of the devil himself, looking down with satanic satisfaction on passing events. Here I conceive to be a true picture of America, and I hesitate not to say

This illustration of "The Land of Liberty" in Punch (London) on December 4, 1847, was the subject of Douglass's commentary at the Broadway Tabernacle on May 9, 1848. *Public Library of Cincinnati and Hamilton County.*

SIMPLICITY OF OLD ZACK'S HABITS.

The drawing that accompanied Melville's critique of the Mexican War, printed in Yankee Doodle *(New York), July 31, 1847.* Houghton Library, Harvard University.

that this description falls far short of the real facts, and of the aspect we bear to the world around us.

Douglass's critique of the Mexican War resembles that of Melville in the nine "Authentic Anecdotes of 'Old Zack'" published in *Yankee Doodle*, an American imitation of *Punch*, between July 24 and September 11, 1847. Melville's "Anecdote no. III," about a tack in Old Zack's saddle, was accompanied by a drawing of "Old Zack" that mirrored his own satirical tone.

In May of both 1847 and 1848, Douglass came to New York City primarily for the meetings of the American Anti-Slavery Society at the Broadway Tabernacle and related venues, but in 1849 he arrived in town much earlier and cast his net much wider. As he explained in the *North Star* on April 27, he arrived early in order to "promote the Anti-

Slavery cause and the circulation of the North Star among the colored people of this city and vicinity."

Douglass was disappointed that the Zion Church, which had given him such a heartwarming reception on the evening of his homecoming speech at the Broadway Tabernacle two years before, was not more welcoming. The trustees of the "Colored Methodist Congregation" that owned the church insisted that he pay a thirteen–dollar fee to give an anti-slavery lecture even though they would "throw open their church doors, free of cost, to a white minister who might come among them to plead the cause of the heathen in the Isles of the Pacific."

Fortunately, the Shiloh Presbyterian Church (whose current minister, James W. C. Pennington, had married Frederick and Anna Douglass when they stopped in New York on their way to New Bedford in September 1838) was more accommodating. Douglass spoke at Shiloh Presbyterian at least three times in April 1849, one of these being his celebrated "Slumbering Volcano" speech on April 23. He returned on the evening of May 8, after speaking at another black church, Abyssinian Baptist, the night before.

During the 1849 Anniversary Week of the American Anti-Slavery Society, Douglass's opening address at the Broadway Tabernacle on the morning of May 8 was followed by an evening address on May 9 at Hope Chapel at 718 Broadway. On May 11 Douglass concluded the Anniversary Week by debating Samuel Ringgold Ward on "The Constitutionality of American Slavery" in a combined afternoon and evening session in the Minerva Rooms at 460 Broadway. All five New York venues at which Douglass spoke during the week of May 7 were in the neighborhood of Melville's daily walk between his Fourth Avenue home and the New York Society Library. Abyssinian Baptist and the Broadway Tabernacle were in the immediate vicinity of the library itself, whereas Hope Chapel was on upper Broadway near Herman's Fourth Avenue home. The Minerva Rooms and Shiloh Presbyterian were midway between the two poles of his daily walk.

While Douglass was speaking in New York from April 20 to May 11 in Melville's near environs, Melville was writing *Redburn*, his fourth novel. He had spent January, February, and March with his Shaw in-laws in Boston, where his wife Elizabeth gave birth to their first child, Malcolm, on February 16. After returning to New York on April 11, Herman wrote *Redburn* in April, May, and June (to be followed by *White-Jacket* in July, August, and September). He was also attending to reviews of *Mardi*, his third and most ambitious book. Richard Bentley had published *Mardi* in London on March 15; the New York edition by Harper and Brothers followed on April 13.

By April 23, the day of Douglass's "Slumbering Volcano" speech at Shiloh Presbyterian, Melville had seen enough reviews to be able to send this interim report to Lemuel Shaw:

> I see that Mardi has been cut into by the London Athenaeum, and also burnt by the common hangman in the Boston Post. However the London Examiner & Literary Gazette; & other papers on this side of the water have done differently. These attacks are a matter of course, and are essential to the building up of any permanent reputation—if such should ever prove to be mine.

Anxiety over the reception of *Mardi* would have given an extra edge to his daily visit to the commodious tables of the reading room of the New York Society Library. Several of the New York newspapers in which he was searching for reviews of his work were covering Douglass's extended visit to the city

in April and May. Horace Greeley's New York *Tribune* had been attentive to the careers of both young men. On May 10 the *Tribune* reported on the talk that Douglass had given two days earlier at Shiloh Presbyterian. The same issue contained a devastating review of *Mardi*.

The reviewer, George Ripley, has high praise for *Typee* and *Omoo*, each "written under the immediate inspiration of personal experience," but "the present work aims at a much higher mark and fails to reach it." Once the mariners arrive at the fanciful locale of Mardi, the reader "is presented with a tissue of conceits, fancifully strung about the personages of the tale, expressed in language that is equally intolerable for its affectation and its obscurity." Ripley echoes other reviewers in declaring that Melville "has failed by leaving his sphere, which is that of graphic, poetical narration, and launching out into the dim, shadowy, spectral, Mardian region of mystic speculation and wizard fancies."

Adding to the personal and professional challenges that Douglass and Melville each faced during the Anniversary Week of the Anti-Slavery Society in May 1849 was the sudden, public trauma of the Astor Place riots during the same week. These occurred only a few short blocks from Melville's house at 103 Fourth Avenue and just around the corner from the Hope Chapel, where Douglass spoke on May 9. Both Melville and Douglass were involved in the drama.

On May 7 a crowd of nativist New Yorkers led by "Captain" Isaiah Rynders disrupted a performance of *Macbeth* by the British actor William Macready at the Astor Place Opera House. On May 10 an even more riotous scene at the same venue resulted in the death of twenty-two persons in a crowd of twenty thousand who had converged upon the Opera House to protest another Macready performance. Melville and Douglass each helped to provoke the rioters, though at different stages in the drama and in entirely different ways. Melville did so by signing a petition; Douglass, by taking a stroll.

At the performance of *Macbeth* on May 7, Rynders and his followers, in "a well-orchestrated attack,[drove] Macready from the stage with catcalls, rotten eggs, and the vile-smelling drug asafoetida." In response to Macready's announcement that he would cancel the rest of his New York engagement, Herman Meville, Evert Duyckinck, Washington Irving, and more than forty other New Yorkers signed a letter, published in the New York *Herald* on May 9, protesting the "outrage at the Astor Place Opera House" on May 7 and encouraging Macready to continue his performances as planned. When Macready agreed to perform again on May 10, Rynders brought his rioters back

in force. This time they were supplemented by thousands of New Yorkers who had been encouraged by handbills to show up in force "this night, at the English ARISTOCRATIC Opera House!"

The original protest on May 7 had been fueled by Macready's feud with the American Shakespearean actor Edwin Forrest, who was playing *Macbeth* concurrently at the Broadway Theater. Its sequel on May 10 became a class war as well as a theatrical one, in part because of the conspicuous aristocratic standing of many of Melville's fellow petitioners. Inside the theater Rynders and his working-class recruits so thoroughly disrupted the performance that Macready was forced to flee the building (and the city). Outside, the gathering crowd, which had thrown paving stones and brickbats through the window of the opera house during the performance, was estimated at twenty thou-

"The Riot at the Astor Place Opera House, New York," *from the* Illustrated London News, *June 2, 1849.* National Archives.

sand by the time the militia tried to disperse it, resulting in the twenty-two deaths that shocked New Yorkers and people throughout the nation.

Douglass's role in the Astor Place agitation showed how volatile his presence had become in New York by May 1849. As Dennis Berthold pointed out, "the nativist Democrats who hated Macready also hated blacks, abolitionists, and foreigners, making Macready into a complex political symbol of Whig elitism and comparative racial tolerance." This explains one of the ironic cries with which Rynders and his supporters disrupted the May 7 performance: "Three cheers for Macready, Nigger Douglass, and Pete Williams." The rioters included "Nigger Douglass" because he had "scandalized New Yorkers on May 5 by walking down Broadway arm-in-arm with two white women." Douglass gave his own account of the bi-racial stroll in the essay "Colorphobia in New York!" published in the *North Star* on May 25, 1849.

Defining colorphobia as a strange plague that had broken out on May 5, Douglass explained that it was caused simply by the fact that "two *English* Ladies" who had "taken apartments at the Franklin House were not only called upon at that Hotel by Mr. Douglass, but really allowed themselves to take his arm, and to walk many times up and down Broadway, in broad day-light, when that great thoroughfare was crowded with pure American ladies and gentlemen." How did Americans respond to seeing "two ladies, elegantly attired, . . . actually walking, and leaning upon the arm of a person, with a skin not colored like their own?" With a kind of "delirium tremens" of the mind, in which its victims would "point with outstretched arms towards us, uttering strange exclamations as if startled by some terrible sight."

Merchant card for the Franklin House, 1849. *National Archives.*

In spite of this shocking behavior by his fellow pedestrians (not to mention those who were shouting "Nigger Douglass" two days later at the opera house) Douglass did not despair. He concluded the essay by declaring that increasing numbers of New Yorkers were willing to associate "irrespective of all complexional differences." This was emphatically true of audiences who had been attending his speeches during the previous three weeks. A "mixed audience of white and colored persons" had gathered at Shiloh Presbyterian on April 20 to hear him deliver an address "distinguished by unusual force and beauty," as James McCune Smith reported in the *North Star* on May 4. The New York *Tribune* reported that Douglass's speech to the New York State Vigilance Committee at Shiloh Presbyterian on May 8 was "well-attended by white and colored people." W. C. Nell reported that the debate between Douglass and Samuel Ringgold Ward on May 11 included many of the city's most "intelligent, refined, and reformatory" citizens, "both white and colored."

According to Nell, that spirited debate provided a "brilliant finale" to the Anniversary Week in New York. It featured Ward's proposition that "the Constitution of the United States, in Letter, Spirit, and Design, is Essentially Anti-Slavery." Although no transcript survives, the *Tribune* reported that Ward defended his own proposition and that Douglass contested it. At this point Douglass still agreed with Garrison, Wendell Phillips, and Quincy (and, technically, with Chief Justice Shaw) that the founding fathers had supported slavery and that the Constitution itself offered no way around it.

Did the son-in-law of Chief Justice Lemuel Shaw hear this unique Constitutional debate on May 11? Was Melville among the racially integrated audiences who heard Douglass speak at the Hope Chapel on May 9, at the Broadway Tabernacle on May 8, or at Shiloh Presbyterian on April 20, April 23, or May 8?

Each speech was delivered by the man who had published "Tattooing" from *Typee* in the *North Star* eleven months earlier. Each was delivered in the immediate vicinity of Melville's daily walk between his house and his library. Again, whether Melville attended any of these talks (he was extremely busy writing *Redburn* and attending to Macready), he would certainly have seen many references to them in the New York newspapers he was scanning for reviews of *Mardi*.

The Franklin House, where Douglass began his walk with the "two *English* ladies" in the "Colorphobia" essay, was on Broadway at Dey Street, downtown from the New York Society Library and the Broadway Tabernacle. The two ladies, not identified in the essay, were Julia and Elizabeth Griffiths, newly landed from England and soon to be working for the *North Star* in Rochester. The uptown part of their conspicuous stroll with Douglass would have taken them into the environs of Melville's daily walk; its downtown part would have taken them past the office of *The Literary World* toward the Battery. Melville probably heard of their promenade up and down Broadway as early as May 8, when the *Herald* discussed it as the cause of the "Nigger Douglass" cheer at the Astor House the night before. His awareness of both the

walk and the immediate, vociferous, nativist response to it appears to have influenced a passage in *Redburn*.

Redburn is a fictional account of Melville's own first voyage from New York to Liverpool in 1839. His characterization of Lavender, the steward on Redburn's ship, would have a contemporary resonance for any reader aware of Douglass's bi-racial Broadway stroll. Lavender is a "handsome, dandy mulatto" who had at one time been a barber on West Broadway in New York. After his ship lands in Liverpool, young Redburn is surprised at the manner in which

> negro-sailors are regarded when they walk the Liverpool streets. . . . In Liverpool indeed the negro steps with a prouder pace, and lifts his head like a man; for here, no such exaggerated feeling exists in respect of him, as in America. Three or four times, I encountered our black steward, dressed very handsomely, and walking arm in arm with a good-looking English woman. In New York, such a couple would have been mobbed in three minutes; and the steward would have been lucky to escape with his whole limbs.

The reference to "such a couple" in New York would certainly seem to reflect Melville's awareness of the colorphobia that Douglass had so conspicuously endured and defined as Melville was writing *Redburn* in May 1849.

In 1850 Douglass and his same two English ladies were actually attacked, not just harassed, as they walked together near the Battery. This brutal event followed a violent week in which Rynders and his fellow rioters had disrupted an anti-slavery meeting at Shiloh Presbyterian, personally confronted Douglass at the Broadway Tabernacle, and shut down two successive meetings in the lecture hall of the New York Society Library.

A pleasant afternoon on Broadway, circa 1890. National Archives.

Douglass's personal confrontation with Rynders on May 7, 1850, was one of the finest and most memorable events in his public life. It was remembered as remarkable a half-century later in memoirs by Thomas Wentworth Higginson and John Hutchinson (of the Hutchinson Family Singers). For people living in New York at the time, it was one of those larger-than-life moments that brought deep social forces into absolute clarity—challenging a society and its ruling powers to choose between two conflicting visions. At the Tabernacle in 1850, Douglass won the day, but Rynders won the week.

It was clear in advance that serious violence was possible at the opening meeting of the Anniversary Week on May 7. Both the New York *Globe* and the New York *Herald* had called on rioters to "attend and attempt to break up the Abolitionist meeting at the Tabernacle." The *Globe* had even accused

Douglass of treason and invited its readers to "STRIKE THE VILLAIN DEAD." Several days before the May 7 meeting at the Broadway Tabernacle, Rynders and his followers had disrupted a meeting of the New York Vigilance Committee at Shiloh Presbyterian. During the morning meeting at the Tabernacle, they made "loud and repeated calls for Frederick Douglass, and were evidently anxious to wreak their violence upon him." Douglass's own account of the confrontation in the densely packed hall emphasizes the courage displayed by William Lloyd Garrison, the Hutchinson Family Singers, and Samuel Ringgold Ward, all of whom refused to be intimidated by the "hisses, groans, and other hideous noises" from Rynders and his men.

Readers of the *North Star* had to turn to the reprint from the New York *Evangelist* to appreciate the remarkable self-possession that Douglass showed when called upon to speak. As he

> advanced to the front of the stage [it] was now completely covered with the mob. We shall give no sketch of this speech, which considering the occasion and circumstances, was one of the most masterly which we ever heard. To every interruption from the mob he replied with a keenness of wit which drew down repeated bursts of applause from the mob.

Douglass did this with Rynders himself delivering constant abuse from "within a yard of the speaker." When Rynders shouted that Douglass was "only half a nigger," Douglass immediately replied, "And so half-brother to yourselves." When Rynders complained that slaves wanted to "cut their master's throats," Douglass declared that the "worst they had done was to cut hair." The next day the New York *Tribune* declared that "Frederick Douglass took them in hand and skinned them."

Douglass's quick wit, presence of mind, and physical courage helped preserve enough order to allow the morning meeting in the Broadway Tabernacle to be duly adjourned after Ward's speech. In Douglass's words, "the rude disturbers" had "annoyed and hindered, but had not defeated the celebration." In the afternoon meeting "at the New York Society Library Rooms," the rioters did succeed in "breaking up the meeting . . . by a wild chaotic tumult and other rowdy demonstrations."

Although the meeting reconvened the next morning in the hall of the library, the result was the same. "All sense of decency and propriety seemed to have forsaken the poor and despicable creatures, and their behavior even proved them destitute of all respect for women." Garrison, Phillips, and others "essayed to speak, but in vain. The mob triumphed again, and that, too, in the presence of the police."

The *Tribune* estimated that some 200 to 250 persons had assembled for the morning meeting on May 8 in the New York Society Library. Of these, "some 50 or more were ladies, and about the same number of colored persons." As soon as Garrison entered, "close at his heels came the 'Law and Order' party, headed by Rynders." Before long, the police had no option but to "clear the place. Thus closed Anti-Slavery free discussion in New York for 1850."

After returning home to Rochester, Douglass informed his readers about the attack by "five or six men" who had assaulted him and the two English women while they were walking together near the Battery. Their physical blows had been preceded by "all sorts of coarse and filthy language" directed at both him and his female companions. After two of the attackers "struck the ladies on the head," another struck Douglass "in the face" before "[I could] put myself in a position to ward off the assassin's blow."

Melville was still a member of the New York Society Library when Rynders and his fellow rioters shut down the two successive meetings in its lecture hall on May 7 and 8. On April 17 he had renewed his library membership. On May 1 he wrote Richard Henry Dana, Jr., in Boston that he was about "half way" in writing the "whaling voyage" that was to become *Moby-Dick*. As Melville worked on his new novel in New York for the rest of the spring and summer, he would have been keenly aware of the riotous activity that had disrupted the year's anti-slavery meetings at Shiloh Presbyterian and the Broadway Tabernacle as well as in the lecture hall of the library.

Whether or not he had witnessed Douglass face down Rynders or had been one of the 150 white men in the library who witnessed the bedlam in which the rioters had "triumphed,"

Melville would have learned a great deal about them in newspapers as well as by word of mouth. Some of what he learned influenced what he wrote in *Moby-Dick* and *Benito Cereno*, as will be seen in Chapter 5.

The way in which "Captain" Isaiah Rynders entered Melville's world in May 1849 and 1850 must have sparked sharp memories of his first encounter with the man. On November 1, 1844, soon after returning to Lansingburgh from the South Seas, Melville had come down to New York City to hear his brother Gansevoort speak at a massive City Hall rally for the Democratic presidential candidate James Polk. The rally was followed by a "torchlight procession of twenty thousand New York Democrats" led by "Captain Rynders, mounted on a white charger" and followed by his newly formed "Empire Club, one thousand strong." Although Rynders was a fellow Democrat, Gansevoort Melville took exception to the tactics he and his followers had used in harassing their Whig opponents during the campaign, and on October 26, he had complained in a letter to Polk that the "Empire Club [is] one of those fighting and bullying political clubs which disgrace our city politics."

The disgrace that Rynders had brought to Melville's Astor Place neighborhood in May 1849 he had now brought to his New York Society Library in May 1850. A native of Waterford, a small town directly across the Hudson River from Lansingburgh, Rynders, like Melville, "attended school until about the age of twelve"—when he became a deckhand on a riverboat operating between Troy and New York City. Later he "either owned or commanded a small Hudson River sloop," thereby acquiring the title of Captain that he retained in his subsequent pursuits as a "New York City gang leader and Tammany Hall boss of the sixth ward."

The fact that the police had let Rynders and his mob shut down free speech within the walls of the New York Society Library delivered some harsh truths about the city in which Melville and his family had made their home. One wonders if the anti-abolitionist riots in his library in May 1850, following directly upon the Astor Place riots in his neighborhood in May 1849, contributed to his seemingly sudden decision to move his family from New York to Pittsfield in September 1850. For both Douglass and Melville the volatile events of May 1850 were a sudden, undeniable rupture in the Anniversary Weeks of the three previous years. They deepened each man's understanding of the intensity of racism in the North.

Unless specific biographical evidence becomes available, it may never be known whether Douglass and Melville met for the first time in New York in 1847, 1848, 1849, or 1850; whether they resumed an earlier acquaintance from Albany or even New Bedford; or whether they still had not met in person but simply would have noticed each other intermittently in the newspapers. A better idea of some of the possibilities and probabilities will come in Part II, which examines what each knew of the other's work. One thing is certain, however: They did *not* meet each other in New York City in May 1851.

Melville was then living in Pittsfield, finishing *Moby-Dick* in the house he called Arrowhead. Douglass went to Syracuse, not New York City, for the fifteenth annual meeting of the American Anti-Slavery Society in May 1851, as no venue in either New York City or Brooklyn was willing to host that year's gathering. By June, Douglass had broken with Garrison on anti-slavery policy and changed the name of *the North Star* to *Frederick Douglass' Paper*.

Part II

DID DOUGLASS AND MELVILLE
KNOW EACH OTHER'S WORK?

Herman Melville, *carte-de-visite, 1861*.
Rodney Dewey photograph, Berkshire Athenaeum.

Frederick Douglass, *ambrotype, 1856*.
National Portrait Gallery, Smithsonian Institution.

*U*ntil the publication of John Stauffer's *Black Hearts of Men* in 2002, most students of either Douglass or Melville would have answered the above question in the negative. Stauffer's discovery of a quote from *Moby-Dick* in a March 1856 issue of *Frederick Douglass' Paper* has led to additional discoveries to be presented in Chapter 4 about what Douglass and his circle knew about Melville and his work. Although these discoveries do show that Douglass was aware of Melville, they do not necessarily reveal the full extent of that awareness. Nor do they include any direct testimony from Douglass as to what Melville and his work may have meant to him.

Apart from any subjective meaning that Melville may have had for Douglass, the mere fact that Melville's work was quoted and alluded to in both the *North Star* and *Frederick Douglass' Paper* indicates that there was an anti-slavery and non-white audience for Melville's work. The existence of such an audience, whatever its size, opens new possibilities for recognizing allusions either to Douglass or to African American life in Melville's fiction.

Although Douglass's name does not appear in Melville's fiction from *Typee* through *Benito Cereno*, all of the major novels in this period contain sympathetic attention to non-white characters. All of them contain possible allusions to Douglass, his writings, or his environs. Such elements, in themselves, suggest that Melville was attentive to African American experience and was conscious of writing for an audience that included non-white readers.

Chapter 5 examines traces of Douglass and his world in seven novels from *Typee* through *Benito Cereno*. Each work addresses major American themes such as race, freedom, identity, and nationhood in ways that invite comparison with the words that Douglass was speaking, writing, and publishing in close physical or intellectual proximity to Melville. By the time of *Moby-Dick* and *Benito Cereno*, some of the specific language in which Melville was addressing such themes suggests that his consciousness and artistry may have been profoundly influenced by such events as the "Slumbering Volcano" speech of 1849 and the confrontation with Rynders in 1850.

The next two chapters present evidence which does show that Douglass and Melville were aware of each other's work. They also explore similarities that may simply result from the two men's proximity in time and place as they address the major issues of the day. Such similarities are significant whether they resulted from "fast-fish" influence or "loose-fish" affinity. They help us to see a variety of ways in which Douglass and Melville, while aware of each other's work, spoke to each other's world.

The office of the North Star, Rochester, New York, *mid-19th century.* Courtesy of Moorland-Springarn Research Center, Howard University.

CHAPTER FOUR

MELVILLE IN THE *NORTH STAR* AND *FREDERICK DOUGLASS' PAPER*

In the March 7, 1856, issue of *Frederick Douglass' Paper,* John Stauffer discovered a quotation from Melville's *Moby-Dick* in a commentary on the 1856 presidential election written by James McCune Smith, the paper's New York City correspondent, who signed himself "Communipaw." At the time Smith was one of Douglass's closest intellectual associates. Their connection went back to the first issue of the *North Star* in December 1847, when Smith was listed as an agent for the paper at 93 West Broadway in New York City. In 1852 and 1853 Smith had contributed a series prose portraits entitled "Heads of the Colored People" to *Frederick Douglass' Paper* in addition to his letters from New York. In 1855 Douglass chose him to write the Introduction to *My Bondage and My Freedom.* Like Douglass, Smith was of mixed racial heritage. He was the first "colored" physician in New York City, having earned his medical degree at Glasgow in Scotland after being denied admission to American medical schools. He also operated a pharmacy called Apothecary's Hall on West Broadway in New York.

When Smith quotes from *Moby-Dick* in 1856, he is discussing the role of Horace Greeley and William Seward in the upcoming Presidential election. He cites a speech by Stubb to illustrate his view of Greeley as the "boat-steerer of the Whig party," who, on "the eve of an election, whether State or National,"

> shrieks out like Stubb in Moby-Dick, "Start her, start her, my men! Don't
> hurry yourselves; take plenty of time—but start her; start her like thunder
> claps, that's all—start her, now; give 'em the long strong stroke, Tashtego.
> Start her, Tash, my boy—start her, all: but keep cool, keep cool—cucumbers
> is the word—easy, easy—only start her like grim death and grinning devils,
> and raise the buried dead perpendicular out of their graves, boys—that's all.
> Start her!"

Smith admires Greeley and Seward, for "their ability to act, and their power to command the confidence of the nation." However, neither is "morally fitted to advance the cause of Human Freedom [when] tried by the only just standard" in Smith's mind—"a full and cordial belief that all men are by nature *free* and *equal.*"

Smith's quotation from *Moby-Dick* is notable for several reasons. One is that he refers to the book as if his readers are familiar with it. This alone suggests two things: that Douglass and his circle were part of a non-white and mixed-race audience for *Moby-Dick* and that the book was still current with this audience in 1856, five years after it was published. The latter point is of particular interest because *Moby-Dick* had already fallen out of favor with influential white readers by 1853. Not only did Smith find *Moby-Dick* of literary interest in 1856, but he also found its characters directly applicable to that year's presidential election. Nearly a century later, in 1953, another non-white author, C. L. R. James, cited the same speech by Stubb, calling it "a masterpiece of poetic exhortation."

Beyond the explicit comparison of Stubb and Greeley, Smith's quotation may suggest further connections with the 1856 election. The passage is from Chapter 61, "Stubb kills a Whale," the first successful chase scene in the book in which Stubb and his crew come upon a large sperm whale "tranquilly spouting his vapory jet" as though a "portly burgher smoking his pipe of a warm after-noon." Then follows the horrific process by which this peaceable creature, whose back is of "an Ethiopian hue," is chased, captured, and killed. By the end of the chapter, the whale's black back runs with a "red tide . . . like brooks down a hill." The once tranquil creature now shoots "gush after gush of clotted red gore" from his spout until "His heart had burst!"

For some readers of *Frederick Douglass' Paper* in 1856, the chase and capture of this whale might have called to mind the chase and capture of those humans subject to the Fugitive Slave Law, a law that continued to divide the nation as the new national election approached. For readers such as Frederick Douglass and James McCune Smith, the

James McCune Smith.
Engraving by Patrick Reason, New-York Historical Society.

legalized capture of fugitive slaves like George Latimer in 1842, Thomas Sims in 1851, and Anthony Burns in 1854 was the essential reality against which the American political system was to be judged. After passage of the new and more draconian Fugitive Slave Law in September 1850, Chief Justice Shaw was again at the heart of the controversy over its implementation; he was the Massachusetts judge in the 1851 case that sent Thomas Sims back to Georgia.

James McCune Smith's use of *Moby-Dick* for political commentary in 1856 opens a larger question: To what degree was Melville aware of an anti-slavery, non-white audience for his writing? Melville probably knew of an anti-slavery audience from the time of "B's" exceptional praise for *Typee* in the *National Anti-Slavery Standard* on May 27, 1847. One year later, on June 2, 1848, Frederick Douglass published three consecutive paragraphs on "Tattooing" from Chapter 30 of *Typee* in his *North Star*. (In the illustration below, note the misspelling of Melville's name in the credit line of the published article.)

TATTOOING.

I beheld a man extended flat upon his back on the ground, and despite the forced composure of his countenance, it was evident that he was suffering agony. His tormentor bent over him, working away for all the world like a stone-cutter with mallet and chisel.— In one hand he held a short slender stick, pointed with a shark's tooth, on the upright end of which he tapped with a small hammer-like piece of wood, thus puncturing the skin, and charging it with the coloring matter in which the instrument was dipped. A cocoa-nut shell containing this fluid was placed upon the ground. It is prepared by mixing with a vegetable juice the ashes of the ' armor,' or candle-nut, always preserved for the purpose. Beside the savage, and spread out upon a piece of soiled tappa, were a great number of curious black-looking little implements of bone and wood used in the various divisions of his art. A few terminated in a single fine point, and, like very delicate pencils, were employed in giving the finishing touches, or in operating upon the more sensitive portions of the body, as was the case in the present instance. Others presented several points distributed in a line somewhat resembling the teeth of a saw. These were employed in the coarser parts of the work, and particularly in pricking in straight marks. Some presented their points disposed in small figures, and be-

ing placed upon the body, were, by a single blow of the hammer, made to leave their indelible impression. I observed a few, the handles of which were mysteriously curved, as if intended to be introduced into the orifice of the ear, with a view perhaps of beating the tattoo upon the tympanum. Altogether, the sight of these strange instruments recalled to mind that display of cruel-looking mother-of-pearl-handled things which one sees in their velvet-lined cases at the elbow of a dentist.

The artist was not at this time engaged on an original sketch, his subject being a venerable savage, whose tattooing had become somewhat faded with age and needed a few repairs, and accordingly he was merely employed in touchi:g up the works of some of the old masters of the Typee school, as delineated upon the human canvass before him. The parts operated upon were the eyelids, where a longitudinal streak like the one which adorned Kory-Kory, crossed the countenance of the victim.

In spite of all the efforts of the poor old man, sundry twitchings and screwings of the muscles of the face denoted the exquisite sensibility of these shutters to the windows of his soul, which he was now having repainted. But the artist, with a heart as callous as an army surgeon, continued his performance enlivening his labors with a wild chant, tapping away the while as merrily as a wood-pecker.—*Mellville's Typee.*

Douglass reprints "Tattooing," from Melville's Typee, *in the* North Star, *June 2, 1848.* Boston Public Library.

"Tattooing" shows that Douglass was aware of Melville's writing beginning with his first published book. Lacking any of his commentary, however, it does not reveal why he reprinted it. At the least, one can imagine that he, like Melville, saw the human skin as a site of anxiety for the projection of cultural power and fear. If Douglass read all of *Typee*, he would surely have been interested in the depiction of the oratory and persona of Marnoo (whose back displayed the "best specimen" of tattooing Tommo had seen). Probably he would have recognized a number of his own most striking attributes in Melville's depiction of Marnoo's "Native Oratory."

When *Typee* was published in London in February 1846, Douglass was lecturing in Great Britain. He may have encountered Melville's South Sea novel—and the effusive British reviews of it—during his travels in England and Scotland. Or he may have learned about it after returning to America in April 1847 and reading the review by "B" in the *National Anti-Slavery Standard.* Perhaps his discovery of the book was closer to when

Maori village tattooing. Spinner Collection.

he began the *North Star* in December 1847 or reprinted "Tattooing" in June 1848. In any case, Douglass's reprint came two years after publication of both the English and American editions of *Typee*. This shows that Melville's first book, too, had some staying power with Douglass and his circle.

For readers of the *North Star* who were non-white, Melville's depiction of the physical process by which the skin of one man is punctured by another might have had a sharper sting than for some of the paper's white readers. The latter may have been more affected by the psychic threat of having one's skin color changed through the use of such "dentistical" instruments.

In the novel the strong desire of Karky, the Nukuhevan tattooer, to practice his art upon Tommo's white face prompts the psychological crisis in which Tommo suddenly decides to leave Fayaway and his earthly paradise in the Typee valley. He is "horrified at the bare thought of being rendered hideous for life" and would never more "have the *face* to return to my countrymen, even should an opportunity offer." Therefore, "half wild

with terror and indignation, [he succeeds] in breaking away" from Karky and his designs. As Samuel Otter has recently shown, the fear of being tattooed is actually stronger that of being cannibalized in *Typee*.

After this extensive quotation from *Typee* in the *North Star* in 1848, the next significant allusion to Melville's work appears in the August 11, 1854 edition of *Frederick Douglass' Paper*. Under the headline "Moby Dick Captured," Douglass reprints a story from the New Bedford *Standard* updating its earlier account of the whaleship *Ann Alexander* "being attacked and stove by a sperm whale" in 1851. The *Standard* had learned from a Honolulu newspaper that "five months subsequent to the catastrophe, the same whale [had been] taken by the Rebecca Sims, of this port. Two harpoons were discovered in him marked 'Ann Alexander.' The whale's head was found seriously injured, and contained pieces of the ship's timbers."

It is interesting that Douglass would consider this distant maritime event to be newsworthy in 1854. Equally interesting is the fact that the whale is called "Moby Dick" in Douglass's headline but not in his excerpt from the New Bedford story. Douglass was either making his own connection between the news story and Melville's whale or following others who had compared Moby Dick with the *Ann Alexander* whale beginning in November 1851.

Like Smith's direct quote from the novel in his political column in 1856, Douglass's headline "Moby Dick Captured" indicates that he expected his readers to be familiar with Melville's book. His equating of the two whales was not based on color, for the *Ann Alexander* whale was black, not white. Rather, the attribute that this whale shares with Moby Dick is resistance to the men and ships that hunt him. Just as the real-life whale "attacked and stove" the *Ann Alexander,* swimming away with two of its harpoons and "pieces of the ship's timbers," so Moby Dick attacked and stove the *Pequod,* swimming away with its harpoons in its body and Captain Ahab at the end of the line. By providing to his readers in August 1854 this new information about the resistance of the *Ann Alexander* whale, and linking it implicitly with Moby Dick's resistance to the *Pequod,* Douglass may have been offering yet another warning to those who would enforce the Fugitive Slave Law—and further encouragement to those who would defy it.

Three months before Douglass published "Moby Dick Captured," the capture of Anthony Burns in Boston had inspired intense new resistance to the Fugitive Slave Law. Like Thomas Sims in 1851, Burns was sent back to his Southern owner on June 2, 1854. On June 16 *Frederick Douglass' Paper* reported on two kinds of resistance. One

story reported the arrest of the Rev. Thomas Wentworth Higginson "on the charge of participating in the recent attempt in Massachusetts to rescue Anthony Burns." The other, "Crime against Humanity," was the impassioned sermon that the Rev. Theodore Parker had delivered in Boston on June 4, two days after Burns was shipped back to Virginia.

Near the end of the sermon, Parker characterizes the Fugitive Slave Law as "a long wedge, thin at one end, wide at the other; it is entered between the rotten planks of our SHIP OF STATE; a few blows thereon, will enforce more than the South thinks of—a little more, and we shall go to pieces." Parker's apocalyptic, nautical imagery provides a political as well as journalistic context for the "news" story that Douglass reported on August 11 about a real-life Moby Dick that had been captured years ago after stoving in the side of a ship.

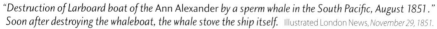

"Destruction of Larboard boat of the Ann Alexander *by a sperm whale in the South Pacific, August 1851." Soon after destroying the whaleboat, the whale stove the ship itself.* Illustrated London News, *November 29, 1851.*

The one other mention of *Moby-Dick* that I have so far found in *Frederick Douglass' Paper* appeared soon after the novel was published, on December 25, 1851. The table of contents for the December issue of *Holden's Dollar Magazine* includes *Moby-Dick; or the Whale*, the full title of the novel. The *Dollar* was edited by Charles Briggs, the "B" who had praised both Melville and Douglass so highly in the same issue of the *National Anti-Slavery Standard* in 1847. The item in his December issue was a reprint of the review of *Moby-Dick* that Evert Duyckinck had published in the November 15 issue of *The Literary World*—the first to equate Moby Dick with the *Ann Alexander* whale.

Duyckinck begins his review by calling attention to the "singular coincidence" between the "catastrophe" at the end of the book and the "staggering" act that had made the *Ann Alexander* whale familiar to readers "throughout the United States." In the process of comparing Melville's whale with the *Ann Alexander's*, Duyckinck calls Moby Dick the "hero" of the novel.

Earlier in November 1851 Melville had made his own connection between his fictional whale and the real one in a reply to a letter from Duyckinck about the *Ann Alexander* whale. "Crash! Comes Moby Dick himself (as you justly say) & reminds me of what I have been about for part of the last year or two. . . . Ye Gods! what a Commentator is this Ann Alexander whale. What he has to say is short & pithy & very much to the point. I wonder if my evil art has raised this monster." Douglass, whether he knew it or not, would have had Melville's own sanction for the headline in which the *Ann Alexander* whale and Moby Dick are equated.

Because copies of the *North Star* and *Frederick Douglass' Paper* are very rare, I have not been able to do a page-by-page search through each one for any other allusions to Melville or his work. Fortunately, the Accessible Archives recently created an electronic data base by which individual words or phrases can be searched in these papers from 1847 to 1855 (not yet reaching James McCune Smith's 1856 allusion to *Moby-Dick*). Typing Melville's titles into this data base revealed another significant allusion to Melville's writing in *Frederick Douglass' Paper*.

After the critical and financial failure of his novel *Pierre* in 1852, Melville began writing short stories for periodical publications that paid by the page. From 1853 to 1856 all of his new fiction appeared in one of two monthly magazines, *Harper's* and *Putnam's*, founded in 1850 and 1853, respectively. In its "Literary Notices" section, *Frederick Douglass' Paper* closely followed the monthly issues of both publications. On December 8, 1854 Douglass informed his readers that the December issue of *Putnam's* "has come, and a very good number it is." Among the pieces singled out is "a new edition of ISRAEL POTTER." On March 2, 1855, *Frederick Douglass' Paper* notes that "Israel Potter" is continued in the March issue of *Putnam's*, which is again "a very interesting and entertaining number."

Israel Potter, a novel-length story, was published serially in *Putnam's* from July 1854 through March 1855, before it appeared in book form. Because contributions in *Putnam's* were anonymous, some readers would not have known that these monthly installments were by Melville. However, Melville's authorship was widely acknowledged in other publications, so Douglass is likely to have known that Melville had written the story. As an editor himself, he closely followed such developments in the trade. He would also have known that Charles Briggs had been the chief editor of *Putnam's* since its first issue in January 1853.

Putnam's was the perfect outlet for such Melville stories as *Israel Potter* and *Benito Cereno.* In his first editorial in January 1853, Briggs promised to present American writers who would critique both national and international affairs through "the acutest observation, and the most trenchant thought, illustrated by whatever wealth of erudition, of imagination, and of experience" could be brought to bear. These are exactly the qualities that Briggs had brought to his own comparison between cannibalism in *Typee* and slavery the South in the *National Anti-Slavery Standard* in 1847. As Sheila Post-Lauria has shown, *Putnam's* deliberately set out to challenge the more conventional expectations that *Harper's* had established for its readers.

Notice of *Israel Potter* in *Frederick Douglass' Paper* offers a new perspective from which to view this work and its reception. Like *Benito Cereno* a year later, *Israel Potter* is Melville's rewriting of another man's story—in this case *The Life and Remarkable Adventures of Israel R. Potter,* published by Henry Trumbull in 1824, in which the real-life Israel, after fighting the British in the Battle of Bunker Hill, became a prisoner of war and ended up living in abject poverty in a London slum for more than forty years.

Melville's fictionalized account of the story received favorable attention while it was serialized in *Putnam's,* but it later became one of the last of Melville's novels to emerge from a century of obscurity. Not until after the Vietnam War did this episodic, anti-heroic story about an "anonymous private" begin to inspire some sustained attention. Only after the Civil Rights agitation of the 1960s did *Benito Cereno* begin to receive the kind of sustained attention that has recently raised it to a masterpiece. In this respect Briggs's trenchant editorial eye has served this age as well as his own.

Beyond its untraditional, anti-heroic glimpse into the era of the Revolutionary War (its first two installments were entitled "A Fourth of July Story"), *Israel Potter* would have had contemporary resonance for non-white, anti-slavery readers in 1854–55. Israel spends the most dramatic moments of his life, in New England as well as in Old England, as a "fugitive." Melville's use of that word invites comparison to Anthony Burns and other fugitives at the mercy of the Fugitive Slave Law, especially in Massachusetts. The real-life Israel grew up in Rhode Island, but Melville transplants his fictional counterpart to Massachusetts. Growing up in the Berkshire mountains, young Israel could never have imagined that "he himself like a beast should be hunted through half of Old England, as a runaway rebel."

Such carefully modulated language in the first chapter extends even to the Berkshire birds. Permanent residents include the "lordly eagle" that rules the Housatonic valley, the "ruffian" hawk that circles "lazily" below him, and an "audacious" crow that "pecks" at the hawk. In the summer these are supplemented by "smaller and less famous fowl," including yellow and blue birds that "flit" and "sport," whereas "the red robin seems an incendiary putting torch to the trees. . . . But in autumn those gay northerners, the birds, return to their southern plantations." Published one month after Anthony Burns had been forcibly returned to Virginia, such linguistic modulations would have registered with some abolitionists. So would the statement that Israel, having "deemed his father's conduct unreasonable and oppressive . . . emancipated himself from his sire."

The reprint from *Typee* in the *North Star* in 1848, the references to *Moby-Dick* in *Frederick Douglass' Paper* in 1851, 1854, and 1856, and the notices of *Israel Potter* in

First installment of "Israel Potter" in the July 1854 issue of Putnam's Monthly *magazine.*

ISRAEL POTTER; OR, FIFTY YEARS OF EXILE.

A FOURTH OF JULY STORY.

CHAPTER I.

THE BIRTHPLACE OF ISRAEL.

THE traveller who at the present day is content to travel in the good old Asiatic style, neither rushed along by a locomotive, nor dragged by a stage-coach ; who is willing to enjoy hospitalities at far-scattered farmhouses, instead of paying his bill at an inn ; who is not to be frightened by any amount of loneliness, or to be deterred by the roughest roads or the highest hills ; such a traveller in the eastern part of Berkshire, Mass., will find ample food for poetic reflection in the singular scenery of a country, which, owing to the ruggedness of the soil and its lying out of the track of all public conveyances, remains almost as unknown to the general tourist as the interior of Bohemia.

Travelling northward from the township of Otis, the road leads for twenty or thirty miles towards Windsor, lengthwise upon that long broken spur of heights which the Green Mountains of Vermont send into Massachusetts. For nearly the whole of the distance, you have the continual sensation of being upon some terrace in the moon. The feeling of the plain or the valley is never yours ; scarcely the feeling of the earth. Unless by a sudden precipitation of the road you find yourself plunging into some gorge; you pass on, and on, and on, upon the crests or slopes of pastoral mountains, while far below, mapped out in its beauty, the valley of the Housatonic lies endlessly along at your feet. Often, as your horse gaining some lofty level tract, flat as a table, trots gayly over the almost deserted and sodded road, and your admiring eye sweeps the broad landscape beneath, you seem to be Boötes driving in heaven. Save a potato field here and there, at long intervals, the whole country is either in wood or pasture. Horses, cattle and sheep are the principal inhabitants of these mountains. But all through the year lazy columns of smoke rising from the depths of the forest, proclaim the presence of that half-outlaw, the charcoal-burner ; while in early spring added curls of vapor show that the maple sugar-boiler is also at work. But as for farming as a regular vocation, there is not much of it here. At any rate, no man by that means accumulates a fortune from this thin and rocky soil ; all whose arable parts have long since been nearly exhausted.

Yet during the first settlement of the country, the region was not unproductive. Here it was that the original settlers came, acting upon the principle well-known to have regulated their choice of site, namely, the high land in preference to the low, as less subject to the unwholesome miasmas generated by breaking into the rich valleys and alluvial bottoms of primeval regions. By degrees, however, they quitted the safety of this sterile elevation, to brave the dangers of richer though lower fields. So that at the present day, some of those mountain townships present an aspect of singular abandonment. Though they have never known aught but peace and health, they, in one lesser aspect at least, look like countries depopulated by plague and war. Every mile or two a house is passed untenanted. The strength of the framework of these ancient buildings enables them long to resist the encroachments of decay. Spotted gray and green with the weather-stain, their timbers seem to have lapsed back into their woodland original, forming part now of the general picturesqueness of the natural scene. They are of extraordinary size, compared with modern farm-houses. One peculiar feature is the immense chimney, of light gray stone, perforating the middle of the roof like a tower.

On all sides are seen the tokens of ancient industry. As stone abounds throughout these mountains, that material was, for fences, as ready to the hand as wood, besides being much more durable. Consequently the landscape is intersected in all directions with walls of uncommon neatness and strength.

The number and length of these walls is not more surprising than the size of some of the blocks comprising them. The very Titans seemed to have been at work. That so small an army as the first settlers must needs have been, should have taken such wonderful pains to inclose so ungrateful a soil ; that they should have accomplished such herculean undertakings with so slight prospect of reward ; this is a consideration which gives us a significant hint of the temper of the men of the Revolutionary era.

Nor could a fitter country be found

1854 and 1855, raise questions about what Douglass thought of Melville and his writing during this extremely intense period in his own editorial, oratorical, and political life. If he owned copies of these or other Melville works, it would be most illuminating to see markings or annotations he may have written. Tragically, any books by Melville may well have perished in the fire at his house in Rochester in 1872 that destroyed much of his early library along with complete runs of the *North Star* and *Frederick Douglass' Paper*. Still, the evidence presented in this chapter does establish that Frederick Douglass and his circle were aware of Herman Melville and his fiction from *Typee* up through the presidential election of 1856.

Although Melville scholars since the 1950s have scoured nineteenth-century newspapers and periodicals for the smallest mention of Melville or his works, no one, until John Stauffer in 2002, noted James McCune Smith's politically acute quotation from *Moby-Dick* in *Frederick Douglass' Paper* in 1856. Nor did any Melville scholars, so far as is known, notice the "Tattooing" passage that Douglass reprinted in the *North Star* in 1848, or the several references to *Moby-Dick* and *Israel Potter* that appeared in *Frederick Douglass' Paper* between 1851 and 1855.

Similarly, no sustained attention has yet been given to the reception of Melville's works in other anti-slavery publications. These range from general-circulation newspapers with a strong anti-slavery emphasis, such as Weed's Albany *Evening Journal* and Elizur Wright's Boston *Chronotype*, to publications explicitly dedicated to anti-slavery issues, such as the *National Anti-Slavery Standard* in New York City and the *National Era* in Washington, D.C. Commentary from such publications has only irregularly been included in compilations of nineteenth-century responses to Melville, and

seldom with attention to the abolitionist or anti-slavery context in which it appears.

I can give one example here of why a broader focus of this kind is needed. Douglass's decision to publish "Tattooing" from *Typee* in the *North Star* on June 2, 1848, is noteworthy in itself. It takes on additional meaning in view of the fact that a year earlier, on June 3, 1847, the *National Era* had printed "The Tattooers of La Dominica," an entire chapter of *Omoo*, Melville's sequel to *Typee*. Douglass's "Tattooing" was therefore responding not only to Melville's first novel but to the reception of his second novel in the most literary of the *North Star's* anti-slavery competitors.

The *National Era* is best known today for having published *Uncle Tom's Cabin* in installments in 1851 and 1852. With the abolitionist poet John Greenleaf Whittier as literary editor from its inaugural issue in 1847, the *National Era* gave much more attention to literary affairs than did the *Liberator* in Boston or the *North Star* in Rochester. The *National Anti-Slavery Standard* greatly expanded its own literary coverage when it hired James Russell Lowell, with considerable fanfare, as its corresponding editor in April 1848.

Douglass, operating with a smaller staff than any of his competitors, did not have a literary editor until Julia Griffiths arrived in Rochester in May 1849. She came from New York, where she and her sister Elizabeth had been the two English ladies whose walk on Broadway with Douglass resulted in his "Colorphobia" essay. Griffiths was responsible for the "Literary Notices" section of *Frederick Douglass' Paper* until she returned to England in the fall of 1855. Her work allowed his paper to take note of interesting features in monthly publications such as *Holden's, Harper's,* and *Putnam's,* but made no attempt to compete with the high-profile literary ambitions of Whittier in the *National Era* or Lowell in the *Standard*.

Frederick Douglass, carte-de-visite, circa 1862. S. M. Fassett photograph, New Bedford Whaling Museum.

Herman Melville, carte-de-visite, after 1860 ambrotype. Berkshire Athenaeum.

CHAPTER FIVE

TRACES OF DOUGLASS IN MELVILLE'S WRITING

Melville and Douglass were extremely well read. Each often alluded to Biblical phrases and Shakespearean dialogue, although without identifying his source. When Ishmael confesses to having "little or no money in my purse" in the second sentence of *Moby-Dick*, he is making a silent allusion to Iago's "Put money in thy purse" in *Othello*. He extends that allusion a few pages later when he declares that "a purse is but a rag unless you have something in it."

When Douglass writes of "Charms, conjuration—mighty magic" in "Colorphobia in New York!" he is using Othello's words from the same scene from which Ishmael borrows Iago's purse. A year later he borrows a different phrase from the same speech when describing the attack on himself and the two English ladies at the Battery. Of course, Melville and Douglass were not the only self-educated Americans in their generation on such familiar terms with Shakespeare. Isaiah Rynders also "effortlessly quoted" from the Bible and Shakespeare's plays.

Douglass, in his newspaper, occasionally refers to Melville or his works directly. Melville, writing fiction, tends to allude to Douglass in the silent manner of the above Shakespearean allusions. The reader needs to know about Douglass's life or writing in order for the allusion to be meaningful. The same is true with the references to African and African-American culture that Sterling Stuckey uncovered in *Moby-Dick* and *Benito Cereno*—or with those in *Moby-Dick* to the painter J. M. W. Turner this author discovered. As Stuckey notes, Melville achieved his deepest aesthetic effects "by fusing models from widely divergent cultural worlds before concealing them deep beneath surface appearances." Douglass's cultural world is another of those that Melville fused beneath the surface with a "subtlety beyond the bounds familiar to his readership."

This chapter suggests a variety of ways in which "traces" of Douglass appear in Melville's writing even if his name does not. Some of the "fast-fish" connections lurking beneath the surface are closer to Ishmael's "strand of cobweb" than to his "nine-inch cable." Other possible connections may simply be similarities in the writing of two men who addressed shared subjects in "neighborly style." By the time Melville was writing *Moby-Dick* and *Benito Cereno* in the 1850s, however, his cumulative response to the cultural world of Douglass was resulting in a more profound level of engagement. Certain turns of phrase and thematic insights seem as close to those of Douglass as was the head of the harpooned whale to the ship's timbers of the *Ann Alexander* in the news story that Douglass printed as "Moby Dick Captured" in 1854.

Typee

Earlier we saw that Melville's character Marnoo in *Typee* may have been modeled on Douglass, especially given the visibility of Douglass himself as an author and orator in Albany in June and July 1845. Melville writes in a way that suggests Douglass's most prominent physical, oratorical, and social characteristics whether or not he actually heard Douglass speak. Such a silent allusion would be a very significant connection between the two men at the beginning of Melville's career. Rereading Chapter 18 of *Typee* with an awareness of Douglass's visits to Albany and Troy reveals certain elements of Tommo's response to Marnoo that raise additional questions as to whether Melville may actually have met Douglass at that time.

Tommo, although he admires Marnoo's physical beauty, oratorical skill, and social ease, feels considerable unease in his presence. He confesses to being jealous of this celebrated personage even before Marnoo

arrives in the village ("so vain had I become by the lavish attention to which I had been accustomed"). Even so, he cannot help being impressed by his first sight of "one of the most striking specimens of humanity that I ever beheld." Tommo overcomes his envy enough to offer Marnoo a seat next to him. "But without deigning to notice the civility, or even the more incontrovertible fact of my existence, the stranger passed on, utterly regardless of me. . . . Had the belle of the season, in the pride of her beauty and power, been cut in a place of public resort by some supercilious exquisite, she could not have felt greater indignation than I did at this unexpected slight." The intensity of Tommo's emotion is so disproportionate to the cause that one wonders if Melville is responding to some personal slight that he received—either on Nukuheva or in Albany.

As soon as Marnoo begins his oration, Tommo is again deeply impressed with the man, even though he is ignorant of the lan-

Review of Typee *in* The United States Democratic Review, *May 1846. Note misprint of Melville's first name.* National Archives.

1846.] *Notices of New Books.*

Typee; a Residence in the Marquesas. By SHERMAN MELVILLE. Wiley & Putnam, 161 Broadway, New-York.

These volumes are perhaps of the most interesting of Wiley & Putnam's deservedly popular " Library of American Books." The adventures are of a youth in the romantic islands of the Pacific Ocean, among a strange race of beings, whose manners and modes of life are by no means familiar to us. ' The scenes, described with peculiar animation and vivacity, are of a description that must task the credulity of most plain matter of fact people; yet they are without doubt faithfully sketched, and afford evidence of " how little half the world knows how the other half lives." The fairy vales of ·the Marquesas are represented as presenting all that nature and a most favored clime can contribute to the happiness and enjoyment of man, and inhabited by a primitive race with whom the intercourse of the author appears to have been on the best possible terms. The volumes are of a most amusing and interesting description.

guage in which he is speaking. Following the oration, after working his way through all of the male and female natives in the crowd, Marnoo finally sits down next to him. "As soon as our palms met," Tommo recalls, Marnoo "bent towards me, and murmured in musical accents,—'How you do?' 'How long you been in this bay?' 'You like this bay?'" Tommo's jealous indignation quickly melts into admiration. He asks Marnoo how he came to speak English so well when raised on a Polynesian island. Marnoo asks Tommo how he suddenly became a resident in a Polynesian valley after having come from far across the sea. If Melville did meet Douglass in Albany or Troy in June or July 1845, his own complex emotions may be embedded in Tommo's response to Marnoo.

Such possible biographical residue is only one of the ways in which Douglass might have left his "trace" in *Typee*. Thematically there are striking similarities between Douglass's autobiography of 1845 and Melville's novel of 1846. In the Appendix to his 1845 *Narrative* Douglass gives a spirited defense of the "tone and manner" in which he has attacked the inhumanity of Christianity in the South. He is particularly severe on the those Christians who "love the heathen on the other side of the globe . . . while they despise and totally neglect the heathen at their own doors." Melville, in his Preface to *Typee,* defends certain passages in his book "which may be thought to bear rather hard" upon the missionaries in the South Seas. He has included them because they are "based upon facts admitting of no contradiction." Melville certainly did not need Douglass's attack on southern Christianity to make his own critique of South Seas missionaries, but Douglass's forthright example might have given Melville the courage to offer his own critique even in the face of certain opposition.

The Christian resistance that each encountered in 1846 sometimes came from the

same publication. On April 9 the New York *Evangelist* so severely objected to the depiction of missionaries in *Typee* that Wiley and Putnam forced Melville to remove all offending passages from the revised New York edition that was published in August. On August 8 the same *Evangelist* published a bitter attack by the Reverend Samuel Hanson Cox on Douglass's activity in England, to which Douglass replied in a restrained, scathing letter published in the *Liberator* in November.

Neither author's social criticism was limited to Christianity. Each was incensed, and even astounded, by the degree to which men who thought themselves civilized could be capable of the cruelest savagery. Although Douglass's autobiographical narrative dealt primarily with the domestic issue of slavery in the southern United States, and Melville's fictional narrative dealt primarily with the international issue of colonialism in the South Seas, there was plenty of room for common ground given the talent and temperament of each.

Melville's strongest anti-colonial assertion in *Typee* appears in Chapter 17 (which comes immediately before the arrival of Marnoo): "the fiend-like skill we display in the invention of all manner of death-dealing engines, the vindictiveness with which we carry on our wars, and the misery and desolation that follow in their train, are enough of themselves to distinguish the white civilized man as the most ferocious animal on the face of the earth." Wiley and Putnam cut this and all other passages critical of colonial imperialism, too, from the revised New York edition.

Melville's rhetorically bold declaration that "the white civilized man" is "the most ferocious animal on the face of the earth" would have found plenty of domestic support in Douglass's *Narrative*—even in the parts extracted in the June 9, 1845 edition of the Albany *Evening Journal*. In addition to Gore's cold-blooded murder of his slave Denby by shooting him through the head as he stood in the river, and Beal Bondy's cold-blooded murder of a neighbor's slave by shooting him as he hunted for oysters, the extracts in that day's issue also included the sentence describing the murder by Mrs. Hicks of her fifteen-year-old enslaved baby-sitter for the crime of falling asleep during the night. "Mrs. Hicks, finding the girl slow to move, jumped from her bed, seized an oak stick of wood by the fireplace, and with it broke the girl's nose and breast-bone, and thus ended her life." Passages such as these (whether Melville had heard them when Douglass lectured in Albany or Troy, read them in the *Narrative*, or simply read them in Weed's paper) might have enabled Melville to general-ize much more broadly about the "ferocity" of "white civilized man" than his own experience in the South Seas would have allowed.

Douglass's 1845 *Narrative* may have left stylistic, as well as biographical and thematic, traces upon *Typee*. Melville and Douglass were both adept at abstract rhetorical formulations such as the one about the ferocity of the white man. But each was also a master of the telling anecdote. Along with Denby, Gore, and Mrs. Hicks, Mrs. Thomas Hamilton is one of those who make an unforgettable cameo appear-ance in Douglass's *Narrative*. The owner of two female slaves, Henrietta and Mary, Mrs. Hamilton lived "directly opposite" the Auld house in which Douglass had lived on Philpot Street in Baltimore, and young Frederick vis-ited that house

> nearly every day. Mrs. Hamilton used to sit in a large chair in the middle of the room, with a heavy cowskin always by her side, and scarce an hour passed during the day but was marked by the blood of one of those slaves. The girls seldom passed her without her saying, "Move faster, you black gip!" at the same

time giving them a blow with the cowskin over the head or shoulders, often drawing blood. She would then say, "Take that, you black gip!"—continuing, "If you don't move faster, I'll move you."

Mrs. Hamilton's counterpart in *Typee* is "a robust, red-faced, and very lady-like personage, a missionary's spouse" in Honolulu. Every day "for months together [she] took her regular air-ings in a little go-cart drawn by two islanders, one an old grey-headed man, and the other a rogueish stripling." Drawn "through the streets of the town in this stylish equipage, the lady looks about her as magnificently as any queen driven in state to her coronation. A sudden ele-vation, and a sandy road, however, soon disturb her serenity. The small wheels become imbed-ded in the loose soil." Does this "tender-hearted lady . . . think a little" about the bodies of these "poor heathen" whose souls she has crossed an ocean to save? "Not she; she could not dream of it." Instead, "she retains her seat and bawls out, 'Hookee! Hookee!' (pull, pull.) . . . At last the good lady loses all patience: 'Hookee! Hookee!' and rap goes the heavy handle of her huge fan over the naked skull of the old savage, while the young one shies to one side and keeps beyond its range." Her "*draught* bipeds" are in this manner "civilized into draught horses, and evangelized into beasts of burden."

Not only the anecdotes themselves but the manner of their telling and their moral import are strikingly similar. Perhaps this is simple coincidence. Or perhaps Douglass's story about Mrs. Hamilton in Baltimore reminded Melville of a missionary spouse he had actually seen in Honolulu. If so, he may have consciously or unconsciously shaped her story to resemble Douglass's story of Mrs. Hamilton, each ending with the white woman's imperative refrain ("Move faster, you *black gip!*" and "Hookee! Hookee!"). Regardless, the degree to which the Baltimore and Honolulu anecdotes deliver an identical message in a similar style shows a striking affinity between the two authors. John S. Wright recently wrote that Douglass's 1845 *Narrative* "succeeded by intuitively alternating onrushing picturesque episodes with essayistic digressions." The same is emphatically true of Melville's 1846 *Typee*.

Two anti-slavery publications responded to *Typee* in ways already noted: the *National Anti-Slavery Standard* by publishing "B's" highly appreciative review on May 27, 1847; the *North Star* by reprinting "Tattooing" on June 2, 1848. On the same day as the review in the *National Anti-Slavery Standard* appeared, the *National Era* in Washington, D. C., published its own high praise for *Typee*. John Smith the Younger, in his "Literary Gossip" column, notes that Melville's new book, *Omoo*, had already "met with a very rapid sale." Yet "[it] is not equal to Typee. The latter is one of the most fascinating books which has ever been composed—full of the most splendid imagery and enchanting description. Herman Melville stands, in my opinion, in the very first rank of American writers." John Smith the Younger was a pseudonym for James A. Houston. His praise of *Typee* has been overlooked by Melville scholars (as has much of the response of the *National Era* to Melville in general).

The praise for *Typee* in the "Literary Gossip" section of the *National Era* was only an appetizer for an enthusiastic review of *Omoo* in its book reviews. Whereas "B" in the *Standard* gave general praise for *Omoo* but wrote more specifically about *Typee*, the *National Era* did the opposite, presenting an extended review of *Omoo* on May 27, 1847, that was followed by additional extracts from the new book on June 3 and again on July 8. Melville's chapter "The Tattooers of La Dominica" was one of the June 3 extracts. It contrasts in interesting ways with the

J. Storer, "An Inhabitant of the Island of Nuku Hiva," from Voyages and Travels, Vol. 1, *by G. H. Langsdorff, 1813. Courtesy of William Reese Company, New Haven.*

"Tattooing" passage that Douglass was to reprint from *Typee* a year later. The narrator gains access to the tattooers of La Dominica through a white man who, unlike Tommo, *had* allowed his face to be tattooed. The tone of this passage is not as anxious as the one Douglass reprints from *Typee*, as the tattoo masters of this island work with the elegance of "genteel tailors" who know that "a suit to be worn for life should be well cut."

Omoo

From an anti-slavery point of view, the most interesting characters in *Omoo* (1847) are Baltimore and Bembo, dark-skinned mariners prominent in the early chapters as the British whaleship *Julia* sails from the Marquesas to Tahiti. Baltimore is introduced as "the poor old black cook." A footnote indicates that he is called Baltimore "from the place of his birth, he being a runaway Maryland slave." Bembo is introduced as a "New Zealand harpooner," and referred to as "the Mowree," Melville's spelling for the Maori—New Zealand natives notorious during the nineteenth century for their fierce resistance to British colonization.

In Chapter 19, called "More about Bembo," the captain and the mate go ashore to consult with the Consul in Tahiti, leaving Bembo in charge of the ship. "Though not yet civilized," Bembo is, "according to sea usages, which know no exceptions, held superior to the sailors." Personally he is "below the ordinary height; but then, he was all compact, and under his swart, tattooed skin, the muscles worked like steel rods. Hair, crisp, and coal black, curled over shaggy brows, and ambushed small, intense eyes, always on the glare. In short, he was none of your effeminate barbarians." His courage as a whaler is attested to by the time he jumped onto a whale's back and delivered the iron in person. Whereas Baltimore embodies the submissiveness that his white shipmates expect, Bembo is capable of fierce resistance.

The anonymous reviewer of *Omoo* for the *National Era* on May 27, 1847, is fascinated by the book and captivated by Bembo. He begins with an eloquent evocation of the romantic appeal of "Life on the ocean wave" to "the imagination of the landsman." Next he addresses Melville's ability to narrate the "wildest adventures" with such an air of reality as to "bewilder the imagination of the reader." In a third paragraph he cites an early chapter of *Omoo* in which a whaling captain shoots at some natives on shore for the sport of it. After quoting Melville's assertion that "wanton acts of cruelty like this are not unusual on the part of sea captains landing at islands comparatively unknown," the reviewer finds it "almost incredible the light in which many sailors regard these naked heathens. They hardly consider them human. But it is a curious fact, that the more ignorant and degraded men are, the

more contemptuously they look upon those whom they deem their inferiors. . . . This is true of landsmen in America as well as sailors in the South Seas." Among "landsmen in America," the masters and overseers in Douglass's 1845 *Narrative* would have been obvious examples of such cruelty and contempt for readers of the *National Era* in 1847.

After this preparation, the reviewer devotes the rest of his review to "Bembo, the Mowree," whose story is "of thrilling interest." In Chapter 23 Bembo is again left in charge of the ship in the absence of Jermin, the mate. When Jermin returns he indulges the entire crew in drink and Bembo is left alone at the helm, deserted by Sydney Ben, an Australian convict who was to have shared the watch with him. When Bembo calls Ben back to duty and the latter strikes him, "the two men came together like magnets," engaging in a furious, evenly matched brawl until "at last the white man's head fell back, and his face grew purple. Bembo's teeth were at his throat." At this point their crewmates "hauled the savage off, but not until repeatedly struck on the head would he let go." Once Bembo is vanquished, his shipmates, thinking him "cowed," leave him on the deck, rejoicing in his humiliation and leaving him alone only "after rating him in sailor style, for a cannibal and a coward."

The extract in the *National Era* begins with the above fight and continues verbatim for a chapter and a half. Bembo at first writhes in agony after being separated from his foe. He then refreshes himself by pouring buckets of water over his head. During the night watch the narrator awakes to see Bembo at the helm, steering the ship in a freshening breeze directly into the broken surf of a coral reef. Only at the last minute, "after a desperate struggle," is Bembo "torn from the helm" and the ship saved from sure destruction. The narrator later surmises that the "only motive" for his "intention to destroy us [was] a desire to revenge the contumely heaped upon him the night previous."

In Chapter 24, when members of the crew realize what the Mowree had tried to do, they grab him and threaten to kill him. First they want to "Strike him down!" and "Hang him at the main-yard!" Then they decide to "give him a sea-toss," shouting "Overboard with him!" They have almost wrestled him overboard when the mate, awakened from his "drunken nap" by the scuffle directly over his head, enters the fray, planting his "iron hand upon the Mowree's shoulder" and crying, "There are two of us now; and as you serve him, you serve me!" Even after learning exactly what Bembo had tried to do, Jermin stands firm: "Ye can't have him; I'll hand him over to the consul; so for'ard with ye, I say; when there's any drowning to be done, I'll pass the word." As Jermin stands his ground, the crowd disperses. The narrator concludes the chapter by declaring that "no one but Jermin could have prevented this murder." These same words conclude the extract in the *National Era*.

This episode works so well as an adventure story because of Melville's narrative flair, Bembo's tenacity in battle, his ruthlessness in revenge, and Jermin's courage in saving him from his shipmates. Its drama would have been heightened for any anti-slavery reader who connected Jermin's action in saving Bembo with Captain Judkins' action in saving Douglass on the *Cambria* in 1845. Douglass's account of the "THE AMERICAN MOB ON A BRITISH STEAMER PACKET" was so widely reprinted that anti-slavery readers in Boston, Albany, New York, and Washington could have been in a position to make such a connection.

Melville's fictional episode with Bembo releases deep racial tensions similar to those of Douglass's real-life episode on the *Cambria*—

the immediate polarization of a ship once race becomes an issue, the suppressed rage of the figure who has been stigmatized, the alacrity with which a white mob attacks a colored person whose words or actions have offended, the courage of a white captain or mate in defending a person of color from a white mob. Melville's account of Bembo's resistance, reprinted with such acclaim in the *National Era* in 1847, opened up a fictional subject that Douglass was to address in *The Heroic Slave* in 1853, followed by Melville's *Benito Cereno* two years later.

By consistently referring to Bembo as "the Mowree," Melville also relates his story to real-life events in the South Seas, of which he would have known simply from reading Thurlow Weed's newspaper in Albany. Bembo has shipped on board the *Julia* at "the Bay of Islands" in New Zealand. On July 19, 1845, the Albany *Evening Journal* reported that "the natives of New Zealand had risen upon the English inhabitants of the Bay of Islands and completely overpowered" them. After killing twenty to thirty people and driving the rest away, they had burned the town. In "Further News from New Zealand" on July 24, Weed printed a letter from the captain of the U.S. *St. Louis*, who rescued the survivors from Kororerika, "the English village" destroyed by the "natives." The American captain fears "that the result of these troubles will be, in future, the extermination of the natives by the English."

Bembo's prospects in the novel are similarly ominous. The mate, after saving him from the mob, "put him in double irons" and "locked him up in the captain's state-room." He is not allowed to go ashore with the rest of the crew in Tahiti. When "the British Colonial Barque Julia" sails away from Tahiti with a new crew, Bembo is "carried to sea in irons, down in the hold. What eventually happened to him, we never heard." This is the chilling sequel to the

Painting of the Lucy Ann *from the journal of Captain Joseph T. Chase, whaleship* Massachusetts, *1850. Lucy Ann was the Australian whaleship on which Melville sailed from the Marquesas to Tahiti. The voyage became the inspiration for his fictional depiction of the* Julia *in* Omoo. *New Bedford Whaling Museum.*

"thrilling" adventure in which Jermin spared Bembo from the mob.

Omoo, like *Typee*, mediates between the "native" and "civilized" worlds. Because its narrator is able to move more freely from place to place than was Tommo, he plays a mediating role similar to that of Marnoo. Melville indicates in the Preface to *Omoo* that "the title of the work ... signifies a rover" in the Marquesas dialect. It applies especially to those natives who are free to "wander from one island to another" because they are *taboo*. Marnoo was the epitome of such a rover in *Typee*. *Omoo* is written in the spirit of Marnoo by a "civilized" narrator who aspires to his condition of fluid movement across spatial, linguistic, political, and psychological boundaries. The book is genial, expansive, and fluid, but it has a chill.

The roving sailor/narrator, however sensitive he may be, is implicated in the actions of that captain who shoots natives for sport, and, however much he may admire Bembo for his tenacity or Jermin for his courage, he can do nothing as the *Julia* sails off with Bembo in irons. Acknowledging that the activities of missionaries have brought some benefits to the natives of Tahiti, Melville's narrator cannot avoid seeing that "intercourse with the Europeans had tended to debase, rather than exalt their condition." Here, as elsewhere in the world, "facts are more eloquent than words." Actual conditions in these Christianized islands suggest that the natives of Imeeo and Tahiti were doomed. Western missionaries preach "salvation" but natives are dying. "Like other uncivilized beings, brought into contact with Europeans, [they] must here remain stationary until utterly extinct."

Having changed his New York publisher to Harper and Brothers for *Omoo*, Melville could again critique the intersection of colonial and missionary impulses in the South Seas in the kind of language that Wiley and Putnam had expurgated from the revised *Typee*. Thurlow Weed's newspaper, in its second notice of *Omoo* on May 3, 1847, defended Melville against future evangelical attacks as stoutly as it had defended Douglass against the slaveholders on the *Cambria*. The reviewer for the *Evening Journal*, not having reached the second volume of *Omoo*, "understands" that it

> *gives an unfavorable account of the character and labors of Missionaries in the Polynesian Islands. In this respect the Book will probably give offense. If, however, Missionaries in that portion of the World are less faithful and devoted than the hundreds of pious and self-sacrificing Christian Philanthropists who teach by example as well as precept, in China, India, Birmah, &c., it is well that the fact be known.*

Mardi

In *Mardi* (1849) Melville abandoned the pretense of writing fact-based narratives about his experiences in the South Seas and let his imagination fly into unabashed romance, rhapsody, and allegory. In some ways this makes traces from Douglass and his fact-based world less likely than what may be present in *Typee* and *Omoo*. *Mardi* does not appear to have been reviewed by "B," or anyone else, in the *National Anti-Slavery Standard*, but on July 12, 1849, the *National Era* declared *Mardi* to be "a failure" simply from the "copious extracts we have seen." It was not alone in wishing that Melville "had confined himself to the kind of writing we find in Typee and Omoo." One of the most stinging rebukes had been George Ripley's May 10 declaration in the New York *Tribune* that Melville "had failed by leaving his sphere, which is that of graphic, poetic narration, and launching out into the dim, shadowy, spectral Mardian region of mystic speculation and wizard fancies."

The disappointment might have been particularly keen for partisans of the anti-slavery movement who had appreciated the direct social criticism in Melville's first two books. One such reader may have been Elizur Wright, the irrepressible abolitionist who was now editor of the Boston *Chronotype*. On June 9 he printed a "Gossip from Gotham" column that began by declaring that "Herman Melville's new work has greatly disappointed his old admirers." It concluded with this personal appeal: "Come back, O Herman, from thy cloudy, supermundane flight, to the vesssel's deck and the perfumed i[s]les, and many a true right hand will welcome thy return." In 1847 the *Chronotype* had reviewed both *Typee* and *Omoo* with an eye for social customs and belief systems, contrasting the "primitive valley of stark paganism" in the former

with the "mongrel mixture of savagism and Christianity" in the latter.

The fanciful flights that carried Melville from the topography of the South Seas into the allegorical realms of *Mardi* actually enabled him to address American slavery more directly than before—for any reader who managed to reach Chapter 162 out of 195 in a six-hundred-page book. In the political allegory near the end of the novel, Melville responds to revolutions in Europe and conditions in America early in 1848 by presenting Great Britain, France, and the United States as the imaginary realms of Dominora, Porpheero, and Vivenza. Taji, the narrator in this allegory, and Media, the Mardian King, are traveling with Babbalanja, Mohi, and Yoomy (who represent the philosopher, the historian, and the minstrel poet, respectively). Chapter 162, "They Visit the extreme South of Vivenza," is a fictional representation of the American South, with Nulli, the South Vivenza statesman, representing Senator John C. Calhoun of South Carolina.

Melville's Vivenza allows us to compare his depiction of slavery directly with that of Douglass in his 1845 *Narrative*, in his May 1848 speech at the Broadway Tabernacle, and in the pages of the *North Star* in 1848, the year in which Melville was writing the allegorical section of the novel in New York. (Melville had begun the novel after moving to New York in September 1847. His awareness of the *North Star* is likely to have increased after Douglass reproduced "Tattooing" from *Typee* in June 1848; the final proofs of *Mardi* were not complete until January 1849.) A comparison of the Vivenza section of *Mardi* with Douglass's depictions of slavery in 1848 shows a variety of ways in which the two men's authorial concerns continued to converge.

As Taji and his fellow Mardian voyagers approach the national capitol of Vivenza, they are at first impressed by the statue of "a helmeted female, the tutelary diety of Vivenza." As they draw nearer, they see an inscription that translates: "In-this-re-publi-can-land-all-men-are-born-free-and-equal." Then they see tiny characters, "Except-the-tribe-of-Hamo." As Media immediately points out, "This nullifies the other." Mohi thinks it "seems to have been added for a postscript." The phrase about the Hamo tribe satirizes not only the reality of slavery in the land of the "free-and-equal" but also the use of Biblical declarations about the "curse of Ham" as divine sanction for slavery itself.

The Biblical proscription against the Tribe of Ham was widely contested in America in the 1840s, but few attacks on the concept had been as devastating as the one Douglass launched in the opening chapter of his 1845 *Narrative*: "If the lineal descendants of Ham are alone to be scripturally enslaved," he argued, "it is certain that slavery at the south must soon become unscriptural." The reason for this is that "a very different-looking class of people are springing up at the south, and are now held in slavery, from those originally brought to this country from Africa; and if their increase will do no other good, it will do away the force of the argument, that God cursed Ham, and therefore American slavery is right." This new class of people consists of the "thousands . . . ushered into the world, annually, who, like myself, owe their existence to their white fathers, and those fathers most frequently their own masters." Douglass continued to undermine the "curse of Ham" concept in the April 7, June 2, June 16, September 22, October 20, and November 10, 1848 issues of the *North Star*.

As Taji and his companions look around the capitol of Vivenza, they see "a man with a collar round his neck, and the red marks of stripes on his back." The banner he is hoisting is "correspondingly striped" (the American flag). Arriving in the deep South of Vivenza in Chapter 162, they see "hundreds of collared men . . . toiling in trenches. . . . Standing grimly over these, were men unlike them; armed with long thongs, which descended upon the toilers, and made wounds. Blood and sweat mixed; and in great drops, fell." The leader of the men with thongs is Nulli, Melville's depiction of Senator Calhoun—"a cadaverous, ghost-like man; with a low ridge of forehead; hair, steel-gray; and wondrous eyes;—bright, nimble, as the twin Corposant balls, playing about the ends of ship's royal yards in gales."

When Babbalanja asks Nulli if the toilers in the trenches have souls, he says no. He also denies that the "collared man," who has warm flesh and a beating heart, is actually a man. When Yoomy and Mardi immediately cry out for God's judgment on "this accursed land," Nulli coolly argues that "these serfs are happier than thine; though thine, no collars wear; more happy as they are, than if free. Are they not fed, clothed, and cared for? Thy serfs pine for food: never yet did these, who have no thoughts, no cares."

All three of Nulli's arguments here—that slaves have no souls, that they are not actually men, and that they are "happier" than wage slaves in the north—had been addressed by Douglass in his 1845 *Narrative* and in untold speeches and essays. All are addressed in the *North Star* in 1848 in articles and reports specifically about Calhoun. One article on August 25 discusses Calhoun's recent "proclamation of nullification." Another reports his recent contention that the Declaration of Independence was in error in declaring all men to be created equal. Douglass's distinctive way of responding to Calhoun's arguments is seen in "Slaves are Happy and Contented!" in the June 2 issue that also contains "Tattooing" from *Typee*.

The June 2, 1848 issue of the North Star in which Douglass reprinted "Tattooing" from Typee. *National Archives.*

This article (signed with the initials of assistant editor John Dick) begins by admitting that "Now and then a case occurs, in which the slave prefers bondage to freedom." Such is a recent case, "paraded throughout the South as testimony in favor of the patriarchal institution." An "aged slave, who had been recently liberated in Virginia, and sent to Indiana when he was too old to work," decided to "to return to his old master. His heart was in 'Old Virginny,' and he had no happiness, even with liberty, in the land of strangers."

"Wonderful generosity!" is the *North Star's* commentary on this scenario. "When this negro was too old to work, he was turned adrift upon the world; when he could not take care of himself, he was sent among strangers!" In contrast is another instance which gives a truer picture of the "happy and contented" slave:

A slave trader from the south purchased a negro man, wife and child, in Covington, Kentucky, and placed them in jail for safe keeping. On Thursday night, the woman, in the excitement of despair, murdered her child, by cutting her throat, after which the man cut the woman's, and then his own. The former are dead—the latter was living at last accounts, with but faint hopes of his recovery.

"How hollow is the profession of Christianity, and how ridiculous it is to boast of freedom," concludes the *North Star* on June 2, "in a land where such scenes occur!"

When Nulli reiterates that slaves in the South "are content [and] shed no tears," Yoomy cries out, "Oh fettered sons of fettered mothers, conceived and born in manacles . . . how my stiff arm shivers to avenge you! 'Twere absolution for the matricide, to strike one rivet from their chains. My heart outswells its home!"

Nulli declares in response that slavery "'tis right and righteous!" He asserts that the church "champions it!—*I* swear it!" Yoomy prays to heaven that the enslaved "may yet find a way to loose their bond without one drop of blood. But hear me, Oro! were there no other way, and should their masters not relent, all honest hearts must cheer this tribe of Hamo on; though they cut their chains with blades thrice edged, and gory to the haft! 'Tis right to fight for freedom, whoever be the thrall!"

Douglass had argued the right of the enslaved to fight for their freedom throughout 1848, but the issue was of special concern during the May meetings of the American Anti-Slavery Society in New York. In the opening session at the Broadway Tabernacle on May 9, Douglass specifically addressed the plight of those slaves who had recently been recaptured after attempting to escape on the schooner *Pearl* in Washington, D.C. In the part of the speech that he reprinted near the passage from *Typee* in the *North Star* on June 2, he praises the courage of the men, women, and children who had attempted to escape from slavery in the national Capitol, only to be recaptured and "brought back in chains." To anyone who supports the slaveholder in a case such as this, he declares, in language anticipating that of Yoomy, "you may expect that the heart that beats against this bosom, will give utterance against you."

Douglass fully endorsed the resolution that was passed the next day in the Minerva Rooms "setting forth the rights of the slaves to escape." He was less sure about the proposal that "Slaveholders, as such, can have no rights . . . " which at first " . . . struck me unfavorably." Yet he did come to agree that those who hold slaves, including "the iron-hearted and brass-browed Calhoun . . . have forfeited all rights to be numbered with [the human] family."

Once Yoomy and his Mardian companions have established the right of the slave to resist, by violence if necessary, they complete their discussion of slavery by hoping against hope that some peaceful solution might still be found. "Humanity cries out against this vast enormity," declares Babbalanja, but "not one man knows a prudent remedy" Mohi warns that "these South savannahs may yet prove battle-fields." Yet, Babbalanja, in spite of seemingly insuperable obstacles, holds to his faith that "Time—all-healing Time—Time, great Philanthropist—Time must befriend these thralls!" Such was the long-range faith of Douglass and most Garrisonian abolitionists in the Anniversary meetings in New York in May 1848.

Douglass appealed directly to time at the end of his talk at the opening session in the Broadway Tabernacle on May 9. In spite of all of the evident opposition to the rights of the enslaved, "there is yet an under-current pervading the mass of this country . . . which shall one day rise up in one glorious fraternity for freedom." He ends his speech with these words: "There's a good time coming, boys, / A good time coming, / Wait a little longer. . . . / Cannon balls may aid the truth, / But thought's a weapon stronger, / We'll win the battle by its aid, / Wait a little longer."

Blassingame correctly identifies these lines as the first verse of Charles Mackay's poem "The Good Time Coming," but Douglass's more immediate allusion would have been to the musical setting of those words by the Hutchinson Family Singers. "There's a Good Time Coming" had been a signature song of these abolitionist singers since their return from England in 1846. When Douglass retold the story of the "mobocrats" on the *Cambria* in his *Life and Times* many decades later, he remembered the Hutchinson Family as "the sweet singers of anti-slavery and 'good time coming.'"

The 1848 Broadway Tabernacle speech that Douglass ended with the words of "There's a Good Time Coming" was immediately followed by the "soul-stirring song" that the Hutchinson Family Singers "poured down upon the audience from the gallery" to close the morning session. As the Hutchinsons often sang upon the inspiration of the moment rather than by a set program at the New York Anti-Slavery meetings, it seems likely that on this occasion they sang "There's a Good Time Coming" in response to Douglass's call.

In his Introduction to *The Story of the Hutchinsons* written shortly before his death in 1895, Douglass still remembered their

Cover to sheet music of "The Fugitive's Song," by Jesse Hutchinson, Jr., in honor of Frederick Douglass, "A Graduate from the Peculiar Institution." Published in 1845. *National Archives.*

Title page to "Slavery is a Hard Foe to Battle," written and published by Horace Waters, 1855. *National Archives.*

singing in the Tabernacle in the late 1840s as embodying

> the divinest gift that heaven has bestowed upon man, the gift of music—the superb talent to touch the hearts and stir the souls of men to noble ends, even when such hearts were encased with the hardest pride and selfishness. No matter how high, no matter how low, this gift of music has, like the all-pervading love of God, the power to reach, melt, and fuse the souls of men into a sense of common kinship, common brotherhood and a common destiny. While it is of no language, it is of all languages, and speaks to the souls of men of all nations, kindreds, tongues and peoples, and like the overhanging firmament ever speaks forth the glory of God.

Melville's Yoomy, throughout the second half of *Mardi*, alternates between the kind of passionate rhetoric that Douglass employed against slavery ("you may expect that the heart that beats against this bosom, will give utterance against you") and the kind of soulful songwriting for which the Hutchinson Family was known (they wrote many of their own lyrics and, like Yoomy, were widely referred to as minstrels). Whether or not Melville was at the Broadway Tabernacle on May 9 to hear Douglass speak and the Hutchinson Family sing, his appeal to "all-healing time" at the end of the Vivenza section of *Mardi* echoes the spirit of "There's a Good Time Coming" in both Douglass's speech and the Hutchinson song. That hopeful spirit continued in the retrospective accounts of the Anniversary Week that Douglass published in the May 19, 26, and June 2 issues of the *North Star*, as well as in another meeting at which Douglass spoke and the Hutchinson Family sang on the evening of May 10.

A year later, when the 1849 Anniversary Week was shadowed by the riots led by

Rynders at the Astor Place Opera House, *Mardi* was being reviewed. The devastating review by George Ripley in the New York *Tribune* on May 10 has been noted. On the same day the *Daily Chronotype* in Boston printed another of those reviews in an anti-slavery publication that has been overlooked by Melville scholars who have otherwise so thoroughly documented the reception of his work. One measure of the standing of the Boston *Chronotype* as an anti-slavery paper is the paragraph about Douglass in Edmund Quincy's July 2, 1847, letter to Caroline Weston. Although Quincy objected bitterly to the fee Douglass proposed for the letters he was asked to contribute to the *National Anti-Slavery Standard*, he preferred to pay Douglass "more than his letters are worth than to put him in a huff, & perhaps sell them to the Era or the Chronotype."

The sophisticated, three-column review of *Mardi* that appeared in the *Chronotype* on May 10, 1849, was by an anonymous writer who noted its strong anti-slavery sentiment and called attention to the declaration that "Your federal temple of freedom, sovereign kings, was the handiwork of slaves." He also savored the ironic force of the "inscription in hieroglyphics" declaring that "In-this-republican-land-all-men-are-born-free-and equal . . . except-the-tribe of Hamo"—even though it would probably seem "meaningless to the critics."

Beyond attending to anti-slavery issues, the reviewer differed from most in actually preferring *Mardi* to *Typee* and *Omoo*. Because each of the two earlier books was "a beautiful picture," readers were expecting the same in the "magic glass" of *Mardi*. Instead, Melville

> gave back . . . a magnificent allegory,
> wherein the world is seen as in a
> mirror. . . . Youth and its impetuosity,
> and its fervid and rose colored dreams,

> are personified. . . . But Philosophy and
> Humanity are the crowning glories of the
> book. We could bear our heart, and bow
> the knee to such humanity as Mr. Melville
> possesses, and we would forgive him if he
> hated us, he so loves and serves his kind.
> Critics may carp, conservatism may cast
> contemptuous glances, bigotry may tuck
> up her garments and "give a wide berth"
> to Mardi, but the live heart of the author
> beats there in love, and sometimes in
> scorn, and it is a life that is immortal.

This reviewer intuited the kind of spiritual and poetical strength that was to find full expression, two years later, in *Moby-Dick*.

The one serious objection the *Chronotype* reviewer had to *Mardi* was that "Mr. Melville seems to lack the faith that God had a purpose in creating the world." His vision "does not fill the heart that asks for a Heaven for a man on the earth, that shall balance the Hell he has formed and made here." A few months after the review in the *Chronotype*, Melville clarified his own resistance to depending on God for deliverance with these words in the last chapter of *White-Jacket*: "There are no mysteries out of ourselves." Douglass made a similar point in his address "Self-Help" at the Abyssinian Baptist Church three days before the review of *Mardi* appeared in the *Chronotype*: "It is a ridiculous and absurd notion to expect God to deliver us from bondage. We must elevate ourselves by our own efforts."

Redburn

Redburn (1849), on the face of it, was not an especially promising book for addressing antislavery concerns. Melville was retelling the story of his own voyage to Liverpool and back in 1839, and only a few chapters at the beginning and end of the book take place in New York City. Redburn, a young cabin boy in his teens, is an unlikely vehicle for the kind of social awareness that Melville did not develop "until I was twenty-five," when he began writing *Typee*. Melville addressed this problem by writing *Redburn* with a double consciousness, preserving the consciousness of Redburn as a young sailor within his first-person narrative yet also registering, in subtle ways, his own acute consciousness of contemporary concerns in New York as he wrote the book in April, May, and June 1849. This double consciousness is perfectly illustrated in Melville's depiction of Lavender's arm-in-arm promenade with his "good-looking English woman" in Liverpool.

Already noted is how Melville relates this event to the contemporary world of 1849 as well as to Frederick Douglass himself by adding that "in New York, such a couple would have been mobbed in three minutes." However, young Redburn himself was not likely to have had the kind of consciousness about this event that Douglass in that same year would express in "Colorphobia in New York!" Melville bridges the gap between Redburn's adolescent experience in Liverpool in 1839 and his own consciousness a decade later by having Redburn confess that "at first I was surprised that a colored man should be treated as he is in [Liverpool]; but a little reflection showed that, after all, it was but recognizing his claims to humanity and normal equality; so that, in some things, we Americans leave to other countries the carrying out of the principle that stands at the head of our Declaration of Independence."

Redburn sees in retrospect his youth and inexperience as "unconsciously swayed in some degree by those local and social prejudices, that are the marring of most men, and from which, for the mass, there seems no possible escape." Melville and Douglass were, each in his own way, trying to address and

reverse those same unconscious prejudices. Melville's unusual phrase for an internal condition, "the marring of most men," matches Douglass's depiction of the exterior condition of those New Yorkers whose gestures show them to be "most horribly cut and marred" by "Colorphobia."

As discussed in Chapter 3, Melville was writing *Redburn* in New York during the three weeks in April and May 1849 in which Douglass was speaking to multi-racial audiences at Shiloh Presbyterian, the Broadway Tabernacle, the Hope Chapel, and the Minerva Rooms, in addition to taking his controversial bi-racial walk up and down Broadway with the Griffiths sisters. Beyond presenting Lavender's Liverpool stroll in such a way as to remind readers of the Broadway stroll that Douglass recounted in the "Colorphobia" essay, Melville addresses other elements of the non-white world in a manner that would have appealed to anti-slavery readers who had responded favorably to his earlier novels in the Albany *Evening Journal,* the *National Era,* the *National Anti-Slavery Standard,* the *North Star,* and the Boston *Chronotype.* Lavender is one of two conspicuously non-white sailors in *Redburn* who are introduced as the joint subjects of Chapter 17, "The Cook and the Steward." The cook is black, the steward mulatto. Melville's characterization of each transcends the stereotype on which it builds.

Redburn explains that "our black cook . . . according to the invariable custom at sea, always went by the name of "the doctor." He was "a . . . serious old fellow, much given over to metaphysics." So serious is he about the Bible that he often reads the Good Book as he cooks, so that "big drops of sweat would stand upon his brow, and roll off, till they hissed on the hot stove before him." Before the ship leaves the dock, young Redburn surmises that *our black cook . . . must have been a member of one of those negro churches, which are to be found in New York. For when we lay at the wharf, I remembered that a committee of three reverend-looking old darkies, who, besides their natural canonicals, wore quaker-cut black coats, and broad-brimmed black hats, and white neck-cloths; these colored gentlemen called upon him, and remained conversing with him at his cook-house door for more than an hour; and before they went away they stepped inside, and the sliding doors were closed; and then we heard some one reading aloud and preaching; and after that a psalm was sung and a benediction given; when the door opened again, and the congregation came out in a great perspiration; owing, I suppose, to the chapel being so small, and there being only one seat beside the stove.*

For Redburn as a young sailor, this "committee of three reverend-looking old darkies" provides some local color for his first voyage in the time frame of Melville's own first voyage in 1839. For Melville and his readers in 1849, the broader reference to "those negro churches, which are to be found in New York" included three at which Douglass had spoken in April and May: Zion Church, which charged him a fee to speak against slavery; Abyssinian Baptist, where he spoke on "Self-Help" to the black community; and Reverend Pennington's Shiloh Presbyterian, where he spoke four times between April 20 and May 8. Just as Ishmael's visit to the negro church in *Moby-Dick* evokes the Zion Church at which Douglass was preaching when Melville visited New Bedford in 1840, so does the shipboard visitation from the negro churches in *Redburn* evoke those churches at which Douglass was speaking during his visit to New York in 1849.

Once Redburn's ship is at sea, he admires the cook's "warm love and affection" for his cookhouse. "In fair weather, he spread the skirt of an old jacket before the door, by way of a mat; and screwed a small ring-bolt into the door for a knocker; and wrote his name, 'Mr. Thompson,' over it, with a bit of red chalk." By writing out his own name, the cook supplants the "customary" term of "the doctor" by which black cooks were known at sea. The name Mr. Thompson also supplants the kind of demeaning designation (by age and place) by which "old Baltimore" is known in *Omoo*. Two Reverend Thompsons happened to be prominent in New York churches in which Douglass preached in 1849: John P. Thompson at the Zion Church and Joseph P. Thompson at the Broadway Tabernacle.

Melville further indicates an awareness of the New York churches in which Douglass was active by referring to the Broadway Tabernacle in the Liverpool section of the book. The Tabernacle is listed as one of three great churches in the world which "any poor sinner" is free to enter. "St. Peter's in Rome is open to him . . . St. Paul's in London is not shut against him; and . . . the Broadway Tabernacle, in New York, opens all her broad aisles to him." This passage occurs in Chapter 41 immediately after Redburn has come to terms with having seen "our black steward, dressed very handsomely, walking arm in arm with a good-looking English woman." Redburn completes his thought about the Broadway Tabernacle, St. Peter's, and St. Paul's by declaring that "this consideration of the hospitality and democracy in churches, is a most Christian and charming thought. It speaks whole volumes of folios, and Vatican libraries, for Christianity."

At the end of its return voyage, the *Highlander* "warps into a berth at the foot of Wall-street." When the crew call upon Captain Riga to collect their wages, Redburn is surprised to see that the old cook, "who had taken no pay in advance, had the goodly round sum of seventy dollars as his due." This is far more than was due any of the white sailors, excepting the captain. "With a scrape of the foot, and such a bow as only a negro can make, the old cook marched off with his fortune; and I have no doubt at once invested it in a grand, underground oyster-cellar."

The most famous oyster-cellar in New York in 1849 was Thomas Downing's "popular oyster house restaurant at 5 Broad Street," a few blocks from the shipping berths at the foot of Wall Street. Downing was a prominent member of the Vigilance Committee that ran the Underground Railroad in New York City, and he was known to have hidden fugitive slaves in his oyster house at the corner

View south on Broadway shows the columned façade and triangular roof of the New York Society Library at the corner of Leonard Street. Further south, the recessed tower of the Broadway Tabernacle is barely visible beyond the intervening buildings and beneath the library's roof. This daguerreotype, circa 1850, is among the earliest known photographs of a New York street scene. It shows a portion of Broadway that Douglass and Melville knew intimately between 1847 and 1850. New-York Historical Society.

Looking uptown on Broadway, stereograph, 1860s. Nearby was George T. Downing's oyster house at 690 Broadway in 1849, a short walk from Herman Melville's Fourth Avenue address until 1850. National Archives.

the self-help within the black community that Douglass advocated in his speech. So was Thomas Van Rensselaer, who spoke after Downing and before Douglass. Van Rensselaer was editor of the *Ram's Horn*, a black anti-slavery newspaper in New York. At the end of the same week, he moderated the May 11 debate between Douglass and Ward on "The Constitutionality of American Slavery." Like both of the Downings, he was a leader of the Vigilance Committee at whose meeting Douglass spoke at Shiloh Presbyterian on the evening of May 8. That night, Douglass humorously made his position toward the Underground Railroad clear in the first words he addressed to George T. Downing: "Mr. Chairman, I am in favor of running away."

Thomas Van Rensselaer had himself run away in 1819, the year of Melville's birth (slavery was not officially abolished in the State of New York until 1827). He had been a slave in the Mohawk Valley near Albany, so his "master" was probably related to the Van Rensselaers of Albany who still lived in the Manor House at the north end of Broadway. This is the same Van Rensselaer family to whom Melville's Gansevoort relatives were related, whose teenage slave Bet had been hanged on Pinsker Hill in 1794, and whose Manor House in the 1840s had become a second home to Herman's sister Augusta. She was "indispensable to the comfort of Stephen Van Rensselaer and his wife Harriet" during her extended visits there.

Doggett's New York City Directory for 1849–50 lists Thomas Van Rensselaer at 81 White Street—near its intersection with Broadway two short streets north of the New York Society Library. Douglass, in the April 21 letter in which he complained about the fee imposed by the Zion Church, assured his readers that "my visit to this city has [not] been mainly unpleasant or unsatisfactory. On

of Broad and Wall. Readers who knew of his role in the Underground Railroad would have appreciated the precision, rather than the redundancy, in Melville's phrase "underground oyster-cellar."

Thomas Downing's son, George T. Downing, was the current president of the New York Vigilance Committee when Douglass addressed that group at Shiloh Presbyterian on the evening of May 8, 1849. The younger Downing also ran an oyster house (presumably also of the "underground" kind) at 690 Broadway, a few short blocks from the Melville family home. His father's Broad Street oyster house was diagonally across from Allan Melville's law office at 14 Wall Street (see these locations on the New York map).

Appropriately, Thomas Downing chaired the meeting at the Abyssinian Baptist Church at which Douglass gave his address on "Self-Help" on May 7, 1849. Both as a "negro restaurateur" and as a leader of the Underground Railroad in assisting fugitive slaves, Downing was a shining example of my arrival I was cordially welcomed to the home and hospitality of my friend Thomas Van Rensselaer. I found him alive to the great cause of freedom, ready to render every aid in his power to make my mission to this city a successful one." As soon as Douglass arrived in New York on April 13, Van Rensselaer took him to a "beautiful and commodious church" in Brooklyn, where he followed Douglass's speech with a "warm and vigorous appeal for the 'North Star.'"

Douglass's April 21 letter acknowledges other "distinguished colored gentlemen" who had already provided invaluable assistance during his stay. These included Reverend James W. C. Pennington, Dr. James McCune Smith, and George Downing, all of whom had joined Douglass's effort the night before to "secure subscribers" for the *North Star* by speaking at Shiloh Presbyterian. Douglass presumably continued to enjoy Van Rensselaer's "home and hospitality" during the next two weeks of anti-slavery activity, which climaxed in his debate with Ward in the Minerva Rooms on May 11. If Melville did meet with Douglass during the four weeks that Douglass spent in his near environs in 1849, it is possible to imagine their sitting down in one of the Downings's underground oyster houses with some of Douglass's associates.

Like Mr. Thompson, the black cook who invests in "a grand, underground oyster-cellar," Lavender, the mulatto steward in *Redburn*, is himself an exemplar of self-help in the very environs in which Douglass was speaking in 1849. His having been a barber on West Broadway before going to sea puts him in the immediate neighborhood of the Broadway Tabernacle, the New York Society Library, Zion Church, and Abyssinian Baptist. West Broadway runs uptown two blocks west of Broadway before it crosses Canal Street, where it continues, as Laurens, up to Washington

Park (see the New York map). Around the corner from Abyssinian Baptist was the pharmacy of James McCune Smith, on West Broadway between Anthony and Thomas. The home of James W. C. Pennington was on West Broadway between Thomas and Duane.

In *Redburn* the references to Lavender's West Broadway roots continue even after the ship sails for Liverpool. Lavender wears a "gorgeous turban" when Redburn first meets him ashore in the captain's cabin, but "he never wore that turban at sea." Instead, he "sports an uncommon head of frizzled hair . . . well perfumed with Cologne water, of which he had a large supply, the relics of his West Broadway stock in trade." His clothes are "mostly cast-off suits of the captain of a London liner, whom he had sailed with upon many previous voyages . . . all in the height of the exploded fashions, and of every kind of color and cut." But Lavender also wears "several full suits of black, which, with his dark-colored face, made him look quite clerical; like a serious young colored gentleman of Barbadoes, about to take orders."

Even before the ship sails for Liverpool, Lavender is depicted as a great favorite with the ladies. Nearly every evening he and the cook sit together in the cook-house so that Mr. Thompson can dispense advice to his steward, who admits to being "a sad profligate and gay deceiver" with his female admirers. Lavender listens respectfully to the "edification" from his friend, but he does not feel it is his fault if "his bewitching person turned all heads and subdued all hearts, wherever he went." This passage in New York sets up Lavender's subsequent stroll with the "good-looking English woman" in Liverpool.

In addition to Lavender's West Broadway roots and entrepreneurial flair, he has more than a little resemblance to Frederick Douglass. Most specific is the promenade with the

English woman in Liverpool that matches that of Douglass with his two English ladies on Broadway, but this former West Broadway barber shares other conspicuous attributes with Douglass: a mulatto complexion, intimacy with the captain of a London liner, fastidious dress, and a physical presence that "turned all heads." Douglass never was a West Broadway barber, but he did once play such a role in that neighborhood—in an episode to be discussed in relation to Melville's *Benito Cereno*.

Melville's attention to Redburn's two black shipmates, each a cut above the white sailors in intrinsic merit, provides insight into middle-class negro life that was rare in fiction in 1849. Not only do Lavender and Mr. Thompson embody self-help of the kind that Frederick Douglass advocated in his talk at the Abyssinian Baptist Church, each is depicted with the kind of dignity and individuality found in James McCune Smith's "Heads of the Colored People" in *Frederick Douglass' Paper* beginning in 1852 (one of whose portraits was of "The Steward," a mulatto). Melville's attention to the cook and the steward in *Redburn*, and to the world of negro churches, neighborhoods, barber shops, and oyster-cellars, brings his consciousness even closer to the world in which Douglass was such a conspicuous presence as Melville was writing the book in April and May 1849. So did his daily stroll through the neighborhood in which Douglass was living with Van Rensselaer during at least part of his four weeks in the city.

These traces of Douglass's world in Melville's book make it seem even more likely that the two men might have met during the four weeks in which Douglass was living and lecturing in close proximity to Melville. Chapter 1 asked what, if anything, Melville knew about Douglass and when he knew it, either in 1840 or by 1851. By the time he finished *Redburn* in June 1849, Melville knew a

lot more about Douglass and his world than he had known in New Bedford in 1840 or Albany in 1845. That knowledge was leaving traces in his fiction in ways both large and small.

Given the positive attention to Lavender and Mr. Thompson as middle-class black citizens of New York, does *Redburn* contain any white characters who threaten black dignity in the manner of Isaiah Rynders and his followers during the week of the Astor Place riots? Demographically and by temperament, the answer is yes. A sailor named Jackson, the most frightening man Redburn has ever met, is the novel's equivalent of Rynders. Jackson has no official position of authority over the sailors, yet he terrorizes his crewmates by his tyrannical manner and evil eye. "He was a native of New York city, and had a good deal to say about *highbinders*, and rowdies, whom he denounced as only good for the gallows; but I thought he looked a good deal like a *highbinder* himself. . . . In fact, he was a great bully, and being the best seaman on board, and very overbearing in every way, all the men were afraid of him, and durst not contradict him, or cross his path in any way." Among Jackson's many adventures he "had served in Portuguese slavers on the coast of Africa; and with a diabolical relish used to tell of the middle-passage, where the slaves were stowed, heel and point, like logs, and the suffocated and dead were unmanacled, and weeded out from the living every morning, before washing down the decks."

After terrorizing his crewmates for most of the voyage, Jackson drowns after falling from the yardarm of the main-topsail shortly before the ship reaches New York. As he falls, he coughs up a "torrent of blood" that leaves its stain on the swelling sail and several of his shipmates. Young Redburn cannot forget him even after he has died. Jackson shadows his memory of the voyage as much as Rynders had shadowed the Anniversary Week in May 1849, until the "torrent of blood" finally poured from the Astor Place riots on May 10.

A retrospective of the 1849 "Meetings in New York" in the June 8 issue of the *North Star* characterized them as "the grand Pentecost of the churches." From "the huge dimensions of the Broadway Tabernacle" to "the little negro chapel in Marion Street" (Shiloh Presbyterian), "every place of meeting was crowded with unseated listeners." At the same time, infamous placards inciting "deeds of violence against a portion of their fellow-citizens" appeared "on every conspicuous place" until the voices of anniversary speakers gave way to the "horrible uproar" of the mob at Astor Place. "Such a union of the noblest purposes and most infernal deeds . . . was never before witnessed in our city."

White-Jacket

Melville's next novel, *White-Jacket* (1850), written in July, August, and September of 1849, addresses anti-slavery issues somewhat more directly in its attack on flogging in the U. S. Navy. Its implicit comparison between the mistreatment of the American sailor and that of the southern slave is so strong, Samuel Otter has argued, that the book is "about the extension of black slavery to the decks of the United States naval frigate and to the backs of white sailors." Douglass made a similar comparison in the opposite direction in an editorial on "Flogging in the Navy" in the *North Star* on January 26, 1849. He saw flogging as "but an off-shoot of the system of slavery" and hoped that Americans, after "contemplating the gross inhumanity of cutting the backs of white men," might eventually recognize the foul brutality of cutting the backs of black men."

After writing *White-Jacket*, Melville sailed to England in October 1849 to find a British publisher for his man-of-war manuscript. By the time he returned in early February, Congress was seriously considering a law against flogging in the Navy. The *National Era*, in its review of *White-Jacket* on April 25, 1850, declared that "the book should be placed in the hands of every member of Congress." Melville's account of the flogging inflicted with "the cat-o'-nine-tails . . . must arrest the attention of the nation. [It] gives a clearer insight into the abuses prevalent in our navy, and a better conception of the necessary remedies, than any work within our knowledge. It entitles its author to the warmest thanks of every American."

On September 28, 1850, Congress did indeed abolish flogging. Early in October Melville wrote Duyckinck of his "devout jubilations for the abolition of the flogging law." At the end of the same month, Douglass saw the abolition of flogging in the Navy as the "one concession to the humane spirit of the age" by a Congress that had otherwise "served their master, the Slave Power, to the full extent of their ability." Congress had most fatefully served the "Slave Power" by passing a new and more punitive Fugitive Slave Act on September 18. The relief to be granted to the sailor was emphatically denied to the slave.

Otter has effectively argued that *White-Jacket* itself, though positing powerful connections between the situations of the sailor and the slave, sidesteps some of their fuller implications (see his chapter "Jumping Out of One's Skin"). Yet Melville does continue to explore issues of slavery, and sailors of color, in new and impressive ways. One of the most striking elements of *White-Jacket* is its legal analysis of the use of the Articles of War to suppress sailors in general and to justify flogging in particular. Melville's legal argument is sustained and sophisticated, occupying two sequences of three chapters each (Chapters 34–36 and 70–72). Legally, as well as emotionally, his arguments apply to the Fugitive Slave Act as well as to the Articles of War.

In the first three-chapter sequence, Melville pictures the "dazzlingly white back" of a sailor being "stripped like a slave; scourged worse than a hound. And for what? For things not essentially criminal, but made so by arbitrary laws." His chapter entitled "Flogging not Lawful" reveals that "in the American Navy there is the everlasting suspension of the Habeas Corpus." For this and other reasons, "every American man-of-war's man would be morally justified in resisting the scourge to the uttermost."

In "Flogging not Necessary" Melville goes beyond the letter of the law and the rule of precedent to consider the claims of "natural law." He decides that the issue of flogging provides one of those "occasions where it is for America to make precedents, and not to obey them." The chain of argument he uses attacks exactly the kind of legal reasoning used by Judge Shaw to deny habeas corpus to George Latimer in the fugitive slave case of 1842. It anticipates as well the kind of legal reasoning by which Captain Vere will hang Billy in *Billy Budd*.

As he was writing these chapters against the legality of flogging between June and September of 1849, Melville was working out his own attitude toward the Constitutional issues that Douglass and Ward had debated with regard to slavery in May. His legal acuity in *White-Jacket* no doubt reflects discussions that he would have had with Judge Shaw in January, February, and March, when he and Elizabeth were living in her father's home in Boston. The sophistication of Melville's legal argumentation is probably also indebted to his growing acquaintance with Richard Henry Dana, Jr., in Boston.

Richard Henry Dana, Jr., circa 1840.
Etching by S.A. Schoff, National Archives.

Dana had long been familiar to Melville as the author of *Two Years before the Mast* (1840), which Herman had read before his whaling voyage from New Bedford. But now Dana was a Boston lawyer who was becoming increasingly prominent in anti-slavery affairs. Douglass had praised Dana in the *North Star* in November 1848, after hearing him speak against slavery with "great power and clearness" at a rally at Faneuil Hall. He described Dana as "small of stature, but large in intellect."

Melville met Dana at two parties in Boston in the summer of 1847, before his marriage to Elizabeth Shaw. Their relationship appears to have blossomed in July 1848, when Dana met Melville at Judge Shaw's house and then gave him a dinner party attended by some of Dana's closest legal (and anti-slavery) associates. The relationship resumed when Melville was in Boston in March 1849, with Dana hosting two more dinner parties for him, writing his brother in Heidelburgh that Melville "is incomparable in dramatic story telling." These sociable occasions were followed by correspondence about *Redburn, White-Jacket,* and *Moby-Dick*—all of which are alluded to in the letter Melville wrote to Dana on May 1, 1850. To Dana's query about "the real names of the individuals who officered the frigate" in *White-Jacket*, Melville promises to "tell you all, when next I have the pleasure of seeing you face to face."

Unlike Melville's whale ships in *Typee, Omoo,* and *Mardi,* and the merchant ship in *Redburn,* the naval frigate in *White-Jacket* is a "floating metropolis" of more than five hundred people. The scale of this ship precludes the intimate view that Melville's narrators had of certain black characters in earlier works, but it offers a wider range of non-white sailors. Within the constraints of the gigantic ship and the regulations on shipboard life, Melville shows a keen attention to the individual personalities and the collective plight of non-white sailors—an unusual focus for a white writer at this time. One such sailor is the "fine negro" who is "captain of the gun" in *White-Jacket's* gun crew. He has named the gun "*Black Bet* . . . in honor of his sweet-heart, a colored lady of Philadelphia."

Another non-white sailor who makes only a cameo appearance is Wooloo, a Polynesian from the Society Islands. "Of a sedate, earnest, and philosophical temperament," Wooloo has a minimal role in the plot, but provides a striking illustration of cultural relativity. "His tastes were our abominations: ours his. Our creed he rejected: his we. We fancied him a loon: he fancied us fools. Had the case been reversed; had we been Polynesians and he an American, our mutual opinions of each other would still have remained the same."

Douglass made a similar case for the reversibility of experience when he and the Hutchinson Family Singers appeared before a largely white audience on the evening of May 10, 1848. Challenging a number of whites who got up to leave as soon as he began to speak, Douglass asked them, "Suppose you yourself

were black . . . would you not feel as I do? There is no use being offended with me, I have a right to address you. There is no difference, except of colour, between us."

The cooking for the entire crew of the frigate *Neversink* is "all done by a high and mighty functionary, officially called the '*ship's cook*,' assisted by several deputies. In our frigate, this personage was a dignified colored gentleman whom the men dubbed 'Old Coffee'; and his assistants, negroes also, went by the poetical appellations of '*Sunshine*,' *Rose-water*,' and '*May-day*.'" Although "the *ship's cooking* required very little science . . . old Coffee often assured us that he had graduated at the New York Astor House, under the immediate eye of the celebrated Coleman and Stetson." Of the assistants, Sunshine, "the bard of the trio," accompanies his songs with "some remarkable St. Domingo melodies." A double standard on the ship allows "these jolly Africans" to "make gleeful their toil by their cheering songs," whereas regular sailors are forbidden to sing when "pulling the ropes, or occupied at any other ship's duty."

The most memorable moments with Rose-water and May-day come when they are ordered by Captain Claret to perform the spectacle of "*Head-bumping*." This activity

> *consists in two negroes (whites will not answer) butting at each other like rams. . . . In the Dog-Watches, Rose-Water and May-Day were repeatedly summoned into the lee waist to tilt each other, for the benefit of the Captain's health. May-Day was a full-blooded "bull-negro," so the sailors called him, with a skull like an iron tea-kettle, wherefore May-Day much fancied the sport. But Rose-Water, he was a slender and rather handsome mulatto, and abhorred the pastime. . . . I used to pity poor Rose-Water from the bottom of my heart. But*

my pity was almost aroused into indignation at a sad sequel to one of these gladiatorial scenes.

The sequel turns Captain Claret's entertainment into a scene whose multiple ironies anticipate some of those in the "Battle Royal" in the opening chapter of Ralph Ellison's *Invisible Man* one hundred years later. After the two men

had been bumping one evening to the Captain's content, May-Day confidentially told Rose-Water that he considered him a "nigger," which, among some blacks, is held a great term of reproach. Fired at the insult, Rose-Water gave May-Day to understand that he utterly erred; for his mother, a black slave, had been one of the mistresses of a Virginia planter belonging to one of the oldest families in that state. Another insulting remark followed this innocent disclosure; retort followed retort; in a word, at last they came together in mortal combat.

The two men are separated by the master-at-arms, and the captain announces that, although "I now and then permit you to play, I will have no fighting." So "the negroes were flogged." Forced to witness this scene with five hundred other "compelled spectators," White-Jacket feels great sympathy at "the scourging of poor Rose-Water. . . . Poor mulatto! thought I, one of an oppressed race, they degrade you like a hound. Thank God! I am a white." Yet whites are not exempt, and White-Jacket is suddenly called before the mast himself for failing to follow an order that he had never been given.

Until now White-Jacket had remained "unscourged" after almost a year on the *Neversink*. As he sees "the boatswain's mate . . . curling his fingers through the *cat*" that will soon be cutting into his own back, he is overcome by an irresistible urge to charge Captain

Claret and plunge overboard with him to a double death. This instinct is not simply to escape the scourge. White-Jacket is discovering a "man's manhood so bottomless within me, that no word, no blow, no scourge of Captain Claret could cut me deep enough for that." The "instinct in me" is the same one that "prompts even a worm to turn under the heel." White-Jacket justifies the murderous element of this instinct by claiming "the privilege, inborn and inalienable, that every man has, of dying himself, and inflicting death upon another. . . . These are the last resources of an insulted and unendurable existence."

In this passage Melville identifies entirely with the same kind of instinct that finally drove Frederick Douglass to fight back against Edward Covey, the notorious slave-breaker, at the climactic point in his 1845 *Narrative*. Before White-Jacket can act on the impulse to charge Captain Claret and carry him overboard, however, he is saved from himself, and from the lash as well, by the intervention of a corporal of marines who comes to his defense and convinces the captain to desist.

This physical reprieve for the narrator is one of the ways in which Melville's story evades a fuller conjunction between the sailor and the slave. But certainly the narrator's consciousness has been raised by emotional sympathy, even though his white skin has not been raised by the cat. In the words of Douglass's editorial on flogging in the *North Star* in January 1849, the fictional sequence in which the "cat" that cuts the black backs of May-Day and Rose-Water is about to cut into the "white back" of White-Jacket does challenge Melville's reader to "contemplate" the "foul brutality" of the one condition in conjunction with the "gross inhumanity" of the other.

The second round of legalistic chapters that follows hard upon White-Jacket's last-minute reprieve shows both a sarcastic edge and a wider sympathy. The edge shows in this cartoon-like image of Captain Claret: "With the Articles of War in one hand, and the cat-o'-nine-tails in the other, he stands an undignified parody upon Mohammed enforcing Moslemism with the sword and the Koran." This satire is very much in the spirit of Douglass's commentary on *Punch's* caricature of America in his talk at the Broadway Tabernacle in May 1848.

The wider sympathy in these chapters comes in Melville's argument against blaming the victim for the situation his oppressors have created. "Nor," White-Jacket declares, "is the general ignorance or depravity of any race of men to be alleged as an apology for tyranny over them." Indeed, most of the "iniquities practiced" by the sailor on a man-of-war "are indirectly to be ascribed to the morally debasing effects of the unjust, despotic, and degrading laws under which the man-of-war's man lives." Douglass had been making this argument on behalf of the slave throughout his career as an orator, writer, and editor.

Immediately after the second round of legalistic chapters, another non-white sailor, Tawney, comes to the fore. Now "a sheet-anchor-man" on the *Neversink*, he is an elderly negro who had fought against this very ship when he had been impressed on the British frigate *Macedonia* in the War of 1812. Tawney is "a staid and sober seaman, very intelligent, with a fine, frank bearing, one of the best men in the ship, and held in high estimation by everyone." Through his decades of experience, he had come to have an exceedingly realistic view of war. In almost every case he has witnessed, victory has been achieved not through heroism or valor but rather through "a very great disparity" in firepower.

For this reason, "were the secret history of all sea-fights written, the laurels of sea-heroes

would turn to ashes on their brows." Too often the crew of a frigate "must consent to being slaughtered by the foe" simply to glorify "some brainless bravo" of a captain. Tawney had come to the conclusion that war "and every thing connected with it is utterly foolish, unchristian, barbarous, and brutal, and savoring of the Feejee Islands, cannibalism, saltpeter, and the devil."

Taking White-Jacket on a tour of the *Neversink*, Tawney points out all the "ineffaceable indentations and scars" hidden under the black paint of the war ship, especially in the area of the main mast, which he and his mates, in earlier battles, had come to know as the "*slaughter-house*" of a frigate. In this section of the warship, he had seen "the beams and carlines overhead . . . spattered with blood and brains. About the hatchways it looked like a butcher's stall; bits of human flesh sticking in the ring-bolts." Overall, "Tawney's recitals were enough to snap this man-of-war world's sword in its scabbard."

Tawney's denunciations of war are as unsparing as the one Douglass had recently delivered at Hope Chapel on Broadway in May 1849. After denouncing America in general for conferring its "blessings on war-makers" rather than on "peace-makers," Douglass evoked a storm of hisses when he referred to President Zachary Taylor as a "legalized cutthroat," a man who had recommended himself to the American public primarily by "blowing out the brains of the Mexicans."

The most anomalous non-white sailor on the *Neversink* is Guinea, the purser's steward, introduced in Chapter 90, "The Manning of Navies." The chief anomaly is that he occupies the condition of both a sailor and a slave since he is the purser's property. Melville was working directly from life with this character, for Robert Lucas, the steward of the *U. S. United States* was in fact enslaved to its purser,

Edward Fitzgerald. Although enslaved sailors were illegal in the Navy at the time, the purser, in life as well as in fiction, got permission from the Secretary of the Navy to bring his slave on board as a steward and collect a double salary.

When the ship carrying Melville and Lucas landed in Boston in October 1844, two of Lucas's shipmates, still unidentified, took his case to abolitionist lawyers. They in turn filed a writ of Habeas Corpus with Chief Justice Shaw, who decided the case in favor of Lucas on October 11. His main argument was that Lucas was not a fugitive slave but rather one who had been voluntarily transported out of the State of Virginia by Fitzgerald. Shaw ruled that once the ship left the waters of Virginia, the master lost legal authority over the slave, and so Lucas became free as soon as he stepped ashore in Massachusetts, a state which did not recognize slavery within its own borders.

In this 1844 case, Robert Lucas joined a series of slaves from southern states to whom Shaw had granted freedom. Shaw was opposed to slavery in principle and he acted accordingly when he felt the law allowed it. He simply felt that, in the case of a fugitive slave, the U. S. Constitution offered him no recourse but to return the slave to its lawful owner. Because Frederick Douglass had himself been a fugitive, Shaw presumably would have sent him back to Maryland if a legal claim had been made against him in Massachusetts between his arrival in New Bedford in 1838 and the purchase of his freedom eight years later.

How does Melville handle the fictional situation of Guinea in *White-Jacket*? The narrator, after explaining that Guinea is at once a sailor and a slave, admits that he and other white sailors often envied him. "Never did I feel my condition as a man-of-war's man so keenly as when seeing this Guinea

freely circulating about the decks in citizen's clothes, and, through the influence of his master, almost entirely exempted from the disciplinary degradation of the Caucasian crew." (The emotion here is somewhat similar to the jealousy Tommo feels when seeing Marnoo moving freely among the natives of Typee Valley without giving him the time of day.) The "disciplinary degradation" from which Guinea is exempted is the flogging inflicted on sailors time and time again. All hands are required to be on deck to witness each flogging, but Guinea, through the influence of the purser, is exempt from even this requirement.

One difference between Guinea in the novel and Robert Lucas in real life is that the *Neversink* ends its voyage in Norfolk, not Boston. For abolitionists in Boston who were familiar with the Robert Lucas case (which had been reported in the Boston *Post* as well as in the *Liberator* immediately after Judge Shaw's decision), this might have seemed a jarring departure from the strong anti-slavery tenor of the novel as a whole. Melville, for those in the know, was consigning the fictional counterpart of Robert Lucas to a life of continued enslavement, which is especially curious since Melville's narrator goes out of his way to praise the fictional purser for his generous treatment of Guinea "under circumstances peculiarly calculated to stir up the resentment of a slave-owner." In Boston, in real life, generosity came in Fitzgerald's willingness, declared in advance, to abide by whatever ruling the court would make about the freedom of Lucas. In Norfolk at the end of the novel, there would have been no legal "circumstances" which would have required such generosity.

At the end of "The Manning of Navies" Melville makes what I take to be the most direct allusion to Douglass himself in the novel. It is only a "cobweb" connection perhaps, but a significant one nevertheless. White-Jacket has been discussing Landless, a white sailor who is flogged time and time again but who never displays the least amount of manly resistance: "Landless always obeyed with the same invincible indifference." Because of this, he is the kind of man whom "most sea-officers profess to admire; a fellow without shame, without a soul, so dead to the least dignity of manhood that he could hardly be called a man."

Such a lack of dignity is now an issue for White-Jacket after the inner resistance he felt when about to be flogged himself. In contrast to Landless, White-Jacket now describes the kind of sailor whom the officers "instinctively dislike." A seaman of this kind "exhibits traits of moral sensitiveness" and his "demeanor shows some dignity within." Officers "feel such a man to be a continual reproach to them, as being mentally superior to their power. . . . To them there is an insolence in his manly freedom, contempt in his very carriage. He is unendurable, as an erect, lofty-minded African would be to some slave-driving planter." The word "unendurable" links this image of "an erect, lofty-minded African" with the sudden rush of manhood that White-Jacket, in the expectation of being flogged, had felt deep within himself when forced to draw upon "the last resources of an insulted and unendurable existence."

Douglass, in his persona as well as in his writing, had become the epitome of the "erect, lofty-minded African" by the time Melville wrote these words in the summer of 1849. In his 1845 Narrative he had been unforgettably "erect" in the way he stood up to Covey, who was himself the epitome of the "slave-driving planter." At the same time Douglass was remarkably "lofty-minded" in recounting this and other experiences as a slave.

Self-evident to any reader of the *Narrative* in 1845, these qualities became even more strikingly visible during Douglass's subsequent years of speaking and writing. Never were they more so than in late April and early May of 1849, when he gave at least nine speeches in Melville's immediate vicinity while also walking up and down Broadway with his English ladies on either arm.

Douglass is not directly depicted among the non-white sailors on the *Neversink,* but he is spiritually present in the image of the "erect, lofty-minded African." Like Bulkington in *Moby-Dick,* he is a "sleeping-partner" ship-mate, "so far as this narrative is concerned." "Unendurable" to those in power, he is a living symbol of the moral sensitivity, inherent dignity, mental superiority, and manly freedom that are needed for resisting obdurate oppression. Those exact qualities were to make him increasingly unendurable to Rynders and his followers in New York in May 1850.

One passing comment in *White-Jacket* shows Melville's increasing sensitivity to the situation—and history—of black citizens in New York City. In Chapter 16, shortly after introducing the "fine negro" captain who had named his gun *Black Bet . . . in honor of his sweet-heart,"* White-Jacket tries to imagine what the ship might look like if he and his gunmates were currently taking their training in a real battle rather than a "sham" one. In such a case as that, "our bulwarks might look like the walls of the houses in West Broadway in New York, after being broken into and burnt out by the Negro Mob."

This is an allusion to the race riot that destroyed property up and down West Broadway fifteen years before Melville wrote his novel. On July 4, 1834, white New Yorkers attacked black New Yorkers at the Chatham Street Chapel. On July 7 white rioters attacked Chatham Chapel itself, and on July 9, 10, and 11 they "roamed the city almost at will. First they concentrated on the homes and businesses of white abolitionists and 'amalgamators'; then they attacked the churches of prominent black abolitionists; and finally they razed and ransacked the negro quarters."

Lewis Tappan was one of the abolitionists whose homes and churches were attacked. He objected to the "perversion of justice" by which the New York *Courier and Enquirer* used the term "Negro riot" to characterize the actions of white rioters against negro churches, homes, businesses, and sympathizers. Among the "colored churches" seriously damaged by the rioters were Zion Church and Abyssinian Baptist, both in the West Broadway neighborhood of the Broadway Tabernacle, then under construction and itself damaged in rioting.

Paul Gilje's recent reconstruction of the 1834 riot in *The Road to Mobocracy* includes a map showing that the mob violence ran from Broadway to West Broadway along Anthony, Leonard, and Franklin streets. Abyssinian Baptist, on Leonard near West Broadway, had been one of its main targets—which made it an appropriate venue for Douglass's address on "Self-Help" on May 7, 1849. Tappan and Gilje both describe additional rioting against negro targets along Laurens Street, the extension of West Broadway that runs north from Canal Street to Washington Square.

Melville's allusion to "the walls of the houses in West Broadway in New York, after being broken into and burnt out by the Negro Mob," is so specific that one wonders if someone in the spring or summer of 1849 had walked him through the neighborhood, as Tawney had done for White-Jacket aboard the *Neversink*, to see exactly where the damage had been done. If Melville attended any of Douglass's lectures at the Broadway Tabernacle, Abyssinian Baptist,

Zion Church, or even up Broadway a bit at Shiloh Presbyterian, he could have easily met individuals well informed about this local history within the black community. Among them were Reverend Pennington, from his home on West Broadway between Duane and Thomas; James McCune Smith, at his pharmacy on West Broadway between Thomas and Franklin; Thomas Van Rensselear, with whom Douglass was staying only a few blocks away on White Street; and the "underground oyster-cellar" entrepreneurs Thomas Downing and his son George.

The passage in *White-Jacket* about the destruction of homes by the "Negro Mob" on West Broadway, no less than the one in *Redburn* about how Lavender and his English lady would be "mobbed in three minutes" in New York, shows Melville's keen attention during the spring and summer of 1849 to the kind of "colorphobia" that Douglass had recently endured on Broadway and addressed in the *North Star*. Each passage was written within a few months of the chants of "Nigger Douglass" in the Astor Theater on May 7, 1849. Each predicted, in effect, the even more riotous behavior by which Rynders and his white confederates were to confront Douglass and "shut down anti-slavery free speech" in May 1850.

In the May 16, 1850, issue of the *North Star*, Douglass reflects upon the white rioters who had broken up the Anti-Slavery meetings at Shiloh Presbyterian, the Broadway Tabernacle, and the New York Society Library, asking why have they "reappeared after the lapse of fifteen years?" (Here he is alluding to the same 1834 riots to which Melville had alluded in *White-Jacket*.) He further asks, "Why were they not promptly suppressed by the municipal authority? What does it all mean? Have we to refight the battle for liberty of speech, and the right of peacefully assembling?"

Douglass assigns the most immediate responsibility for the riots to that "portion of the New York press" that "for weeks past" has "teemed with the most inflammatory appeals to the vindictive passions of the people of this city against the abolitionists." The *Herald*, The *Globe*, and the *Journal of Commerce* have used every possible means to "appeal to the mob" in the name of "self-interest . . . the Constitution . . . the Church . . . [and] patriotism." Beyond the local newspapers, Douglass believes that "Daniel Webster and other recreant Northern Senators" who had joined Southerners to agitate for a new Fugitive Slave Law "ought to be held responsible. It would be a shame to fix the blame upon the ignorant and misguided men who only acted the part marked out for them."

Writing two weeks later in the *North Star* about the actions of those who had actually assaulted him and his two lady friends on the Battery, Douglass took a similarly forgiving attitude toward the "immediate actors" in this attack. "I felt no indignation towards the poor miserable wretches who committed the outrage. They were but executing upon me the behests of the proslavery church and clergy of the land; doing the dirty work of the men who despise them, and who have no more respect for them in reality than they have for me." At the same time, he declares that he will not give "an inch" in spite of "the almost unprecedented abuse . . . persecution . . . insults . . . violence . . . scorn and contempt" that have been "heaped upon me, in the city of New York, during the past three weeks."

In his response to both the public riots and the personal attack in 1850, Douglass remains both "erect" and "lofty-minded" after being the personal focal point of the worst race riots the city had seen in fifteen years. His only crime, he declares on May 30, is

that I have assumed to be a man, entitled to all the rights, privileges, and dignity, which belong to human nature. . . . The very "head and front of my offending hath this extent—no more" . . . I have walked the streets of New York, in company with white persons, not as a menial but as an equal. . . . The right to associate with my fellow worms of the dust, on terms of equality, without regard to color, is a right which I will yield only with my last breath.

This statement, published in the *North Star* two months after *White-Jacket* had been published in New York City, was Douglass's most recent assertion of the kind of "man's manhood" that White-Jacket had suddenly discovered deep within himself when "Arraigned at the Mast" in Melville's new book. When Douglass writes that the "head and front of my offending hath this extent— no more," he is silently alluding to Othello's speech to Brabantio in Shakespeare's 1604 play (the same speech from which he had borrowed "Charms, conjurations—mighty magic" for his "Colorphobia" essay a year before). When he writes of "the right to associate with my fellow worms of the dust," he may be alluding to the passage in which White-Jacket celebrates that instinct which "prompts even a worm to turn under the heel."

Douglass comes closer to Melville's actual phrasing in the "Lecture on Slavery" that he gave in Rochester on December 8, 1850: "There is a point beyond which human endurance cannot go. The crushed worm may yet turn under the heel of the oppressor." Not only does Douglass directly echo Melville's worm that "turns under the heel." His emphasis upon that "point beyond which human endurance cannot go" echoes Melville's use of "unendurable" in the identical context of resisting oppression. By the end of 1850, Douglass and Melville are "anchored together" in heart and mind on issues large and small.

Moby-Dick

White-Jacket was very favorably reviewed in American publications in March and April 1850, immediately before the anti-abolitionist riots broke out in New York as Melville was writing *Moby-Dick* in May. On May 1 Melville wrote Dana in Boston that he was "half way" in his work about the "whaling voyage." Confessing that he had felt "tied & welded to you by a sort of Siamese link of affectionate sympathy" ever since reading *Two Years before the Mast* before his own whaling voyage, Melville was moved to find these feelings reciprocated in the way Dana had responded to *Redburn* and *White-Jacket*. He was also very glad that Dana's unspecified "suggestion" about the new book "so jumps with mine."

Whatever Melville was feeling about his new book on May 1, it is certain to have been affected by the riots one week later that shut down free speech within the walls of his own New York Society Library. The national crisis over slavery had already reached a new stage of intensity when Daniel Webster of Massachusetts spoke in favor of a new Fugitive Slave Act on the floor of the U.S. Senate on March 7. The riots in New York on May 7 and 8 would have deepened the intensity of the national crisis in an unforgettable way as Melville was writing *Moby-Dick*.

The crisis continued to escalate as Melville wrote more of *Moby-Dick* in the summer of 1850, moved his family to Pittsfield in September, and wrote the rest of the book by June of the following year. Passage of the Fugitive Slave Act on September 18, 1850, gave renewed Congressional sanction to the former act of 1793 while adding many new, draconian features. The new law explicitly denied a jury trial to any accused fugitive, overrode state private liberty laws, subjected

The Fugitive Slave Law of 1850 allowed slave hunters to seize alleged fugitive slaves without due process of law and prohibited anyone from aiding escaped fugitives or obstructing their recovery. National Archives.

THE FUGITIVE SLAVE LAW.

citizens in the North to harsh penalties for assisting a fugitive, and provided financial incentives for commissioners who ruled against a fugitive accused.

In October Douglass spoke against the new law in a rally at Faneuil Hall in Boston, where he shared the platform with Dana, Phillips, Parker, and Charles Francis Adams. Reporting on this heartening rally in the *North Star*, he strongly disagreed with those "arch compromisers" such as Senators Clay and Webster who argued that the Union has been "saved" and "restored" by the passage of the new Fugitive Slave Act. "Our wise men have attempted to get respect for their laws by trampling upon the laws of God, and to heal the wounds of the confederacy, by inflicting wounds on the negro's back. Their efforts are in vain." Douglass's optimism was right in the long run, wrong in the short run.

From October 1850 through June 1851, as Melville continued to write *Moby-Dick* in Pittsfield, events in Boston escalated as dramatically as they had in New York the previous May, over a longer period of time but with the same result. The two most explosive cases occurred in the court room of Chief Justice Shaw. In February 1851 Shadrach Minkins was arrested as a fugitive slave. As his case was being heard, a group of black Bostonians "liberated" him by breaking into court and carrying him to freedom.

One result of this dramatic kidnapping was the high-profile trial of Elizur Wright, the editor of the *Chronotype,* who was sympathetic to Minkins and those who had stolen

Boston Court House is cordoned off with chains for the trial of Thomas Sims, Chief Justice Lemuel Shaw presiding, From Gleason's Pictorial Drawing Room Companion, May 3, 1851.

BOSTON COURT HOUSE.

Thomas Sims sails back to Georgia. From Gleason's Pictorial Drawing Room Companion, May 3, 1851.

him away. Another was the decision to "wrap" Boston's Court House "in chains" while Judge Shaw was hearing the fugitive slave case of Thomas Sims in April 1851. Judge Shaw denied the habeas corpus petition that Dana filed on behalf of Sims; and Sims, marched to the wharf under federal protection, was sent back to Georgia on the brig *Acorn*.

Municipal and state officials in Boston supported the decision of Judge Shaw in April 1851 as fully as the authorities in New York had supported the actions of Isaiah Rynders in May 1850. Under the pressures of these times and places, Melville wrote *Moby-Dick*. He would have been fully aware of the competing claims of Douglass and Dana on the one side and of Shaw and Webster on the other. *Moby-Dick* was, among other things, his own deep, interior response to the public, societal tensions depicted by E. C. Del in his *Practical Illustration of the Fugitive Slave Law*. Del's drawing shows a Southern slave-

holder riding the back of a kneeling Webster and holding out a noose, with the sanction of the Constitution, intended for the neck of a female fugitive. She is being supported by Garrison and Douglass, each of whom has been driven by the new law to take up arms in spite of his strong preference for a non-violent end to the institution of slavery through moral suasion.

This chapter is not the place for a full-scale analysis of *Moby-Dick* in the context of the Fugitive Slave Law and other abolitionist issues. Its primary purpose is to look at those portions of the book that pertain to Douglass and Melville as their lives and works have been examined thus far. Pertinent passages will be addressed in the sequence in which they appear in the novel, with primary emphasis on the early land-based chapters.

"Loomings," Chapter 1 of *Moby-Dick*, is preceded by "Etymology" and "Extracts," the latter being Ishmael's "glancing bird's eye

PRACTICAL ILLUSTRATION OF THE FUGITIVE SLAVE LAW.

Original illustration by E. C. Del, 1851. National Archives.

view of what has been promiscuously said, thought, fancied, and sung of Leviathan, by many nations and generations, including our own." Not until I read through Ishmael's eighty extracts with the Fugitive Slave Law in mind did I notice the presence of both whales and men prepared to resist those who would capture or control them. One resistor is the sperm whale that stove the whaleship *Essex* in Owen Chase's 1821 *Narrative*. Another is the "infuriated Sperm Whale" in Thomas Beale's 1839 *Natural History*. "Mad with the agonies he endures," this whale "snaps" at the boats with his jaws and "rushes" at them with his head, sometimes "utterly destroying" them. The extract from Frederick Bennett in 1840 emphasizes the sperm whale's unique "disposition" to employ the "formidable weapons at either extremity of its body . . . offensively,

and in a manner at once so artful, bold, and mischievous, as to lead to its being regarded as the most dangerous to attack of all the known species of the whale tribe."

These accounts of resistant whales are soon followed by three accounts of whalers who mutinied against their captains and ships. One extract alludes to the "horrid transactions" related in the 1828 "Narrative of the Globe Mutiny." In "Another Version of the whale-ship Globe narrative," a mutineer is quoted directly. Finally, an extract taken from a "Newspaper Account of the Taking and Retaking of the Whale-ship Hobomock" cites the passage in which "the whites saw their ship in bloody possession of savages enrolled among the crew." Even before Ishmael begins his narrative per se, he has made an implicit analogy between the whale who furiously resists its would-be captors and the mutineer who fights for his own life on a ship that denies him his rights.

In "Loomings" three passages are of particular interest in view of the above discussion of Douglass and Melville. The first is the first sentence, "Call me Ishmael," an obvious allusion to the Ishmael of Judeo-Christian tradition, the archetype of the outcast or scapegoat. A few recent interpreters have also called attention to the Ishmael of the Koran, a figure highly honored in Islamic cultures. Proposed here is a third association that would have had special meaning for the anti-slavery and non-white element of Melville's audience—and that can be traced to Frederick Douglass himself.

In his "Self-Help" lecture at the Abyssinian Baptist Church on May 7, 1849, as reported in the New York *Herald* the next day, Douglass declares that "Colored people are now beginning to exercise their gifts. They are now in a position to be heard. But we have no organization among ourselves, in the Ishmaelitish situation in which we are." When Melville's narrator invites his reader to "Call me Ishmael," he identifies with Douglass and other black Americans in their "Ishmaelitish situation" while also declaring his own separation from the mainstream white American culture.

When Ishmael explains that he likes to go sea "as a simple sailor, right before the mast," he admits that taking orders and being made to "jump from spar to spar . . . is unpleasant enough. It touches one's sense of honor, particularly if you come of an old established family in the land, the Van Rensselaers, or Randolphs, or Hardicanutes."

The Van Rensselaers are an obvious reference to Melville's own Van Rensselaer relatives in the Mansion House at the head of Broadway in Albany. This is the family to whom Herman became a poor relative when his father died in 1832 but with whom his sister Augusta restored warm relations in the 1840s.

Melville may also be silently alluding to the enslaved portion of the Van Rensselaer family that had presided over the confluence of the Mohawk and Hudson Rivers for well over a century. Two Van Rensselaer slaves have been part of this story. One is Bet, the teenage girl who was hanged on Albany's Pinsker Hill in 1794 for setting fire to Leonard Gansevoort's stable. The other is Thomas Van Rensselaer, the former slave from the Mohawk Valley with whom Frederick Douglass stayed in New York City in April and May 1849.

Thomas Van Rensselaer was one of the organizers of the meeting at Abyssinian Baptist on May 7 at which Douglass spoke of the "Ishmaelitish situation" of black Americans. After Thomas Downing opened the meeting, Van Rensselaer briefly stated its purpose. Douglass then delivered his address on "Self-Help" within the black community, in which he celebrated Thomas Van Rensselaer as a leading example of that concept. He included him in an honored list similar to the one that Melville's Ishmael presents in *Moby-Dick*.

At present, Douglass declares, "the colored people do not appreciate sufficiently the instrumentalities which have brought about a great change in public opinion. They do not understand what the Downings, the Remonds, the Van Rensselaers, the Sweets, have done by moral force." Douglass's 1849 list of a pioneering generation of black leaders is a perfect foil for Melville's 1851 list of "old established families in the land." Douglass surely would have savored the appearance of "the Van Rensselaers" in each list as much as Melville would have. So, one imagines, would Thomas Van Rensselaer, the Downings, and James McCune Smith.

In the next paragraph of "Loomings," Ishmael asks the reader, "Who aint a slave?" Ishmael uses this somewhat casual question in its local context as further justification for going to sea as a common sailor: "however the old sea-captains may order me about . . . I have the satisfaction of knowing that . . . everybody else is one way or the other served in much the same way . . . and so the universal thump is passed around, and all hands should rub each other's shoulder-blades, and be content."

Asking "Who aint a slave?" is also a jocular way of announcing, on the very surface of the text, that slavery will be an essential subtext for the novel. When Melville wrote to Dana on May 1, 1850 that he was "very glad that your suggestion" about his whaling book "so jumps with mine," that suggestion is very likely to have had something to do with the anti-slavery movement and the fugitive slave agitation, given Dana's current, passionate involvement in those causes. Unfortunately, no copy of the letter containing Dana's suggestion appears to have survived.

When Ishmael arrives in New Bedford in "The Carpet-Bag" chapter, he stumbles into the negro church whose real-life equivalent was the Zion Church on Second Street where Douglass was a preacher when Melville arrived in the city. Chapter 1 of this book explored the possibility that Melville, like Ishmael, might have entered Douglass's church and either heard him preach or seen his face among the "hundred black faces turned around in their rows to peer" at the white intruder. Also touched on was the possibility that Melville might have based the passage upon subsequent knowledge he had acquired about Douglass rather than any immediate experience in 1840. Chapters 2 and 3 showed that Melville had ample opportunity to learn about Douglass almost constantly after his return from whaling in 1844, beginning with the publication of the *Narrative* in 1845 and continuing with newspaper accounts

in Albany and New York City for the rest of the decade. This is apart from any lectures by Douglass that Melville may have attended or any meetings they may have had.

If the two men did get to know each other in Albany in 1845 or in New York in 1847, 1848, 1849, or 1850, they are likely to have compared notes about what each was doing during Melville's short visit to New Bedford at the end of 1840. If Melville had not in fact entered Douglass's church in 1840, he might have written the scene into the novel a decade later as a tribute to what he had learned about Douglass since—in the same spirit in which he wrote "those negro churches, which are to be found in New York" into *Redburn*. Either way, the fictional scene remains true to what young Ishmael's response would have been before he went whaling or met Queequeg—discomfort, embarrassment, a quick exit. In this sense Ishmael's discomfort in the negro church resembles that of Redburn when he first sees Lavender and the English woman walking arm in arm, or of White-Jacket when he envies Guinea's relative ease even though a slave. Melville leaves his young sailors room to grow—especially when it comes to interracial relations.

Melville's presentation of Father Mapple's sermon in the Seaman's Bethel in Chapter 9 of *Moby-Dick* gains in complexity and specificity when viewed from an anti-slavery perspective—as Carolyn Karcher showed in "A Jonah's Warning to America" in 1980. The hymn with which Father Mapple introduces the sermon also has anti-slavery implications. Like the sermon itself, its subject is the delivery of Jonah from captivity into freedom. As David Battenfeld pointed out in a 1955 essay, resurrected in 2002, Melville created the words of this hymn, adapting them from Psalm 18, subtitled "Deliverance from despair" in the "psalms and hymns of the Reformed Protestant Dutch Church . . . in which Melville was brought up."

Printing Mapple's five-stanza hymn alongside the verses of the psalm from which they derive, Battenfeld shows the skill with which Melville adapted Psalm 18 to the situation of Jonah. The opening lines of the hymn are an excellent example. Where the psalmist had written, "Death, and the terrors of the grave, / Spread over me their dismal shade," Melville writes, "The ribs and the terrors in the whale, / Arched over me a dismal gloom."

One change that Battenfeld notes is *not* required by the Jonah story. Melville changes "In my distress, I call'd my God" to "In black distress, I called my God." Melville's change to "black" distress adds a racial—as well as emotional—dimension to the spiritual deliverance being celebrated in Mapple's hymn. It weaves another subtle thread into the anti-slavery subtext of the novel as a whole. Melville did not have to be thinking of Frederick Douglass when he inserted "black" before "distress." Yet the fact that Douglass had found his own deliverance from the despair of slavery in the city in which the hymn is being sung particularizes the blackness that has been added to the psalmist's despair. So does the fact that Ishmael had already accidentally visited the negro church in New Bedford where Douglass himself had been a preacher in 1840 and where "the preacher's text was about the blackness of darkness."

After the hymn with its "black distress," the congregation in the Seaman's Bethel hears the "two-stranded lesson" of Father Mapple's sermon. Certain words in the sermon, too, invite attention from an anti-slavery point of view. At Jonah's first appearance, "how plainly he's a fugitive! no baggage, not a hat-box, valise, or carpet-bag,—no friends accompany him to the wharf with their adieux." As they would with a fugitive slave, the suspicious sailors consult "the bill that's stuck against the spile upon the wharf to which the ship is moored, offering five hundred gold coins for the apprehension of a parricide, and containing a description of his person."

The captain "knows that Jonah is a fugitive" when he comes to pay for his passage, and therefore extorts additional money from him. Even when seemingly secure in his stateroom, Jonah is a "thus far successful fugitive [who] finds no refuge for his restless glance." When the storm hits the ship, and the mariners prepare to cast lots to see who has brought this commotion upon them, Jonah becomes the "God-fugitive" whose shipmates "mob him with their questions" before they "not unreluctantly lay hold of Jonah" and drop him "as an anchor" into the sea.

The point of the Jonah story in Father Mapple's sermon, of course, is not to celebrate Jonah's life as a fugitive but to emphasize his need as a sinner to follow God's law. The second strand of his sermon addresses "the more awful lesson which Jonah's lesson teaches to *me*, as a pilot of the living God." The essence of that responsibility is "to preach the Truth to the face of Falsehood!" From here Father Mapple launches into a series of declarations that can apply to all truth seekers, whether they are ministers, writers, or orators. They are as applicable to the young professional lives of Douglass and Melville as they are to Mapple himself.

"Woe to him who seeks to pour oil on the waters when God has brewed them into a gale! Woe to him who seeks to please rather than to appall!" "Delight is to him, who gives no quarter in the truth, and kills, burns, and destroys all sin though he pluck it out from under the robes of Senators and Judges." "Delight is to him whom all the waves of the billows of the seas of the boisterous mob can never shake from this sure Keel of the Ages."

Surely Melville is declaring his own truth-seeking aspirations in this section of the sermon. Relative to most writers, he had held firm to such principles—except when he had allowed Wiley and Putnam to expurgate the first edition of *Typee*. But Frederick Douglass was much more prominent than Melville as a fearless, truth-seeking embodiment of Mapple's words. In Albany in 1845 and in New York from 1847 through 1850, Douglass had "preached Truth in the face of Falsehood" in close physical and intellectual proximity to Melville himself. At the Broadway Tabernacle in New York in 1850 he had quite literally held firm against "all the waves of the billows of the seas of the boisterous mob." When Melville in *Moby-Dick* has Mapple speak of "plucking out" sin from "under the robes of Senators and Judges," his anti-slavery readers in Massachusetts would have had no difficulty seeing Senator Daniel Webster and Judge Lemuel Shaw as the chief sinners, as Carolyn Karcher pointed out in 1980.

When Queequeg and Ishmael leave New Bedford for Nantucket in the packet boat in the "Wheelbarrow" chapter, they pass the very wharves on which Douglass performed the kind of labor represented by Ishmael's "piled" casks, "moored" ships, and "blended noises of fires and forges." Whereas the view of the wharves depicts the site of Douglass's life as a laborer ten years earlier, Ishmael's account of the boat as it plunges into the open water under a "bracing breeze" embraces the spirit of Douglass's more recent speeches and experiences in New York.

For Ishmael the separation from land inspires these impassioned words: "how I spurned that turnpike earth!—that common highway all over dented with the marks of slavish heels and hoofs; and turned me to admire the magnanimity of the sea which will permit no records." Ishmael's "slavish

heels and hoofs" need not be taken as literal references to slavery (though certainly an anti-slavery reader could read them as evocative of mounted slave-catchers chasing their prey). However, his "sea which will permit no records" does have a precise anti-slavery meaning—especially for readers familiar with Douglass's widely reprinted "Slumbering Volcano" speech at Shiloh Presbyterian on April 23, 1849.

Douglass's address that evening had a "three-stranded" lesson. First was his argument that "the slaveholders are sleeping on slumbering volcanoes, did they but know it" (a declaration he supported with these words from Thomas Jefferson: "I tremble for my country when I reflect that God is just, and that his justice cannot sleep forever"). Second was his tribute to Madison Washington, that "noble-minded and noble-hearted" black man who had led the successful slave revolt on the *Creole* in 1840 (and to whom Douglass would return in writing *The Heroic Slave* in 1853). The third strand of the "Slumbering Volcano" speech celebrated the ocean itself, first in a poem in which human freedom is represented by the spirit of an eagle soaring freely over "some cliff on ocean's lonely shore . . . round whose base the billows roar," then in a closing paragraph that weaves all three strands of the argument together through a personification of the Atlantic Ocean.

In his oceanic conclusion, Douglass thanks God that there is one surface "upon which the bloody statutes of Slavery cannot be written. They cannot be written on the proud, towering billows of the Atlantic. The restless waves will not permit those bloody statutes to be recorded there." This is the antislavery context for Ishmael's own tribute to "the magnanimity of the sea which will permit no records."

For the listener who has not fully caught his metaphorical drift, Douglass spells out his thought in more literal terms. "You may bind chains upon the limbs of your people if you will; you may place the yoke upon them if you will; you may brand them with irons, you may write out your statutes and preserve them in the archives of your nation if you will; but the moment they mount the surface of our unsteady waves, those statutes are obliterated, and the slave stands redeemed, disenthralled." The words spell out, as clearly as any, Douglass's literal equivalent for what Ishmael calls our "turnpike earth . . . all over dented with the marks of slavish heels and hoofs."

That Ishmael has more than the pure ocean in mind is immediately clear in the next paragraph. As Queequeg "seemed to drink and reel" at the "same foam-fountain" with Ishmael, he is described in conspicuously racialized language: "His dusky nostrils swelled apart; he showed his filed and pointed teeth." Because the ship is plunging this way and that, "for some time we did not notice the jeering glances of the passengers, a lubber-like assembly, who marveled that two fellow beings should be so companionable; as though a white man were anything more dignified than a whitewashed negro." When Queequeg does notice "one of these young saplings mimicking him behind his back," he tosses him up and over in an airborne "somerset." This is the same young sapling that Queequeg saves from the waves minutes later, when the tempest parts the "weather-sheet" and the swinging boom sweeps the young man overboard.

The "jeering glances" from the white passengers will remind some Douglass scholars of the racial discrimination on a packet boat from New Bedford to Nantucket that Douglass had himself protested in 1841. Melville may have known about that earlier discrimination, either from Douglass himself or from accounts in the press. However that

may be, of most interest is how Melville's depiction of Queequeg in the "Wheelbarrow" chapter relates to Douglass's depiction of Madison Washington in the "Slumbering Volcano" speech.

In the one sentence of the speech devoted to the successful conclusion of the slave revolt on the *Creole*, Douglass goes out of his way to emphasize the racially conspicuous features of Washington's personal appearance: "in a very few minutes Madison Washington, a black man, with woolly head, high cheek bones, protruding lip, distended nostril, and retreating forehead, had the mastery of that ship, and under his direction, that brig was brought safely into the port of Nassau, New Providence." Ishmael gives similarly conspicuous attention to Queequeg's non-white features as the Nantucket packet plunges into the Atlantic.

As Karcher has pointed out, Queequeg is a composite non-white figure whose physical appearance partakes of Polynesian, African, or multi-racial features at various points in the story. It most resembles that of a black American—and of Madison Washington— during the moment in which the Nantucket packet "spurns that turnpike earth" for "the magnanimity of the sea which will permit no records." Madison Washington's "distended nostrils" are echoed in Queequeg's "dusky nostrils" that "swelled apart." His "retreating forehead" had already been matched by the "long retreating slope" of Queequeg's forehead in "A Bosom Friend." That is the feature that "reminds" Ishmael of George Washington and prompts his assertion that "Queequeg was George Washington cannibalistically developed." Returning to the "Wheelbarrow" chapter, perhaps the most interesting phrase in the paragraph featuring Queequeg's "dusky nostrils" is Ishmael's term "whitewashed negro."

This term resembles "Negro Mob" used for the riots on West Broadway in *White-Jacket*: Seemingly applied to blacks, it actually applies to whites. Technically the phrase is not used to describe Queequeg at all but rather the "whiteness" of the passengers who are shooting "jeering glances" at Ishmael and Queequeg simply for being "companionable, . . . as though a white man were anything more dignified than a whitewashed negro." A cruder version of Ishmael's "whitewashed negro" had been conspicuously used in a "jeering" way by the white rioters who had shut down the meeting of the American Anti-Slavery Society in the New York Society Library on May 8, 1850. According to the New York *Globe*, when Wendell Phillips tried to address the audience, a voice cried out that he was "a white-washed nigger instead of a real black one; put him out; put the red-head down; we won't listen to him."

Phillips replied in kind to this and other insults from the crowd, declaring that "In Boston, where I come from, such scenes are not permitted." But he was soon drowned out by hisses, cheers, and groans from Rynders and his followers. Garrison had been treated similarly at the beginning of the session, one voice from the crowd asking, "Say, old Judge, are you going to give your daughter to that nigger Douglass?" In *Moby-Dick* Melville turns the tables on the protesters themselves when he asks "whether a white man were anything more dignified than a whitewashed negro."

A similar turnaround had actually been inflicted on the white rioters in Library Hall on May 8 before the police finally shut down the meeting. Although the crowd continued to yell "Douglass, Douglass," he did not come forward to speak. The one black man who did was "a frosty-headed old darkie" whom Garrison announced to the crowd as "a citizen of your city." When "the old fellow attempted to speak," he could only occasionally be heard through the noise of the crowd. What he did say, as reported by the *Globe*, was "I'm ashamed of yer. Why, you as worse dan the colored folks. You is a disgrace to dis 'spectable community. Dar, I meant to say dis to yer, and now you can go on." Hereupon "the speaker withdrew, amid a perfect storm of laughter and hisses."

The *Herald* and the *Tribune*, in their accounts of the event, both identified this "aged colored man, with gray hair" as Thomas Van Rensselaer, and each gave a less colloquial account of what he said to the crowd. In the words of the *Tribune*, Van Rensselaer told the whites "that if negroes should act as they did, they would be mobbed and exterminated." The *Herald* treated the same remarks more expansively. In its account Van Rensselaer said, "You see, by my skin, that I am one of the proscribed race. Suppose the blacks came into your meetings and disturbed them, what would you think of them? Why, you are worse than blacks. Are you the enlightened race that we negroes are to follow? I am ashamed of you. (Immense laughter.) I am ashamed to be in company with men who act like brutes. (Renewed laughter.)"

With this speech Van Rensselaer had the last word for "the trustees of the Library, on a representation that the books and property overhead were endangered by the meeting," prevailed upon the Chief of Police to close it down, which Garrison, "under protest," agreed to do. According to the account from the New York *Express*, there were cries of "tear down the building" and "set fire to it" before the hall was cleared.

I have presented several accounts of Van Rensselaer's speech to the rioters at the New York Society Library because each accords with Melville's presentation of Fleece's "sermon to the sharks" in *Moby-Dick*. Fleece, the "old black cook" on the *Pequod*, makes his only appearance in Chapter 64 ("Stubb's Supper"), when he is awakened in the middle of the night to cook a whale steak that Stubb has cut from the "tapering extremity" of the whale he has just killed. Claiming to be unhappy with the taste of the steak, Stubb attempts to humiliate Fleece with the kind of abuse that white men in power could, usually with impunity, inflict upon black men beneath them. First, he commands Fleece to "preach" to the sharks who are noisily feasting on the flank of the whale to "be quiet," instructing and critiquing him every step of the way. Then he puts the cook through an excruciating catechism on every reason that the whale steak has been overcooked.

Fleece, in addition to being old, "has something the matter with his knee-pans . . . shuffling and limping along, assisting his step with his tongs." He speaks to the sharks in exactly the kind of dialect that the *Globe* attributes to Van Rensselaer in Library Hall: "Fellow-critters: I'se ordered here to say dat you must stop dat dam noise dare." But at the end of this painful scene, in which Stubb persists in harassing the old man in every possible way, Fleece has the last word: "Wish, by gor! whale eat him, 'stead of him eat whale. I'm bressed if he ain't more of a shark dan Massa Shark hisself."

Fleece's sermon in "Stubb's Supper" is as memorable as Van Rensselaer's in Library Hall, and for much the same reason. Each turns jeering white oppression back on the white man himself, in colloquial language whose intelligent use doubly undercuts the supposed superiority of his oppressor(s). Again Melville has written a purely fictional scene that would have very specific meaning for the anti-slavery and non-white portion of his audience—and especially for Douglass,

Van Rensselaer, the Downings, James McCune Smith, and any others in Douglass's circle who might have directly experienced the debacle in the New York Society Library on May 8, 1850.

I remember being disturbed and bored by "Stubb's Supper" when I first read *Moby-Dick* in the 1960s. I wondered why a book celebrating the friendship between Ishmael and Queequeg would include a chapter that appears to condone Stubb's race-baiting of Fleece. On subsequent readings I came to appreciate the way in which Fleece's body language and colloquial thought eloquently express resistance to Stubb's oppression. Only after I read contemporary press accounts of Van Rensselaer's sermon to the "sharks" in the New York Society Library, however, could I appreciate the full range of Melville's artistry and nuance in this scene. The nuance even extends to Fleece's double role as a cook and a "preacher." Even though Thomas Van Rensselaer is correctly listed as an "editor" in the New York City Directory for 1849–50, the *Tribune* and the *Herald* both call him a "preacher" in their accounts of his speech to the rioters. Van Rensselaer had also been a "cook" of sorts, for he "operated a restaurant in New York City" before becoming editor of the *Ram's Horn*.

So far I have encountered only one writer who has discussed *Moby-Dick* in relation to the 1850 riots in the New York Society Library to which Melville belonged. Willie Weathers, in a 1960 essay, rightly suggests that if Melville did not "witness" these riots in person he "certainly would have read full accounts of them" in the local press. Weathers speculates that the occurrence of these riots while Melville was writing *Moby-Dick* in May 1850 "supplied the initial impulse for the new direction taken by Melville's whaling-adventure novel." Melville's transformation of Van Rensselaer's speech in the Library Hall into Fleece's sermon to the sharks is one very specific example of that "new direction" in *Moby-Dick*. The Anti-Slavery riots in both the Broadway Tabernacle and the New York Society Library were also to leave their mark on *Benito Cereno* five years later.

If Fleece shows seemingly submissive, underground resistance to abusive oppression in the novel, Steelkilt's resistance is overt, courageous, and even mutinous. (In this way these two characters are powerful updates of the roles played by Baltimore and Bembo in *Omoo*.) Steelkilt is not a sailor on the *Pequod*. He is instead the protagonist of Chapter 54, "The Town-Ho's Story," the longest digression in the novel. Steelkilt responds to unendurable abuse by Radney, the first mate, by "stoving" his jaw with his fist. When the captain threatens to flog him for striking an officer, he and his followers physically resist until they are overpowered by superior force and confined to the hold. Even after he is betrayed by his followers, Steelkilt holds firm in his will. When the time comes for the flogging, he "hisses" something to the captain that makes the captain desist, leaving it to Radney to pick up the "cat" and lay on the lash.

In the context of the voyage of the *Pequod*, Steelkilt embodies the kind of resistance to unjust authority that Starbuck, Captain Ahab's first mate, sorely lacks. Were Steelkilt in Starbuck's position, he would have had the physical and moral force to wrench the ship away from Ahab. In the context of the dispute over the Fugitive Slave Law as Melville was writing the novel in 1850-51, Steelkilt symbolizes the courage to resist an unjust law and to defy abusive authority. Unlike Bembo in *Omoo*, he is ultimately successful in his resistance. Just as Steelkilt is about to murder Radney after the flogging scene, Moby Dick suddenly appears near the ship. Radney is swallowed by the White Whale during the ensuing chase, enabling Steelkilt and his fol-

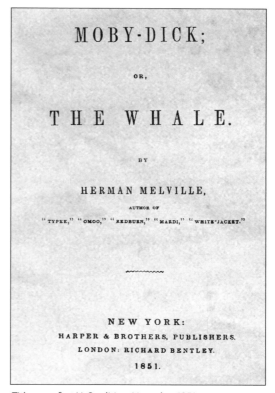

MOBY-DICK;

OR,

THE WHALE.

BY

HERMAN MELVILLE,

AUTHOR OF

"TYPEE," "OMOO," "REDBURN," "MARDI," "WHITE-JACKET."

NEW YORK:
HARPER & BROTHERS, PUBLISHERS.
LONDON: RICHARD BENTLEY.
1851.

Title page, first U. S. edition, November 1851. National Archives.

lowers to desert the ship as soon as they reach port. That they succeeded in achieving their freedom is attested by Ishmael at the end of the chapter: "I trod the ship; I knew the crew; I have seen and talked with Steelkilt since the death of Radney."

This interpolated account of successful, sustained resistance to abusive authority within *Moby-Dick* received additional visibility in the larger culture when Melville selected "The Town-Ho's Story" as the only part of the novel to be published in advance of the book itself, in the October 1851 issue of *Harper's Monthly Magazine*. *Harper's* introduced "The Town-Ho's Story" with a note indicating that it is part of "a new work by Mr. Melville, in the press of Harper and Brothers, and now publishing in London by Mr. Bentley." That Melville chose this story of fierce resistance as the vehicle for introducing *Moby-Dick* would have sent a clear message to the anti-slavery, abolitionist, and non-white element of his audience in a year that had featured the kidnapping of Shadrach from Judge Shaw's court room in February, the return of Thomas Sims to Georgia in April, and the battle at Christiana, Pennsylvania, in September.

In Christiana three fugitive slaves, with local reinforcements, had violently resisted the slaveholder and federal marshals who were pursuing them, killing slaveholder William Gorsuch. Frederick Douglass gave shelter to the fugitives when they reached Rochester and, with the aid of Julia Griffiths, helped them escape to Canada. One week before "The Town-Ho's Story" appeared in *Harper's*, Douglass published a stirring account of "Freedom's Battle at Christiana" in *Frederick Douglass' Paper*, defending the right of fugitives to resist, and even kill, their kidnapping pursuers.

For this and other reasons, it would be interesting to know what Douglass might have thought of Melville's account of Steelkilt's resistance in the October 1851 issue of *Harper's*. In "The Town-Ho's Story," Melville was introducing his White Whale to America's reading public not as the nemesis of Ahab but rather as the savior of Steelkilt and the terminator of Radney. Ishmael presents the the death of Radney as "a certain wondrous, inverted visitation of one of those so called judgments of God which at times are said to overtake some men." The "secret part of the story" involving Steelkilt's plan to murder Radney is so "potent" that it "never reached the ears" of the captain of either ship, remaining the "private property" of the crewmen of the *Town-Ho* and the *Pequod* in much the same way that secrets of the Underground Railroad were kept.

In a brief notice on October 16, *Frederick Douglass' Paper* declares that the October issue of *Harper's* "is very attractive." The "reader is sure of variety" and "several of the

"The Town-Ho's Story" appeared in Harper's New Monthly Magazine as a preview of Moby-Dick. *National Archives.*

original articles are of considerable merit." One of those original articles would have been "The Town-Ho's Story," for most of the feature articles in *Harper's* were reprints from British publications. Douglass's notice does not, however, mention "The Town-Ho's Story" by name (as was to be the case with "Israel Potter" in notices about *Putnam's* in 1854 and 1855). Specific mention of *Moby-Dick* in *Frederick Douglass' Paper* would have to wait until the notice about *Holden's Magazine* in December 1851, the story entitled "Moby Dick Captured" in August 1854, and the quotation from the novel as political commentary by James McCune Smith in March 1856.

Before leaving Steelkilt we must take a brief look at the sailor for whom he is a foil, Starbuck, the chief mate of the *Pequod*, to whom Chapter 26, the first of two chapters entitled "Knights and Squires," is entirely devoted. Ishmael's analytical commentary here anticipates Starbuck's tragic lack of valor when faced with those "spiritual terrors" that will emanate from an "enraged and mighty" Ahab later. If the "coming narrative" were "to reveal, in any instance, the complete abasement of poor Starbuck's fortitude, scarce might I have the heart to write it. . . . That immaculate manliness we feel within ourselves . . . bleeds with keenest anguish at the undraped spectacle of a valor-ruined man."

The spiritual fall of a man such as Starbuck has tragic implications for a democratic nation whose "abounding dignity [is] not in the dignity of kings and robes" but rather in "that democratic dignity which, on all hands, radiates without end from . . . the great God absolute! The centre and circumference of all democracy!" Melville's image of the "centre and circumference" of America's democracy recalls Douglass's use of a similar phrase in his "Homecoming" speech at the Broadway Tabernacle in 1847, when he declared his intention to *blister* America "*all over, from centre to circumference,*" on the issue of slavery. Douglass used the same phrase at Hope Chapel on May 9, 1849, when he referred to 1836 as a year in which "the question of Slavery was rocking this country from centre to circumference." He and Melville both use the "centre to circumference" imagery to pose central questions about American democracy.

Already noted is the similarity between Melville's worm that "turns under the heel" in *White-Jacket* and Douglass's worm that "may yet turn under the heel" in his "Lecture on Slavery" in Rochester in December 1850. Did imagery from *Moby-Dick* in 1851 reappear in any of Douglass's subsequent speeches? Douglass biographer, William S. McFeely, intuits a connection between *Moby-Dick* and the masterful speech that Douglass gave in Rochester on July 5 the following year, "What

to the Slave is the Fourth of July?" He finds the parallel not so much in the borrowing of a single phrase as in the prophecy of the fate of the nation.

McFeely makes the connection with Melville by declaring that Douglass offered his Rochester audience "only an Ishmael's hope of survival." Douglass expresses that qualified hope through a "bold mixing of metaphors" in one short passage:

> *From the round top of your ship of state, dark and threatening clouds may be seen. Heavy billows, like mountains in the distance, disclose to the leeward huge forms of flinty rocks! That bolt drawn, that chain broken, and all is lost. Cling to this day—cling to it, and to its principles, with the grasp of a storm-tossed mariner to a spar at midnight.*

These metaphors recall three of Ishmael's most memorable maritime images in *Moby-Dick*: his "gallant ship beating against a terrible storm off a lee coast of black rocks and snowy breakers" in the painting above Father Mapple's pulpit; his "storm-tossed ship, that miserably drives along the leeward land" in the "Lee Shore" chapter; and his image of Queequeg in a dark midnight sea after being separated from the ship by a storm, "holding up that imbecile candle in the heart of that almighty forlornness."

One month before Douglass discoursed on "What to the Slave is the Fourth of July?" in Rochester, Austin Bearse launched a yacht named *Moby Dick* in Boston. As advertised in the *Liberator* on July 2, 1852, the *Moby Dick* was a "Fast-Sailing Pleasure-Boat" run by Bearse with assistance by J. B. Smith, "the well-known and popular Caterer." It was "ready, at all times, for Pleasure Parties, or Fishing Excursions in the Harbor." Bearse, in addition to being a captain, was a leading member of Boston's Committee on Vigilance.

Under the guise of running a charter boat, he and Smith were actually on the lookout for fugitive slaves in need of assistance.

In July 1853 Bearse and his associates on the *Moby Dick* rescued Sandy Swan from the brig *Florence* in Boston harbor and spirited him out of town to eventual freedom in Canada. In September 1854 Bearse again used the *Moby Dick* to rescue a slave in Boston harbor, this time from the schooner *Sally Ann*. Later that month Bearse sold his *Moby Dick*, for "the boat had become too well known for its abolitionist work." By then, ironically, its name would have become "anathema" to Chief Justice Shaw and other "Boston defenders of the Fugitive Slave Law."

In 1880 Bearse published a sketch of the *Moby Dick* as the frontispiece to his *Reminiscences of Fugitive-Slave Law Days in Boston*. He did not, however, reveal why he

THE FAST-SAILING PLEASURE-BOAT,
MOBY DICK,
AUSTIN BEARSE, Master,
Lying at the North side of Central Wharf, Boston,
IS READY, AT ALL TIMES, FOR
Pleasure Parties,
—OR—
FISHING EXCURSIONS IN THE HARBOR.

☞ J. B. Smith, 16 Brattle street, the well-known and popular Caterer, is prepared to furnish such supplies as may be desired, for these Excursions.

References. Marston & Sampson, head of Philadelphia Packet Pier; Cook & Wood, head of Long Wharf; Norris & Hallett, Eating-House, head of Central Whf.

Advertisement in the Liberator *for the speedy pleasure boat, Moby Dick, July 2, 1852. National Archives.*

had chosen *Moby Dick* as its name. One imagines that when Douglass published his story "Moby Dick Captured" in *Frederick Douglass' Paper* in August 1854, he would have been aware of the other *Moby Dick* that, for one month more, would be rescuing fugitive slaves in Boston Harbor.

On a moonlit July night in 1853, yacht Moby Dick, *captained by Austin Bearse, lands a fugitive slave at Drake's Wharf, South Boston. A. C. Russell etching from Bearse's* Reminiscences of Fugitive Slave-Days in Boston, *1880. Boston Public Library.*

Benito Cereno

Just as the May 27, 1847, issue of the *National Anti-Slavery Standard* was an early manifestation of Douglass's and Melville's joint visibility in American culture, so was the November 1855 issue of *Putnam's Magazine* a culmination of that joint visibility. The same man, Charles Briggs, was largely responsible for each of these moments. In 1847, he was the "B" who had given Douglass's "rare talents" and Melville's fictional "revelations" the highest possible praise in the same issue of the *Standard*. Now, eight years later, he was the editor who had made *Putnam's* the only American magazine in which one could imagine seeing a highly appreciative review of *My Bondage and My Freedom* in the same issue as an installment of *Benito Cereno*.

Briggs had been the chief editor at *Putnam's* since the inaugural issue in January 1853. Then he had pledged to support "the acutest observations, and the most trenchant thought" that American writers could devote to American life. Briggs's implementation of this vision had already led Melville to publish in *Putnam's* such challenging stories as "Bartleby, the Scrivener" (1853), "The Encantadas" (1854), and "Israel Potter" (1854–55). *Benito Cereno* was something else again, however. Its acutest observations and most trenchant thoughts were buried far beneath the surface of a story whose overt obfuscations and deferred revelations must have baffled readers of *Putnam's* then as they do college sophomores today. In keeping with *Putnam's* policy, *Benito Cereno* was published anonymously, but other publications did identify Herman Melville as its author.

The review of *My Bondage and My Freedom* in the November 1855 *Putnam's*, like that autobiography itself, is relatively straightforward. Published anonymously, it is printed in the "Editorial Notes" section and may pos-sibly have been written by Briggs (although his editorial role changed at some point after George Putnam sold the magazine to Dix and Edwards in March 1855). The reviewer identifies Frederick Douglass as

> the well-known fugitive slave, who has come to occupy so conspicuous a position, both as a writer and a speaker. . . . The mere fact that the member of an outcast and enslaved race should accomplish his freedom, and educate himself up to an equality of intellectual and moral vigor with the leaders of the race by which he was held in bondage, is, in itself, so remarkable, that the story of the change cannot be otherwise than exciting.

Putnam's reviewer "confesses" to have read the book

> with the unbroken attention with which we absorbed Uncle Tom's Cabin. It has the advantage of the latter book that it is no fiction. . . . Our English literature has recorded many an example of genius struggling against adversity . . . yet none of these are so impressive as the case of the solitary slave, in a remote district, surrounded by none but enemies, conceiving the project of his escape, teaching himself to read and write to facilitate it, accomplishing it at last, and subsequently raising himself to a leadership in a great movement in behalf of his brethren. Whatever may be our opinion of slavery, or of the best means of acting upon it, we cannot but admire the force and integrity of character which has enabled Frederick Douglass to attain his present unique position.

One month later, after reading the third and last installment of *Benito Cereno*, readers of *Putnam's* sympathetic to Douglass would be in a position to compare his "intellectual and moral vigor" and his "force and integrity of character" with that of Babo, another enslaved person whose talent and leadership are "unique."

Melville's story, too, is rooted in fact more than in fiction, taking not only the essence of its plot but the ethos of its overt narrative voice from the real-life story that Captain Amasa Delano told in Chapter 18 of his *Narrative of Voyages and Travels* in 1817. In the first installment of Melville's story, published in *Putnam's* in October 1855, Babo is seen, through the eyes of Captain Delano, as the perfectly submissive servant/slave, who cares for Captain Cereno with all the attentiveness that any Uncle Tom could possibly show to his master. Captain Delano is so taken with Babo's fealty in this part of the story that he envies Cereno "such a friend; slave I cannot call him."

At the beginning of the November installment, Captain Delano is so impressed with Babo's submissiveness that he asks Cereno if he can buy him for "fifty doubloons." His admiration for Babo intensifies even more during the shaving scene, when Babo's debonair air with the blade reminds him that "most negroes are natural valets and hairdressers; taking to the comb and brush congenially as to the castanets." This natural ability, when added to "the docility arising from the unaspiring contentment of a limited mind," brands them as "indisputable inferiors."

Only in the third installment in December does the reader, with Captain Delano, discover that Babo's submissive pose has been an elaborate charade. Babo is in fact a revolutionary Nat Turner/Madison Washington figure who has already liberated his fellow slaves on the ship. He is dictating Benito's every move while appearing to be following him in the guise of a submissive servant. On the plot level Captain Delano, once he understands the true state of affairs, recaptures the ship from the slaves and

"saves" Benito Cereno from his captors. On the symbolic level Babo's decapitated head on a stake at the end of the story challenges the assumptions of Captain Delano and the white society he represents as boldly as Douglass's words do in *My Bondage and My Freedom.*

Here, as with *Moby-Dick*, I will restrict my commentary to those passages of the story that relate to aspects of Douglass and Melville that have been examined in this book. The first such passage occurs in the October installment, when Captain Delano, feeling something amiss on Benito Cereno's ship but not knowing what, asks himself "might not the San Dominick, like a slumbering volcano, suddenly let loose energies now hid?" Melville not only uses the defining phrase from Douglass's 1849 "Slumbering Volcano" speech, but he does so in the context of a shipboard slave revolt like the one by Madison Washington that Douglass celebrates in that speech. Of course, Delano does not yet realize the true state of affairs. He is in the exact position of the Southern slaveholders as Douglass had depicted them in the 1849 speech: "the slaveholders are sleeping on slumbering volcanoes, if they did but know it."

Maggie Sale, in her 1997 book *The Slumbering Volcano: American Slave Ship Revolts and the Production of Rebellious Masculinity*, juxtaposes the "slumbering volcano" passages by both authors at the beginning of her chapter on *Benito Cereno.* She does not, however, address the possibility that Melville might be using that phrase in dialogue with Douglass's earlier use. Her interpretation locates Melville's authorial sympathies closer to the complacent white mentality of Captain Delano than to the trenchant anti-slavery action of Babo, so she would not be likely to imagine Douglass's speech as part of the inspiration for Melville's story. Melville's spatial and intellectual

PUTNAM'S MONTHLY.

A Magazine of Literature, Science, and Art.

VOL. VI.—NOV., 1855.—NO. XXXV.

BENITO CERENO.

THE advancing speck was observed by the blacks. Their shouts attracted the attention of Don Benito, who, with a return of courtesy, approaching Captain Delano, expressed satisfaction at the coming of some supplies, slight and temporary as they must necessarily prove.

Captain Delano responded; but while doing so, his attention was drawn to something passing on the deck below: among the crowd climbing the landward bulwarks, anxiously watching the coming boat, two blacks, to all appearances accidentally incommoded by one of the sailors, flew out against him with horrible curses, which the sailor someway resenting, the two blacks dashed him to the deck and jumped upon him, despite the earnest cries of the oakum-pickers.

"Don Benito," said Captain Delano quickly, "do you see what is going on there? Look!"

"Master wouldn't part with Babo for a thousand doubloons," murmured the black, overhearing the offer, and taking it in earnest, and, with the strange vanity of a faithful slave appreciated by his master, scorning to hear so paltry a valuation put upon him by a stranger. But Don Benito, apparently hardly yet completely restored, and again interrupted by his cough, made but some broken reply.

Soon his physical distress became so great, affecting his mind, too, apparently, that, as if to screen the sad spectacle, the servant gently conducted his master below.

Left to himself, the American, to while away the time till his boat should arrive, would have pleasantly accosted some one of the few Spanish seamen he saw; but recalling something that Don Benito had said touching their ill conduct, he refrained, as a ship-master in-

---

proximity to Douglass at the time of the "Slumbering Volcano" speech, however, along with his subsequent attention to Douglass, his writing, and his environs in *Redburn*, *White-Jacket*, and *Moby-Dick*, combine to suggest that Melville's use of the "slumbering volcano" phrase is more likely to be a conscious tribute to Douglass.

The shaving scene in the November 1855 issue of *Putnam's* is widely regarded as Melville's most brilliant stroke in *Benito Cereno*, one for which there is absolutely no precedent in Captain Delano's 1817 *Narrative*.

While Captain Delano complacently looks on, thinking what natural valets negroes are and entirely oblivious to the realities of the scene, Benito Cereno feels Babo's knife on his throat, knowing that any false move or word could bring immediate death. This pivotal scene in the story alludes in complex and multiple ways to Douglass's confrontation with Isaiah Rynders in the Broadway Tabernacle on May 7, 1850—and to its sequel in the New York Society Library the following morning.

As seen in Chapter 3, when Rynders declared to Douglass that he was "only half a

Thomas Wentworth Higginson, age 23, daguerreotype, 1846. Public Library of Cincinnati and Hamilton County.

famous occasion when the notorious Isaiah Rynders of New York, at the head of a mob, interrupted an anti-slavery meeting, came on the platform, seated himself, and bade the meeting proceed."

Douglass was speaking at the time, and he continued to do so, Higginson recalls, in spite of Rynders's repeated interventions.

> *Nothing loath, [Douglass] made his speech only keener and keener for the interference, weaving around the intruder's head a wreath of delicate sarcasm which carried the audience with it, while the duller wits of the burly despot could hardly follow him. Knowing only, in a general way, that he was being dissected, Rynders at last exclaimed, "What you Abolitionists want to do is to cut all our throats!" "Oh, no!" replied Douglass in his most dulcet tones. "We would only cut your hair;" and bending over the shaggy and frowzy head of the Bowery tyrant, he gave a suggestive motion as of scissors to his thumb and forefinger, with a professional politeness that instantly brought down the house, friend and foe, while Rynders quitted the platform in wrath, and the meeting dissolved itself amid general laughter. It was a more cheerful conclusion, perhaps, than that stormier one—not unknown in reformatory conventions—with which Shakespeare so often ends his scenes: "Exeunt fighting."*

That stormier conclusion came, of course, in the riot that shut down the meeting in the New York Society Library the next day.

Higginson's account is valuable for its appreciation of Douglass's remarkable grace under pressure, a quality he shares with Babo. It is also valuable for the revelation that Douglass gave "a suggestive motion as of scissors to his thumb and forefinger" as he said, "We would only cut your hair." By revealing

nigger," Douglass immediately replied, "And so half-brother to yourselves." When Rynders argued that the slaves wanted to "cut their master's throats," Douglass declared that "they had had the razor in their hands for years and the worst they had done was to cut hair." This latter exchange about cutting hair versus cutting throats is itself of interest in relation to the scenario that Melville creates in which Babo holds the razor to Benito's throat. However, the fictional scene becomes richer yet in the context of other elements of the confrontation with Rynders and its aftermath the next day.

One person who remembered Douglass's confrontation with Rynders fifty years later was Thomas Wentworth Higginson, the abolitionist preacher and editor, who recreates the 1850 session in the Tabernacle in the January 1904 issue of the *Atlantic Monthly* (the successor to *Putnam's Monthly*). Such was Douglass's poise that Higginson presents the confrontation with Rynders as an example of his "inexhaustible sense of humor." This quality "was never better seen than on the once that Douglass mimicked the role of the barber to Rynders and "instantly brought down the house" by doing so, Higginson's testimony increases the likelihood that the encounter in the Broadway Tabernacle helped inspire the shaving scene in which Babo plays the barber to Cereno.

Like the real-life dialogue, the fictional scene moves from the razor at the throat to the scissors in the hair. After Babo's razor has drawn its first touch of blood from Cereno's throat, "his next operation was with comb, scissors and brush; going round and round, smoothing a curl here, clipping an unruly whisker-hair, giving a graceful sweep to the temple-lock, with other impromptu touches evincing the hand of the master."

Melville's story also finds its own equivalent for Higginson's observation that Douglass was "weaving around the intruder's head a wreath of delicate sarcasm which carried the audience with it, while the duller wits of the burly despot could hardly follow him." This is an apt description of the way Babo's masterful speech weaves itself around the head of the unsuspecting Captain Delano—an effect that Melville extends to readers who have not yet realized that Babo is master not only of razor and scissors but of Benito and the ship.

As he watches the shaving scene, especially after the awkward drawing of blood, Captain Delano momentarily wonders if Babo and Benito Cereno are "acting out, both in word and deed, . . . some juggling play . . . of the barber before him." As with his earlier question of whether there might be some "slumbering volcano" ready to erupt from the hold, he dismisses the thought because his mind is unable to imagine the possibility that a negro servant and slave could be a freedom fighter in disguise.

If Melville was in the Broadway Tabernacle on the morning of May 7, 1850, he would have

seen and heard the remarkable encounter that Higginson later described. If he was in the hall of his own library the next morning, he would have seen and heard the aftermath of Douglass's impersonation of a barber the day before. As the *Globe* reported on May 9, this began when "Mr. Burleigh" came on stage. One voice asked, "Say, old dad, how much do you owe your barber?" to which someone else added, "Oh, let Douglass shave that man, and make a wig for Garrison."

The *Globe*, in reporting this episode, identified Mr. Burleigh as "the Hairy Man," adding that he had "a sufficient quantity of red hair on his face and head to supply the reasonable demands of any wig-maker in the city." The *Herald* struck a slightly more dignified tone by identifying C. C. Burleigh as "editor of a Hartford paper, and a poet." In the *Herald* account, the first voice from the crowd declared, "There's the man that cheated the barber." Another asked, "Why don't Douglass shave that tall Christ, and make a wig for him," to which Burleigh "screamed, at the top of his voice, 'You are a God-abandoned people.'"

At this point a group of men invaded the hall, "howling like demons," according to the New York *Express* on May 9. After chasing the women out, they fomented general panic by shouting "Douglass, Douglass, Douglass!" and "Where are the tar and feathers?" Although Burleigh stood his ground a bit longer, he was soon succeeded by Garrison, Phillips, and Van Rensselear in their unavailing attempts to continue the meeting before everything was finally shut down.

If Melville was not actually in the Library Hall on the morning of May 8, he would have had easy access to the banter about Douglass the barber, like the exchange between Douglass and Rynders the day before, in the daily press. (The accounts cited from the *Globe*, *Herald*, and *Express* were all reprinted in the *Liberator* on May 17.) The white hecklers who called out for Douglass to shave Burleigh and make a wig for Garrison are the same ones who moments later jeered Wendell Phillips as a "white-washed nigger" and were then rebuked as "worse than blacks" by Thomas Van Rensselaer in the same newspaper accounts examined in relation to *Moby-Dick*.

When Melville created the shaving scene in *Benito Cereno* in 1855, he was activating a general anxiety among certain white readers in both the North and South over entrusting their hair, beards, and throats to enslaved or free black persons who might well have reasons to hold a grudge. He was also alluding to the elegance and wit with which Douglass played the barber to Rynders in the Broadway Tabernacle on May 7, 1850, echoed in the crude humor of the white rioters who demanded that he extend his services to Burleigh and Garrison the next day. Although such allusions would have been over the heads of many who read the story in the November 1855 issue of *Putnam's*, this New York magazine had many anti-slavery readers for whom the shaving scene in *Benito Cereno* is likely to have reactivated the memory of Douglass as barber to Rynders. Such readers as these would also have savored the rave review of *My Bondage and My Freedom* in the same issue.

Melville's 1855 story also provides a brilliant fictional realization, through the consciousness of Captain Delano, of another point that Douglass had managed to make during his improvised responses to Rynders on May 7, 1850. Douglass tells Rynders that "you do not object to the presence of the negro . . . when he appears in the livery of the servant." He made the same point in the "Colorphobia" essay a year before, noting that New Yorkers are offended not by the presence

of "colored servants" but by that of "colored gentlemen." Melville's Delano, of course, loves Babo in the "livery" of the servant. He cannot tolerate or imagine him in any other role. By extending Babo's servant role to that of a barber, Melville gives Delano's historical story its broadest possible contemporary currency.

In 1994 Sterling Stuckey called the shaving scene in *Benito Cereno* "one of the great moments in world literature." He was responding to the ingenious way in which Melville had seamlessly incorporated elements of Ashantee culture into Babo's performance as a barber to Benito. All of the ways in which that same scene relates to Douglass's improvised moment as a barber to Rynders make it even greater.

Two other details in *Benito Cereno* relate closely to declarations by Douglass during his confrontation with Rynders. Delano's blinders are finally removed in the December installment of the story, when Benito Cereno suddenly jumps into Captain Delano's departing boat and is followed in short order by Babo. Babo, to Delano's surprise, now seems intent on murdering Benito as well as himself. By dint of superior force, Delano is able to "ground the prostrate negro" into the bottom of the boat "with his right foot." In so doing, he embodies the action carved into the stern-piece of Benito Cereno's ship, seen at the beginning of the story, in which "a dark satyr in a mask" is "holding his foot on the prostrate neck of a writhing figure, likewise masked."

These two fictional images of an oppressive foot suppressing a prostrate, writhing figure recall another striking figure of speech voiced by Douglass immediately after the exchange with Rynders about cutting throats, cutting hair, and the "livery of the servant." Responding to Rynders's accusation that negroes are a "doomed race in this country

[who] will soon die out," Douglass declares that instead "there is something about the negro so buoyant, so tenacious of life, that it defies the power of oppression to crush him. . . . Lift your foot from off his neck, and he will smile at you, and try to teach you a lesson of humanity that you would find difficult to learn were it not for the crushed victim that lies writhing at your feet."

Melville, five years later, uses the image of the foot on the neck to offer the same kind of "lesson of humanity" that Douglass offered to Rynders and his followers in the Broadway Tabernacle. Delano, sadly, learns nothing from "the crushed victim that lies writhing under" his foot. Although Douglass's remarks at the Tabernacle were constantly interrupted by the intervention of Rynders and others, they were recorded for posterity in a number of newspapers, including the *Herald* and the *Tribune* on May 8, the *National Anti-Slavery Standard* on May 23, and the *Liberator* on May 24.

Melville's double use of the foot on the neck points to the likelihood of a conscious tribute to the imagery in which Douglass had appealed to the white man's humanity during his confrontation with Rynders five years earlier. The image of the "crushed victim" that is "writhing" under the foot in both Douglass's and Melville's formulations recalls their shared language in 1850 about the "crushed worm" that "may yet turn under the heel of the oppressor."

Delano's foot subduing Babo dominates the early pages of the December 1855 installment in *Putnam's*. Babo's head and brain dominate the last page. In Melville's story, as in Delano's real-life *Narrative*, Babo has been convicted by the courts of the "Holy Crusade" in Lima and executed in the public plaza after being "dragged to the gibbet at the tail of a mule." Babo "uttered no sound, and could not be forced to," ever since his "slight

frame . . . had yielded at once to the superior muscular strength of his captor" in Delano's boat. He was a "black whose brain, not body, had schemed and led the revolt, with the plot" to deceive Delano. After the execution and decapitation, "the body was burned to ashes; but for many days, the head, that hive of subtlety, fixed on a pole in the Plaza, met, unabashed, the gaze of the whites."

Unlike Delano in his telling of the same tale, Melville challenges the reader to engage with the brain of Babo. A careful reading of the deposition reveals that Babo had not only led his fellow slaves to freedom in a revolt as valiant as the one led by Madison Washington in Douglass's "Slumbering Volcano" in 1849 (and again in *The Heroic Slave* in 1853). After doing that, he stage-managed the brilliant charade by which he and all of his fellow rebels on board had contrived to make Captain Delano believe that Benito Cereno was still in charge of his ship, with the submissive Babo at this side.

How does Melville's final image of Babo's head, "that hive of subtlety," meeting "unabashed, the gaze of the whites" relate to Douglass's confrontation with Rynders and his followers in the Broadway Tabernacle? Higginson recalled the "wreath of delicate sarcasm" that Douglass had woven around Rynders's head as he assured him that "we would only cut your hair" while playing the barber. The transcripts of the same speech record his saying to Rynders and his supporters, "You do not object to the presence of the negro . . . when he appears in the livery of the servant," and if "you lift your foot from off [the negro's] neck," he will "try to teach you a lesson of humanity that you would find difficult to learn were it not for the crushed victim that lies writhing at your feet."

Having parried the challenge from Rynders and kept the opening session in the Tabernacle alive for the concluding address by Samuel Ringgold Ward, Douglass finally informs Rynders that "I have a head to think, and I know that God meant I should exercise the right to think—that I have a heart to feel, and a tongue to speak whatever that heart listeth, and God meant that I should use that tongue in behalf of humanity and justice for every man." Melville offers Babo's head, as Douglass had offered his own, to anyone in the white audience capable of learning "a lesson of humanity" from those it had crushed as a victim.

Amasa Delano was not such a man. The most amazing thing about his 1817 narrative to a reader today is that, as generous as he is throughout the story in wanting to aid a ship he thinks in distress, it never crosses his mind, after the true state of things is revealed, to think of Babo as a human being, as a man with a heart and a brain—as anything other than a slave to be physically subdued and legally executed.

In the last sentence of the November installment in *Putnam's*, Captain Delano's ship arrives to retrieve him from the Spanish ship on which he has been offering assistance. The "two vessels, thanks to the pilot's skill, ere long in neighborly style lay anchored together." When Delano suddenly discovers that the blacks, not the whites, are in control of the Spanish ship, the "neighborly" relation ends. The white men from the American ship pursue the "fugitives" in the Spanish ship as fiercely slave hunters would pursue fugitive slaves, until the ship and its human cargo are successfully retaken. The Peruvian court under the laws of the "Holy Crusade," like Judge Shaw's court under the renewed Fugitive Slave Law, offers recaptured fugitives no protection.

Carolyn Karcher in 1980 compares Babo's silence after being captured with "the status of black slaves in America" in the 1850s,

"legally deprived of the right to make themselves heard, even in the court room." She extends the comparison by citing "Frederick Douglass's poignant characterization of the slave's plight" in the "Lecture on Slavery" that he gave in Rochester on December 1, 1850 (and later reprinted in *My Bondage and My Freedom*). Douglass made this challenge to his audience: "Ask the slave what is his condition—what is his mind—what he thinks of enslavement? and you had as well address your inquiries to the *silent dead*. There comes no *voice* from the enslaved."

Melville may possibly have read this characterization of the slave's plight long before it was reprinted in *My Bondage and My Freedom*; the December 1 speech was already printed in the December 5, 1850, issue of the *North Star*. But he did not need access to it to understand Douglass's contention that "there comes no *voice* from the enslaved." Douglass had been conveying this message, and trying to counteract it, ever since he had "spoken for the Slaves" in the Court Room of Albany City Hall, a few rods from Pinsker Hill, in June and July 1845.

Early in 1855, while Douglass was writing *My Bondage and My Freedom* in Rochester and Melville was writing *Benito Cereno* in Pittsfield, the national prospects for "neighborly" relations between blacks and whites, as well as between North and South, were even bleaker than they had been in New York City in May 1850. The two writers were no longer "anchored together" in that section of New York City whose once hopeful Anniversary Weeks in May were long since gone. They were, however, still addressing their common concerns "in neighborly style."

Douglass in *My Bondage and My Freedom* directly informs readers about his experience as a black man in the North as well as in the South, hoping to shame and shock Americans

Frederick Douglass, albumen print, 1870s. National Archives.

Herman Melville, tintype, circa 1870. Bershire Athenaeum.

into the need to see and treat black fellow citizens as free and equal human beings. Melville attacks the same problem by immersing his reader in the mentality of Captain Delano, challenging the reader to fully understand with head and heart, not simply on the plot level, those "energies" which, "like a slumbering volcano," remain hidden in the hold.

It would be nice to think of Douglass and Melville meeting each other late in 1855, when *Putnam's* was praising My *Bondage and My Freedom* at the same time it was publishing *Benito Cereno*. This chapter has shown some of what these two literary works had to say to each other. But what might the two men who had written them have had to say to each other in person?

A perfect opportunity for such a meeting could have been the grand dinner party for America's foremost writers, editors, and publishers that George P. Putnam gave at the Crystal Palace in New York City on September 27, 1855. The meal was to be catered by

Charles Stetson of Astor House, familiar to readers of this book as one of the two celebrated cooks under whom the ship's cook in *White-Jacket* had "graduated." Herman Melville was one of "some 230 authors and editors" who were invited. On September 7 he wrote Putnam from Pittsfield to say that "if [it is] in my power I shall be most happy to be present at so attractive a festival."

Frederick Douglass was the most prominent American author—and editor—*not* to be invited. Ezra Greenspan, reviewing the guest list in his 2000 biography of Putnam, finds not a single "identifiable" African American author or editor among those to whom invitations were sent. The omission of Douglass was even more flagrant given the extremely favorable reception that *My Bondage and My Freedom* was receiving in both publicity and sales. Melville, it turned out, did not attend either. His name was included in a list of those who sent "letters of regret" in advance of the extravaganza.

Frederick Douglass, stereograph, 1885. National Archives.

Herman Melville, cabinet card by Rockwood, 1885. Berkshire Athenaeum

AMERICAN EPILOGUE

Douglass and Melville each lived four more decades after publishing *My Bondage and My Freedom* and *Benito Cereno* in 1855. Melville ceased writing fiction after publishing *The Confidence Man* in 1857. He published *Battle-Pieces*, his first book of poetry, in 1866, but after that he dropped out of visibility as a literary figure, working from 1865 to 1885 as a customs inspector in New York City. When Charles Briggs revived *Putnam's Magazine* in 1868, he asked in the first issue, "And where . . . is Herman Melville? Has that copious and imaginative author, who contributed so many brilliant articles to the *Monthly*, let fall his pen just where its use might have been so remunerative to himself, and so satisfactory to the public?" A note at the end of this first issue indicated that Melville was willing to be included in the list of "probable contributors," but no contributions appear to have been forthcoming. In 1876 Melville published *Clarel*, an epic poem about the Holy Land, financed by his uncle Peter Gansevoort in Albany. Now quite highly appreciated, it was then unnoticed. From his retirement in 1885 until his death in 1891, Melville self-published two slim volumes of poetry and left the manuscript of "Billy Budd, Sailor" unpublished in his desk. He died of heart failure on September 28, 1891, at his home at 104 East 26th Street.

This event was noted in the New York *Press* as the "Death of a Once Popular Author" whose "own generation" has probably "long thought him dead." A brief obituary in the New York *Daily Tribune* declared that Melville's first novel, *Typee*, was "his best work." The *Evening Journal* in Albany was one of several papers in that city that noted the passing of a local boy who had achieved some national notice a half-century earlier. Thurlow Weed was no longer editor, having died in 1882 after retiring from the *Evening Journal* in 1863.

Douglass, unlike Melville, remained in the public eye until the time of his death. His continued celebrity owing to the strong sales of *My Bondage and My Freedom* in 1855 gave way to notoriety of a different kind in 1859 when he was charged as a conspirator in John Brown's raid on Harper's Ferry and escaped to England for a time. During the Civil War Douglass became a personal advisor to President Lincoln (whose Secretary of State Charles Sumner was unable to give Herman Melville a consular appointment for which letters of support had been solicited from Dana and Weed).

After the war Douglass was appointed to official posts by Presidents Grant, Hayes, Garfield, and Harrison while also continuing his activity as an editor, orator, and author. In addition to publishing *The Life and Times of Frederick Douglass* in 1881 and revising it in 1892, he wrote articles for journals such as *Atlantic Monthly* and *North American Review* and introductions to books such as *The Reason Why the Colored American Is Not in the World's Columbia Exposition* (1892) and *The Story of the Hutchinsons (Tribe of Jesse)* (1896).

Douglass's death from heart failure on February 20, 1895, at his Cedar Hill home was a national event. So was the memorial service at the Metropolitan A. M. E. Church in Washington on February 25; Susan B. Anthony was one of the speakers to an audience that included Supreme Court Justice

John Marshall Harlan. After services the next day in Rochester, Douglass was buried in that city's Mount Hope Cemetery near his wife, Anna Murray Douglass.

As Melville became less involved in public life, his feelings on some national issues differed sharply from those of Douglass. The two men responded to the agony of the Civil War in contrasting ways, Douglass embracing it as a necessary step in ending slavery, Melville favoring the Union side for the same reason but fearing more for the fate of a divided nation in the wake of the war. In their private lives, the two aging men had much in common. Each accumulated a large library, assembled an impressive collection of art, and enjoyed the company of his granddaughters.

Among the art collections of each man were images that would have interested the other. Douglass would have had a certain

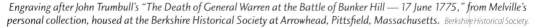

Engraving after John Trumbull's "The Death of General Warren at the Battle of Bunker Hill — 17 June 1775," from Melville's personal collection, housed at the Berkshire Historical Society at Arrowhead, Pittsfield, Massachusetts. Berkshire Historical Society.

interest in Melville's multiple images of Chief Justice Shaw, a personal nemesis since the Latimer case in 1842. He might have taken a somewhat warmer interest in Melville's large, framed engraving after Trumbull's *Battle of Bunker Hill.* During his confrontation with Rynders at the Broadway Tabernacle in 1850, Douglass had declared that "the first blood shed on Bunker's Hill was that of a black man," and a non-white soldier is conspicuous at the far right of Melville's engraving.

Melville would have been interested in Douglass's framed engraving of John Brown, the subject of "The Portent," Melville's first poem in *Battle-Pieces.* He would have been equally intrigued by a huge framed painting of a lee shore scene that still hangs in Douglass's parlor. The artist is unknown, but the image of a ship off the lee shore of a stormy coast would have appealed as much to the author of *Moby-Dick* as to the orator who had delivered "The

Slumbering Volcano" and "What to the Slave is the Fourth of July?" The painting captures the spirit of Melville's "magnanimous" sea and of Douglass's "proud, towering billows of the Atlantic." It pictures a "storm-tossed ship" such as Melville imagines in the "Lee Shore" chapter of *Moby-Dick* off the "huge forms of flinty rocks" such as Douglass imagines to the "leeward" in the "Fourth of July" speech.

Because both men were writers, the final place to look for mutuality in their later years is in the words they wrote. Certainly it is possible that a comprehensive study of the words Douglass wrote late in life might reveal some phrase or image that registers a continuing awareness of the American writer whose *Typee, White-Jacket, Moby-Dick,* and *Israel Potter* had left their mark in *The North Star, Frederick Douglass' Paper,* and occasional Douglass speeches. But one of the places in which Douglass might have

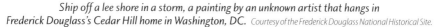

Ship off a lee shore in a storm, a painting by an unknown artist that hangs in Frederick Douglass's Cedar Hill home in Washington, DC. Courtesy of the Frederick Douglass National Historical Site.

made such a recognition late in life does not include it. In Chapter 18 of his *Life and Times,* Douglass compiled a long list of all those friends who had most helped to achieve "the success which has attended my labors in life." Recognizing that he had too often been viewed as a "self-made man," he was eager, now, to acknowledge all those without whose help "the last forty years of my life might have been spent on the wharves of New Bedford, rolling oil casks, loading ships for whaling voyages, putting in coal, picking up a job here and there, wherever I could find one."

Among the white friends, beginning with William Lloyd Garrison, who "took me into their hearts and homes," he lists more than fifty individuals from Parker, Phillips, and Quincy down to John Brown and the Hutchinson Family Singers but not Melville. A lesser number of "fellow citizens of African descent" essential to his success begins with Dr. James McCune Smith and includes Thomas Van Rensselaer, Nathan Johnson, and Thomas Downing. Those "honorable women" to whom he is indebted begin with Lucretia Mott and include Lydia Maria Child,

Harriet Beecher Stowe, and the Mott sisters of Albany.

Melville is also missing from a similar list that Douglass had published in *My Bondage and My Freedom* as part of a lecture on "The Anti-Slavery Movement" he had given earlier in 1855. Among the "poets" who were then aiding the anti-slavery movement, Douglass listed Whittier, Longfellow, Lowell, John Pierpont, and William Cullen Bryant. The fiction writer he mentions is Harriet Beecher Stowe. Would he have included Melville's name, one wonders, after *Benito Cereno* was published later that same year?

Melville, who wrote no autobiography, left his most indelible, and elusive, traces of the people he had known in his fiction. One of the most interesting passages in *Billy Budd, Sailor,* written in his last years of life and not published until 1924, is the conspicuous digression in the second paragraph of the story. Having introduced the concept of the "Handsome Sailor" (of which the blond and blue-eyed Billy Budd, sailing on a British warship in the 1790s, is to be the defining example), Melville stops his new story in its

Frederick Douglass's Cedar Hill home near Washington, DC, circa 1940. National Archives.

tracks to recall a very different sailor whom he saw "in Liverpool, now half a century ago" (at the time of Melville's own voyage to Liverpool in 1839).

This sailor is

so intensely black that he must needs have been a native African of the unadulterated blood of Ham—a symmetric figure much above the average height. The two ends of a gay silk handkerchief thrown loose about the neck danced upon the displayed ebony of his chest, in his ears were big hoops of gold, and a Highland bonnet with a tartan band set off his shapely head. . . . In jovial sallies right and left, his white teeth flashing into view, he rollicked along, the center of a company of his shipmates. These were made up of such an assortment of tribes and complexions as would have well fitted them to be marched up by Anacharsis Cloots before the bar of the first French Assembly as Representatives of the Human Race. At each spontaneous tribute rendered by the wayfarers to this black pagod of a fellow—the tribute of a pause and a stare, and less frequently an exclamation—the motley retinue showed that they took that sort of pride in the evoker of it which the Assyrian priests doubtless showed for their grand sculptured Bull when the faithful prostrated themselves.

Melville acknowledges the digressive nature of this paragraph by beginning the next paragraph with the words, "To return."

This "remarkable" sailor in Liverpool a half century before "seemed to accept the spontaneous homage of his shipmates . . . with no perceptible trace of the vainglorious about him, rather with the offhand unaffectedness of natural regality." He combines the commanding physique and spontaneous ease of Marnoo in the Marquesas, the head-turning panache of Lavender in Liverpool, and the coal-black skin of Daggoo on the *Pequod*. His ease helps a reader of *Benito Cereno* to imagine how figures like Babo and Atufal might have appeared if they had been strolling freely in Liverpool rather than enslaved on Benito Cereno's ship (*Billy Budd* is set in 1797, one year earlier than *Benito Cereno*).

Herman Melville's home at Arrowhead in the Berkshire Mountains, Massachusetts, circa 1940. National Archives.

The strolling sailor of *Billy Budd* combines qualities from throughout Melville's fiction with those of an actual sailor that Melville apparently remembered from 1839, but he also evokes certain associations with Frederick Douglass. Douglass, as we have seen, embodied some of the same qualities that the black sailor shares with such characters as Marnoo and Lavender. Furthermore, he had escaped from slavery in 1838, the year before Melville presumably saw the real-life inspiration for the black "Handsome Sailor" in Liverpool. In his *Life and Times* in 1881, Douglass for the first time revealed how he had escaped from Baltimore to the North in 1838. "In my clothing I was rigged out in sailor style. I had on a red shirt and a tarpaulin hat and black cravat, tied in sailor fashion, carelessly and loosely about my neck."

Is Melville alluding to Douglass's recent revelation about the black cravat tied "loosely about my neck" in his image of the black Handsome Sailor whose silk handkerchief is "thrown loose about the neck?" Whether the similarity is coincidental or intentional, the important thing here (as in the case of the negro church in New Bedford) is that Melville inserts the Liverpool sailor into his story. His striking stroll along the docks of Liverpool, inspiring spontaneous admiration from all who see him, immediately invites non-white as well as white readers into the world of the book. The black sailor seems as free from prejudice in Liverpool as Lavender had been in *Redburn* in 1849—or as Douglass had depicted himself in the Liverpool section of *My Bondage and My Freedom* in 1855 and again in *Life and Times* in 1881.

The publication of *Billy Budd* in 1924 initiated the Melville "revival" in the early twentieth century that coincided with a sharp decline of interest in Douglass's life and works after his death. The remaining sections of this epilogue address enduring issues in American life that Douglass and Melville help illuminate today, a century and a half after their one decade of joint popularity among their own contemporaries.

What Is a Representative American?

James McCune Smith, in his introduction to *My Bondage and My Freedom*, defines Frederick Douglass as a "Representative American man" because he had "passed through every gradation of rank comprised in our national make-up." Smith does not refer to Douglass's race in making this declaration. He does not qualify the term "Representative American man" with any descriptor such as negro, colored, African, black, or mulatto. Surprising as such an omission may have seemed to many of Smith's readers in 1855, we may be slowly approaching an era, 150 years later, in which such un-qualified evaluations of any American's qualities may be becoming somewhat more common.

Herman Melville was a "Representative American man" by McCune Smith's criterion. The difference was that he "passed through every gradation of rank comprised in our national make-up" in the opposite direction. As Douglass was rising from enslavement to freedom, Melville's status was dropping from the heroism of his Revolutionary War ancestors to his ambitious father's fall from prosperity and sanity to his own sudden fall from a prize-winning student at the Academy to a bank clerk to a merchant seaman to a common whaler—in short, all the way down the social ladder to the consciousness of a white man who could, in some situations, envy a slave, as White-Jacket envied Guinea.

The downward tangent in young Melville's social standing relative to Douglass's social ascent was to be felt in their writing lives as well. Douglass had risen from an unlettered slave to an extremely accomplished orator, editor, and author by the time he published *My Bondage and My Freedom* in 1855, at which point Melville was already nearing the end of the literary celebrity that had begun with *Typee. Benito Cereno* has turned out to be a brilliant book for posterity 150 years after its publication date. As Melville had once hoped for *Mardi,* it has "flower[ed] like the aloe, a hundred years hence." In its own day, however, its radical critique of American slavery was too subtle for most readers. *Benito Cereno* was yet another illustration of the frustration Melville felt when he wrote to Hawthorne in 1851, "What I feel most moved to write, that is banned,–it will not pay. Yet, altogether, write the *other* way I cannot." Here, too, Douglass and Melville were Representative Americans in opposing ways.

In 1855 McCune Smith found Douglass representative not only for the gradations he had passed but because he "bears upon his person and upon his soul every thing that is American." Douglass bore upon his person, of course, the scars of flogging. This was another thing of which he informed Rynders during their confrontation in the Broadway Tabernacle in 1850: "I, who have endured the whip of the slaveholder, who bear the marks of the lash upon my back."

Melville, so far as we know, bore no marks of flogging on his back. But his soul was seared by those who did suffer that fate, whether these be the "collared men" in Yoomy's Vivenza or shipmates of every color on White-Jacket's *Neversink.* As the *National Era* wrote of the flogging in *White-Jacket* a week after its first review of the book, "No one can read the description by Herman Melville of the infliction of this devilish mode of punishment, without horror."

Melville's own ability to "bear . . . upon his soul every thing that is American" was enriched by what he learned from the example of Frederick Douglass. Douglass's public persona as an "erect, lofty-minded African" would have been particularly evident to Melville from the time of the June 1845 lecture in Albany to the May 1850 confrontation with Rynders. The traces we have seen of Douglass's persona, voice, language, environs, and example in *Typee, Omoo, Mardi, Redburn, White-Jacket,* and *Moby-Dick* suggest the degree to which Melville's fiction had been enriched by Douglass and his world years in advance of McCune Smith's characterization of Douglass as a "Representative American man" in 1855.

Melville's own most cogent attempt to "bear upon his body and upon his soul every thing that is American" was to come later in 1855 in the three successive installments of *Benito Cereno.* A story that substitutes the skeleton of a slaveholder for the figurehead of Christopher Columbus and contrasts Babo's rebellious soul with Delano's demeaning mind addresses the extremes of the American condition. Three months after *Benito Cereno* ended in the December 1855 issue of *Putnam's,* James McCune Smith quoted the passage from *Moby-Dick* in his commentary on the 1856 presidential election in *Frederick Douglass' Paper.* Perhaps Smith saw Melville also, on some level, as a representative American man.

How Separate are Black and White America?

In writing this book I was surprised to discover the degree to which Frederick Douglass was a celebrity in Albany while Melville was writing *Typee* in 1845—and the degree to which editor Thurlow Weed was embracing both Douglass and Melville in 1846. Similarly surprising is the extent to which Douglass was covered in the daily as well as the anti-slavery press during the Anniversary Meetings in New York in May of 1848, 1849, and 1850 in the immediate environs in which Melville was writing *Mardi, Redburn* and *White-Jacket* and beginning *Moby-Dick*. Who might have expected that such a writer as Charles F. Briggs ("B") would give such exceptionally high praise to both Douglass and Melville in separate articles in the May 27, 1847, issue of the *National Anti-Slavery Standard*? Or that the same November 1855 issue of *Putnam's* that included the shaving scene from *Benito Cereno* would feature such a cogent, appreciative review of *My Bondage and My Freedom*? Similarly, it has been a surprise to discover the kind of attention that was given to Melville's writing in the *North Star* and *Frederick Douglass' Paper*—and to see the degree to which his writing was also treated in a topical manner by other anti-slavery publications such as the *National Era*, the *National Anti-Slavery Standard*, and the *Chronotype*.

Likewise surprising is the extent to which Douglass and his writing left traces in Melville's fiction. Well-publicized elements of Douglass's life appear to have influenced Melville's depiction of Marnoo's oratorical persona, Bembo's rescue from the shipboard "mob," Lavender's Liverpool promenade, and Babo's finesse as a barber. Melville also showed consistent attention to those non-white environs in which Douglass lived and spoke—from Ishmael's visit to the negro church in New Bedford, to Redburn's sensitivity to the negro churches and "underground oyster-cellars" of New York City, to White-Jacket's attention to the damage done to houses on West Broadway by the "Negro Mob." Beyond that Melville appears to have incorporated language that Douglass spoke to largely black audiences at Shiloh Presbyterian and Abyssinian Baptist in 1849, as well as to white rioters at the Broadway Tabernacle in 1850, into both *Moby-Dick* and *Benito Cereno*.

Some of my surprise at the extent of these interrelations may be because I am a Melville scholar who has only recently begun to study Douglass's life and writings. But even as a Melville scholar, thinking of Douglass has greatly opened up my understanding of Melville's own life and writing. If Melville indeed modeled Marnoo on Douglass to the extent that I think he did, this adds an entirely new frame of reference for understanding Melville's literary career all the way to the digression about the black "Handsome Sailor" in the manuscript of *Billy Budd* more than forty years later. Following Douglass's highly visible activities in New York in each successive May as Melville was writing *Mardi, Redburn,* and *White-Jacket* in the same general neighborhood—culminating in the Rynders riots that shut down free speech as Melville was writing *Moby-Dick* in May 1850—provides a whole new context in which to understand issues of race, identity, and nationhood as Melville addressed them in his fiction.

I am guessing that as we learn more about Douglass's and Melville's lives in Albany in 1845 and New York in 1847–50, we will find evidence that the two men actually did meet, either through mutual admirers such as Thurlow Weed, Charles Briggs, and James McCune Smith or simply through mutual awareness of each other's work. Yet it is also interesting, given the various kinds of convergences we have already seen in their intellectual and physical lives, that I have so far found no direct evidence of their meeting in person during these years of fairly close intellectual and physical proximity. If they never did meet, why? And what would this itself tell us about the limitations upon, as well as the possibilities for, interaction among like-minded black and white Americans in the late 1840s?

Beyond the constrictions that an increasingly aggressive "colorphobia" were placing upon any relationships that managed to cross the color line in New York City at the time, Melville faced the additional constriction of his marriage to the daughter of Chief Justice Shaw. Not only was Judge Shaw the most prominent enforcer of the 1793 Fugitive Slave Law, by which he would have felt obliged to send Frederick Douglass back to Maryland if a case involving his bondage had come before him anytime between 1838 and 1846. During the George Latimer case in 1842, some of the public attacks that Douglass and his fellow abolitionists made on Judge Shaw were so severe that his daughter Elizabeth, twenty years old at the time, would surely never have forgotten them. Her father was compared not only to African slave traders but to Judas Iscariot.

Nor would it have been conducive to a social relationship in New York City that Herman's mother Maria, part of the extended Melville family living at 103 Fourth Avenue, had been raised in the prominent Gansevoort slaveholding family in Albany. Melville could have taken Douglass more easily "into his heart" than into his "home" (in Douglass's phrasing from Life and Times). That is one reason I like to imagine the two men meeting at one of those "underground oyster-cellars" run by Thomas Downing and his son George, the one on Broad Street across from Allan Melville's law office, the other on upper Broadway near the Melville family home.

One thing we *have* seen in the course of this book is that Douglass and Melville each wrote for a double audience, black and white. Doing so was a necessity for Douglass as a non-white (or half-white) American confronting an all-white power structure as a speaker, author, and editor. Melville did not face the same necessity as a white writer writing for a primarily white audience, yet he, more than most white writers of his day, consciously incorporated non-white persons, environs, and consciousness into his work, reaching out to a non-white, anti-slavery audience alongside the mainstream white one.

What Are the Boundaries of the Color Line?

In the few strands of Melville's fiction we have had room to examine, crossing the color line often leads to anxiety or embarrassment. Ishmael bumps into the ash-box before he enters the New Bedford church; he makes a quick exit after seeing the hundred black faces "peering" at him. Tommo is deeply attracted to Marnoo's beautiful blend of Grecian and Polynesian beauty, but he is bitterly hurt when Marnoo spurns his offer to sit next to him. When Redburn first sees Lavender arm–in–arm with the English woman in Liverpool, he is shocked—until he thinks about it and realizes that the New Yorkers who would "mob" such a couple are the ones with the problem. White-Jacket uses the "erect, lofty-minded African" as the touchstone for that manliness which is "unendurable" to those who would oppress, but he is jealous of Guinea, an actual slave, for seemingly being more free than the white sailors on the ship.

Shortly after the visit to the negro church in New Bedford, Ishmael breaks through his own anxieties over interracial association through his friendship with Queequeg, but this makes all the more painful Stubb's race-baiting treatment of Fleece and, later, Pip. The ultimate color line in *Benito Cereno* is the one between the two vessels that are anchored together "in neighborly style"—until Captain Delano, with Babo "prostrate" under his foot, finally sees things as they really are. Delano then decisively sends the men from his "white" vessel to capture those in the "black" vessel, literally becoming catchers of fugitive slaves.

Douglass's defining moments along the color line in the pages of this book have come when speaking as a "fugitive slave" in Albany on June 9, 1845; when giving his "blistering" homecoming speech at the Broadway Tabernacle on May 11, 1847; when walking up and down Broadway with an English woman on either arm on May 5, 1849; and when confronting Isaiah Rynders in the Tabernacle on May 7, 1850. To advertise oneself as a "fugitive slave" one month after publishing the *Narrative* that named his Southern "master" in 1845 took tremendous physical, as well as social, courage. So did giving such a "blistering" attack on white America, from "*centre to circumference*," immediately after returning from England in 1847.

To walk arm–in–arm with two English women up and down Broadway in 1849 was to declare one's most basic civil rights without regard to skin color. The psychological violence of the colorphobia that Douglass and his companions encountered on May 5 demonstrated the extraordinary force of white resistance to such simple assertions of racial equality on the streets of New York City. So did the colorphobia with which Rynders and his followers confronted Douglass at the Tabernacle in 1850 before shutting down the two successive meetings at the New York Society Library and actually attacking Douglass and his female companions at the Battery.

The fact that Douglass was ready to meet all such assaults head on, not only in the columns of the *North Star* in 1849 but again in the lecture halls and on the streets of New York in 1850, showed both physical and intellectual courage. When Douglass welcomed Rynders as his "half-brother" at the Broadway Tabernacle in 1850, a split-second after the latter had called him "only half a nigger," he was not only being quick on his feet. He was articulating, under the most intense public pressure, the arbitrary nature of the social construction that separated "white" and "black" into seemingly distinct American races.

In challenging restrictions on public access in his walks on Broadway and the Battery, Douglass was addressing an issue that did not fully engage the nation until the Civil Rights movement of the 1950s and 1960s. In challeng-

ing the social construction of race by calling Rynders his "half-brother," Douglass was addressing an issue that had become widely discussed in academic circles by the 1990s but that has not yet permeated society as a whole.

Nor has society at large as yet assimilated the racial and post–colonial critique implicit in Melville's treatment of "The Whiteness of the Whale" in *Moby-Dick* or of the figurehead of Christopher Columbus in *Benito Cereno*. (We saw what happened to Melville's *explicit* critique of "white civilized man" in exactly those passages that were expurgated in the revised New York edition of *Typee*.) The complexity of the race issue in the lives and writings of Douglass and Melville, and the courage with which each challenged the concepts and boundaries of the color line in his day, are essential elements of their joint legacy for American society in our own time.

How Should We Classify Douglass and Melville?

Douglass and Melville should be classified as Americans. To classify one as black and the other as white creates a false dichotomy between them that, more than anything else, has prevented American society from seeing them in relation to each other. Thinking for a moment of each man individually, the classification of Douglass as black is patently inaccurate. Even Captain Rynders was eager to point out that Douglass was only "half a nigger." The brief exchange in which he did so at the Broadway Tabernacle in 1850 is pertinent to our current concerns with racial classification.

Rynders, not Douglass, injects race into the exchange. Douglass asks "Am I a man?" To which Rynders replies, "*You* are not a black man; you are only half a nigger." Douglass responds, "He is correct; I am, indeed, only half a negro, a half brother to Mr. Rynders (roars of laughter)."

Composing the Crew of the *Ship Acushnet* of *Fairhaven* whereof is Master, *Valentine Pease* bound for *Pacific Ocean*

NAMES.	PLACES OF BIRTH.	PLACES OF RESIDENCE.	OF WHAT COUNTRY CITIZENS OR SUBJECTS.	DESCRIPTION OF THEIR PERSONS.			
				AGE.	HEIGHT. FEET. INCHES.	COMPLEXION.	HAIR.
Joseph Luis	*Fayall*	*Portugal*	*Portugal*	20	5 5	*Light*	*Brown*
Henry Harmer	*Geneva N.Y.*	*Newark N.J.*	*U.S.*	20	5 5	*Light*	*Brown*
William Barnett	*Elizabeth City N.J.*	*Fairhaven*	*U.S.*	25	5 5½	*Light*	*Brown*
George Vliet	*New York*	*New Bedford*	*U.S.*	23	5 6	*dark*	*Brown*
John Adams	*England*	*Fairhaven*	*Portugal*	21	5 6	*dark*	*dark*
Richard T. Greene	*Rochester N.Y.*		*U.S.*	21	5 8½	*auli*	*Black*
John Wright			*U.S.*	18	5 5¾	*Light*	*Brown*
Joseph Broadrick			*U.S.*	18	6 6	*dark*	*dark*
Henry Brent	*Portland*	*Fairhaven*	*U.S.*	17	5 8½	*Light*	*Brown*
Thomas Wolcott	*Stow N.Y.*	*Fairhaven*	*U.S.*	35	5 6¼	*Light*	*Brown*
Carlos W. Green	*New York*	*Fairhaven*	*U.S.*	19	5 5½	*Light*	*Brown*
Wm Maiden	*Philadelphia*	*New Bedford*	*U.S.*	38	5 9¾	*Black*	*Wolly*
Herman Melville	*New York*	*Fairhaven*	*U.S.*	21	5 9½	*dark*	*Brown*
Daniel M. White	*Scotland*	*Fairhaven*	*English*	35	5 7	*auli*	*Brown*
Henry F. Harburg	*Charlestown N.H.*	*Fairhaven*	*U.S.*	20	5 9	*Light*	*Brown*
James Williams	*Smithfield*	*New Bedford*	*U.S.*	24	5 7	*dark*	*dark*

Excerpt from the shipping list (or crew manifest) of the Acushnet, 1840. *New Bedford Whaling Museum.*

This lightning-quick riposte shows the arbitrariness of any separation of American "races" into either black or white. So does the answer that Douglass gave to a further challenge by Rynders, acknowledging that he is "the son of a Slaveholder . . . by a colored mother—a mother as dearly beloved as though she had been white as the driven snow." Only in the most recent census have Americans been allowed to indicate a mixed race heritage.

As we noted in Chapter 1, the shipping list of the *Acushnet* in December 1840 classifies Herman Melville as one of eleven sailors on the ship whose complexion is "dark." Eleven others are listed as "light," with two "black" and one "mulatto." After Judge Shaw ruled against George Latimer in October 1842, Douglass was one of the speakers in a massive October 30 protest in Faneuil Hall. This was probably the first time that he confronted a mob as volatile as he would face at the Broadway Tabernacle in 1850. The Boston *Daily Mail* identified him as "another colored man, by the name of Douglass," in its account of the rally. He

"gesticulated to the noisy audience for about twenty minutes, but not one word in a hundred he uttered was heard."

The audience had previously shouted down another "colored man," Charles Lenox Remond. As soon as they did so, Wendell Phillips told the crowd they should let Remond speak or they would soon be taking away their own rights of free speech. To which they cried out, "We're white!" Already in 1842 American "whiteness" was being defined in response to a socially constructed, biologically diluted "blackness." George Latimer, like Frederick Douglass, was the son of a white man and an enslaved woman, but visually, he was *more* than "half-white." At a rally in Salem, Massachusetts, Latimer's "appearance caused an intense sensation among the audience…. He was whiter, and had straighter and lighter hair, than many of those before him, who are called white men!"

At Faneuil Hall in 1842, Wendell Phillips had been unable to still the boisterous mob that defined itself by its whiteness. At the New York Society Library in 1850, Phillips was himself jeered as a "white-washed nigger" on the day after Rynders had called Douglass "only half a nigger." Writing *Moby-Dick* in 1851, Melville asks "whether a white man were anything more dignified than a white-washed negro" when Ishmael and Queequeg encounter the "jeering passengers" on the packet boat. By then, Melville had joined Douglass and Phillips in facing the fierceness with which the identity of a white race in the American North depended upon classifying others as non-white.

When Toni Morrison explored this issue in *Playing in the Dark* in 1992, she credited Melville as one of those nineteenth-century writers who have helped us to see the ironic degree to which "Africanism is the vehicle by which the American self knows itself as not enslaved, but free." Only the category of the non-white allows the white American self to know that it is "not repulsive, but desirable; not helpless, but licensed and powerful; not history-less, but historical; not damned, but innocent; not a blind accident of evolution, but a progressive fulfillment of destiny." Melville and Douglass were both articulating these darkly ironic American truths a decade before the Civil War.

Artificial academic, as well as racial, classifications have kept Douglass and Melville from being considered in relation to each other. Traditionally, Melville had been viewed as a fiction writer who wrote the kind of imaginary narratives that, since the Melville revival reached the universities in the 1950s, have been taught primarily in literature departments. Until recently, Douglass, in contrast, had been seen as an orator, editor, and autobiographical writer dealing with the kind of factual matters that are more appropriately considered by departments of history, political science, and communications. This separation of academic disciplines in the modern university,

exacerbated by the tendency to treat the two figures as belonging to entirely different racial categories, has contributed to the dynamic by which their lives and writings have been seen within separate American, rather than shared American, traditions.

Reading about Douglass and Melville in the print media of their own time creates a different picture. In the pages of the Albany *Evening Journal* and the Boston *Chronotype*, the *National Era* and the *National Anti-Slavery Standard*, and the *North Star* and *Frederick Douglass' Paper,* Douglass and Melville are part of a common American culture in which the injustice of slavery is the essential national problem to which a solution must be found in the context of the nation's international as well as national destiny.

Melville's anti-flogging chapters in *White-Jacket* address the same subject as do Douglass's anti-flogging editorials in the *North Star* in spite of the different genres in which they are written. The *National Era* recognized this essential truth when it declared, in its April 25, 1850, review of *White-Jacket*, that Melville's book is "reality, not romance." Using contrasting genres to address similar realities is one way in which Douglass and Melville wrote in "neighborly style" (in the phrase I have borrowed from *Benito Cereno*). Another is the extent to which Douglass, in his non-fiction writing, employed some of the fiction writer's most powerful tools: the telling anecdote, the literary allusion, the symbolic implication, the ironic reversal, the scathing satire, the deadpan denunciation.

Consider how Douglass injected the power and pathos of a fiction writer into his speech at Finsbury Chapel, Moorfields, England, on May 12, 1846 (in one of the passages that he later extracted for the Appendix of *My Bondage and My Freedom*). One way in which Douglass informs his English audience about the reality of American slavery is to narrate the story of an enslaved husband and wife who are separated, for life, at the "auctioneer's block." After the male slave is

> at length bid off to another person,[he] asked permission of his new master to go and take the hand of his wife at parting. It was denied him. In the agony of his soul he rushed from the man who had just bought him . . . ; but his way was obstructed, he was struck over the head with a loaded whip, and was held for a moment; but his agony was too great. When he was let go, he fell a corpse at the feet of his master. His heart was broken.

This simple story, ending with "His heart was broken," caused "much sensation" in Douglass's English audience.

Melville achieves a similar effect, with similar means, in his account of the death of the whale in "Stubb kills a Whale" (the chapter from *Moby-Dick* quoted by McCune Smith in *Frederick Douglass' Paper* in 1856). At the beginning of the chapter, this whale is "tranquilly spouting his vapory jet . . . like a portly burgher smoking his pipe of a warm afternoon." After Stubb and his crew have done their work, "gush after gush of clotted red gore . . . shot into the frighted air" and, "falling back again, ran dripping down his motionless flanks into the sea. His heart had burst!" A reader who feels the force of this bursting heart feels differently about whaling for the rest of the book. Even Stubb is seen "thoughtfully eyeing the vast corpse he had made."

One unresolved question about Melville in this study is the degree to which he was or was not an abolitionist. His intellectual, analytical, and spiritual sympathies often resonated with those of Douglass, as we have seen, but he chose not to become involved either in direct political action or in the kind of explicit anti-slavery literary advocacy that characterized

the careers of such writers as Whittier, Lowell, Longfellow, and Stowe in addition to Douglass. One reason may well be the enduring memory of having to remove all of his deepest-felt critique of "white civilized man" from *Typee*. Another may be his financial dependence on Lemuel Shaw and his marital obligation to Elizabeth and to the financial health of their family. Another may be the nature of his own symbolic power as a writer of words.

Melville realized by the time he wrote *Moby-Dick* and *Benito Cereno* that the most powerful messages he was gifted to deliver were those that had to be read between the lines by readers acute enough to discern them. As awkward as it must have been to be positioned between the worlds of Douglass and Shaw during the national crisis over the Fugitive Slave Law, this precarious position gave Melville a double vision comparable to that with which Douglass had learned to address a white and a non-white audience at the same time. Melville symbolizes his own double vision in "The Sperm Whale's Head" in *Moby-Dick*, imploring his reader to develop the imaginative equivalent of the whale's optical ability to see in "exactly opposite directions" in one combining act of vision.

One defining characteristic of each man is that he continued to look for social and psychological cohesion even in the face of the bleakest division. "Colorphobia in New York!" is vintage Douglass in this way. After exposing the common everyday racism he found on the streets of New York in 1849 in the most uncompromisingly vivid way, he concluded the essay with the hopeful declaration that, in spite of this, more and more New Yorkers were showing themselves able "to associate with their fellow creatures irrespective of all complexional differences."

Melville, writing *Redburn* at the same time as Douglass's "Colorphobia," was aware that Lavender and his "good-look-ing" English lady "would have been mobbed in three minutes" if they had been walking "arm and arm" in New York. Yet they are able to walk freely in Liverpool. Moreover, in the docks of that city Melville pictures a "grand parliament of masts" comparable to "the grand Pentecost of the churches" that was celebrated in the *North Star* two weeks after the "Colorphobia" essay.

This "grand parliament of masts" consists of "the collective spars and timbers" of ships representing

> *all the forests of the globe. . . . Canada and New Zealand send their pines; America her live oak; India her teak; Norway her spruce; and the Right Honorable Mahogany, member of Honduras and Campeachy, is seen at his post by the wheel. Here, under the benefi-cent sway of the Genius of Commerce, all climes and countries embrace; and yard-arm touches yard-arm in brotherly love.*

The yard arms of different species touching each other "in brotherly love" are a perfect anticipation of the mulatto American steward "walking arm in arm with a good-looking English woman" a few chapters later. They are a symbolic rebuke to those who would mob such a couple in New York.

After the mob action at the Broadway Tabernacle, the New York Society Library, and the Battery in May 1850, followed by passage of the new Fugitive Slave Act in September of that year, Douglass and Melville had to search much harder for social and emotional harmony than they had the year before. The "Ishmael's hope of survival" generated by the stories that Melville tells in *Moby-Dick* and *Benito Cereno* has to be read and felt against the grain of a plot that leads to physical and spiritual oppression, whether presided over by Ahab's obsession or Delano's complacency.

In "Life as a Slave," the first half of *My Bondage and My Freedom*, Douglass is able to elaborate upon the compelling story of liberation in his 1845 *Narrative*. In "Life as a Freeman," the second half of the book, his narrative thrust is more dispersed, the eventual outcome more unsure. Douglass begins this section by writing, "There is no necessity for any extended notice of the incidents of this part of my life." After conveying in narrative fashion what he is able to say about the anomalies of his life in the Northern states, in contrast to the relative freedom in Great Britain, he concludes the book with extracts from speeches he gave from 1846 to 1855. For Douglass, as for Melville, the fate and nature of the American experiment were still in a precarious state.

In the 1855 speech "The Anti-Slavery Movement" that concludes *My Bondage and My Freedom,* Douglass, even in the political bleakness of that year, still finds hope in the face of despair. He ends his second autobiography with these words: "Old as the everlasting hills, immovable as the throne of God; and certain as the purposes of eternal power, against all hindrances, and against all delays, and despite all the mutations of human instrumentalities, it is the faith of my soul, that this anti-slavery cause will triumph."

Melville ends *Benito Cereno* with Babo's severed head meeting, "unabashed, the gaze of the whites." The silenced head literally embodies Douglass's insight into the enslaved as the "silent dead." *Benito Cereno* offers no rhetorical equivalent to Ishmael's faith in "that democratic dignity which, on all hands, radiates without end from . . . the great God absolute! The centre and circumference of all democracy!" The anti-slavery cause *did* triumph within a decade of 1855, but the challenge of achieving that democratic dignity which would efface the color line remains today.

NOTES

Full citations for the sources cited in this section are provided in Works Cited. Works by Douglass or Melville represented by abbreviations below are listed at the beginning of Works Cited.

Preface

vii *Neither author is known to have kept* ~ The only continuous journals Melville is known to have kept were during his voyages to England and the Continent in 1849-50, to the Mediterranean and the Near East in 1856-57, and around Cape Horn in 1860. These are expertly transcribed and annotated in the Northwestern-Newberry edition of Melville's *Journals* (1989).

viii The first volume of the *Correspondence* series ~ The dates and correspondents for each letter in the future volume are listed on the website for the Frederick Douglass Papers at www.iupui.edu/~douglass/documents_letters.htm.

viii *fire in his Rochester house* ~ As Douglass mentioned in L&T 709.

viii *Sealts estimates that about half* ~ Sealts 5-9.

ix *from centre to circumference* ~ Douglass used this phrase in speeches in New York at the Broadway Tabernacle on May 11, 1847, and at Hope Chapel, May 9, 1849. Melville uses a similar phrase in the first "Knights and Squires" chapter of *Moby-Dick*.

Introduction

4 *the turning point* ~ N 54.

4 *took on the name Douglass* ~ Grover 144.

4 *took its place with me* ~ MBMF 204.

4 *a whale-ship was my Yale College* ~ MD 112.

4 *The ship-yard . . . was our school-house* ~ Editor's column, *New National Era*, July 6, 1871.

5 *he who . . . has caulked ships* ~ "Stop my Paper," FDP, July 24, 1851.

7 *he refused to submit an image* ~ For Melville's 1854 correspondence with George P. Putnam, see C 261, 637. For his rejection of Evert Duyckinck's 1851 request on behalf of *Holden's Magazine*, see C 178-81.

7 *sometimes shocking account* ~ MBMF 207, 214.

8 *past, present, and future* ~ BC 98.

8 *one New York newspaper was surprised* ~ Leyda 836.

9 *Jackson Pollock was painting* ~ Schultz, plates 13, 14.

10 *Andrews was the first* ~ In the introduction to his 1987 edition of *My Bondage and My Freedom*.

10 *Sundquist rightly declared* ~ Sundquist 22.

11 *anchored together . . . in neighborly style* ~ Putnam's 473; BC 95.

Part One

13 *loose fish* ~ MD 396.

Chapter One

15 *City Directory* ~ My addresses and street numbers are from the 1839 and 1841 editions of Henry H. Crapo's *New-Bedford Directory*. No directory was published for 1840.

15 *rolled oil casks* ~ MBMF 201.

15 *little time* ~ L&T 656-57.

16 *intriguing to imagine* ~ McFeely 81.

17 *lacked one large whale* ~ Rodman 214.

18 *rolled oil casks* ~ "Stop my Paper," FDP, July 24, 1851.

18 *huge hills and mountains* ~ MD 60.

18 *I now by instinct* ~ MD 9-10.

19 *Ishmael quickly retreats* ~ MD 18.

19 *tattooed savage* ~ MD 21.

19 *green white sailors* ~ MD 58-61.

20 *all other churches* ~ MBMF 203-5, 374-75.

20 *already been given authority* ~ Thomas James 8-9; Andrews, "Preacher," 593-94.

21 *the days I spent* ~ Andrews, "Preacher," 596.

21 *did not fail* ~ MD 34.

21 *Douglass had already* ~ Thomas James 8.

21 *one white person* ~ MFMF 205.

21 *biographers and poets* ~ Two poems by Laurie Robertson-Lorant, "Melville Stumbles into an African Meeting-House in

New Bedford, Massachusetts" and "Melville Meets a Stranger on New Bedford's Waterfront," are included in *The Man Who Lived Among the Cannibals: Poems in the Voice of Herman Melville* (Spinner Publications).

Chapter Two

23 *throw the MS. into the fire* ~ N 11.

24 *Did Melville hear Douglass lecture* ~ A fourth lecture, in Albany's City Hall on June 12, 1845, is listed in Douglass's "Partial Speaking Itinerary for 1841-1846" (Blassingame 1.1.xciv), but I have not yet been able to document it in the Albany newspapers I have been able to consult.

26 *stories about the horrors of slavery* ~ In addition to Weed's praise of Douglass on June 9, 10, 12, and July 11 and 12, see especially the anti-slavery stories on June 16, 20, 25, 27, and July 7, 9, 10, 11, 12, 15, 18, and 23. One of the more ironic results of Weed's embrace of Douglass came in the June 16 issue of the *Patriot*, Albany's one acknowledged anti-slavery paper. First, the *Patriot* chided the *Evening Journal* for praising Douglass and his *Narrative* only days after having "come down quite sternly upon the ultra-abolitionists of all sorts and upon Birney and Garrison in particular." The *Patriot* then went on to dismiss Douglass himself as "a favorite disciple of Mr. Garrison," one who only "echoes" his opinions. The *Patriot's* own feud with Garrison was so strong that this after-the-fact, backhanded swipe at Weed, Douglass, and Garrison is the only reference to Douglass's June 9 or July 12 lectures that I have found in this anti-slavery newspaper (associated with the Liberty Party).

26 *first best prize* ~ Leyda 48.

26 *Talk not* ~ R 11.

27 *slaves in the family home* ~ Kenney 135-40; Robertson-Lorant 3.

27 *Conflagration of 1793* ~ Munsell 2: 378-81. Munsell reprints his account of "The

Conflagration of 1793" from an issue of the Albany *Evening Journal* whose date he does not give. The original article may well date from the 1845 period in which Weed's newspaper was exploring the history of slavery in Albany as a way of looking toward a better future. Under the title "Times Gone By" on July 9, 1845, Weed reprinted four advertisements for the sale of Negroes from the Albany *Gazette* of 1800. "How strangely would such announcements now read," the paper editorialized. "Will not the next fifty years witness as great a change in moral sentiment on the subject of Slavery in the existing Slave States as the last 50 years has in this State!" The "Conflagration" article from the *Evening Journal* contains considerable information about Bet, the Van Rensselaers, and the Gansevoorts in the 1790s.

27 *Pinsker Hill, where the slaves were executed* ~ Stuckey 1998, 42-43.

27 *Crantz, Kit, and Douw* ~ P 30.

28 *Wilson's Illustrated Guide* ~ Page 51.

28 *June 6 issue* ~ N, "Reader Responses, 1845-49," 172-73.

28 *Marnoo! Marnoo!* ~ T 135.

29 *Never, certainly* ~ T 137-38.

29 *in Blassingame's introduction* ~ Blassingame 1.1.xxviii-xxxv.

29 *the effect he produced* ~ T 138.

30 *his remarks and manner* ~ My citation is from the account in the *Liberator* on December 9, 1842, reprinted from the Salem *Observer*, itself reprinted from the *Register*.

31 *he wrote a note* ~ C 62-63.

32 *Two weeks before* ~ October 2, 1845.

33 *a year earlier* ~ "Portrait Painting," Albany *Evening Journal*, December 27, 1845.

Chapter Three

35 *homecoming address* ~ Douglass's address in the Tabernacle on May 11, 1847, is reprinted by Blassingame as "Country, Conscience, and the Anti-Slavery Cause" (Blassingame 1.2.57-68). Blassingame's headnotes provide invaluable information about the texts of speeches by Douglass that were printed in contemporary newspapers. The text of this May 11 speech was printed in the New York *Herald* and the New York *Morning Express* on May 12, the New York *Daily Tribune* on May 13, the *National Anti-Slavery*

Standard and the *Pennsylvania Freeman* on May 20, the *Liberator* on May 21, and the *Anti-Slavery Beagle* on May 28.

36 *eight different New York newspapers* ~ "The Spirit of the New York Press," *National Anti-Slavery Standard*, May 27, 1847.

37 *remarkable review* ~ "Notes on New Books."

38 *column in defense of Douglass* ~ "Like Master Like Men."

38 *became widely available* ~ Higgins and Parker (112-13) and Parker and Hayford 2002 (484-85).

38 *diary entry by Edmund Quincy* ~ Quincy Family Papers, Massachusetts Historical Society.

39 *July 2 letter* ~ E. Quincy to C. Weston, July 2, 1847 (MS A.9.2.23.32), Boston Public Library, Rare Book Department.

39 *separate paragraphs* ~ For a transcription and analysis of these revealing and somewhat surprising paragraphs, see Wallace, "Douglass, Melville, Quincy, Shaw," 64-67.

40 *became a member* ~ Leyda 269, 276.

40 *reading room* ~ Keep 400-1.

41 *letter in which his wife Elizabeth* ~ Elizabeth Melville to her step-mother Hope Savage Shaw, Leyda 266-67.

41 *withdrew four volumes* ~ Leyda 269.

41 *two small apartments* ~ Keep 400-1.

41 *his own commentary* ~ "The Anniversary at New York."

41 *considerable time with Gansevoort* ~ See the entries for January 23, 24, 25, 27, February 8, 10, 12, 20, 22, and March 6 in *Gansevoort Melville's 1846 London Journal*. ~ Gansevoort attended the Hutchinson Family's London concerts, invited them to dine, and dined with them in return. The Hutchinson Family Singers had a large following in Albany, where Thurlow Weed had helped to launch their career in August 1842.

42 *transcript of his remarks* ~ Douglass's remarks in the Tabernacle on May 9, 1848 are reprinted by Blassingame as "The Triumphs and Challenges of the Abolitionist Crusade" (Blassingame 1.2.117-28). Texts of the speech appeared the next day in the New York *Herald* and the New York *Daily Tribune*, followed in the next few weeks by the *National Anti-Slavery Standard*, the *Liberator*, and the *North Star*.

45 *interim report to Lemuel Shaw* ~ Leyda 300; C 130.

45 *devastating review* ~ Leyda 303.

46 *a well-orchestrated attack* ~ Berthold 429-30.

46 *nativist Democrats* ~ Berthold 430.

46 *Three cheers for . . . Nigger Douglass* ~ Berthold 434, citing the New York *Herald*, May 8, 1849.

47 *James McCune Smith* ~ "Meetings in New York."

47 *Shiloh Presbyterian on May 8* ~ The *Tribune*'s report is reprinted in Blassingame as "Shall Thou Steal?" (Blassingame 1.2.174-76).

47 *W. C. Nell reported* ~ "Communications," dated May 12, published in the *North Star*, May 25, 1849.

48 *at the Hope Chapel on May 9* ~ Nell describes Hope Chapel, only a few blocks from Melville's house, as "up Broadway in a neighborhood of the aristocracy, who were represented in good numbers at the meeting." Melville had aligned himself with that "aristocracy" by signing the Macready petition on May 8.

48 *a handsome, dandy mulatto* ~ R 202.

48 *remembered as remarkable* ~ Higginson in "The Sunny Side of the Transcendental Period" (1904) and Hutchinson in *Story of the Hutchinsons* (1896).

49 *Both the . . . Globe and . . . Herald* ~ Thurlow Weed reported the threats from these two papers in the Albany *Evening Journal*, from which Douglass reprinted them as "Mob Instructions" in the *North Star*, May 16, 1850.

49 *had disrupted a meeting* ~ "The Vigilance Committee Meeting," NS, May 16.

49 *Douglass's own account* ~ "Letter from the Editor," NS, May 16.

50 *the New York Tribune* ~ Reprinted in the *North Star* as "A Dark Business," May 16.

50 *in Douglass's words* ~ "Letter from the Editor," NS, May 16.

50 *the morning meeting on May 8* ~ As reprinted in "Anti-Slavery Society, Second Day," NS, May 16.

50 *Douglass informed his readers* ~ "At Home Again," NS, May 30, 1850.

50 *Melville renewed his library membership* ~ Leyda 372.

50 *he wrote . . . Dana* ~ Leyda 374; C 162.

51 *torchlight procession* ~ Parker 1: 333.

51 *Rynders attended school* ~ Blassingame 1.2.237n1.

51 *seemingly sudden decision* ~ See the discussion in Parker 1: 779-80.

Chapter Four

55 *Stauffer discovered* ~ Stauffer, *Black Hearts*, 66. Smith's column was entitled "Horoscope."

55 *Apothecary's Hall* ~ Visited by W. C. N[ell] in "Gleanings by the Wayside," NS, February 11, 1848.

56 *fallen out of favor* ~ See the section "Burial, Disinterment, and Revival: 1853-1925" in Parker and Hayford, 1970.

56 *C. L. R. James* ~ His 1953 book *Mariners, Castaways, and Renegades* is subtitled *Herman Melville and the World We Live In*. James wrote it while awaiting deportation on Ellis Island.

56 *Stubb kills a Whale* ~ MD 283, 285, 286.

56 *mispelling of Melville's name* ~ The misspelling is silently corrected in the Accessible Archives text of "Tattooing." Melville's original text is part of the section he calls "A Professor of the Fine Arts" in chapter 30 (T 217-18).

57 *whose back displayed* ~ T 136. Tommo devotes a meticulous, highly appreciative paragraph to the "tattooing on [Marnoo's] back in particular," from the "slender, tapering, and diamond-checkered shaft of the beautiful 'artu' tree . . . traced along the course of the spine" to the contrast of bright blue designs against "the light olive color of the skin." One can imagine Douglass, reading this paragraph, thinking of the different kind of tattooing that had been inflicted on his back by Edward Covey.

57 *Native Oratory* ~ T 137. After describing the tattooing on Marnoo's back, Melville uses "Native Oratory" as the sub-heading for the part of the chapter in which Tommo describes and admires Marnoo's oratorical style. The phrase "Native Oratory" would have invited American readers to compare Marnoo's oratory with that of speakers who were native to the United States rather than the South Seas--in which connection some of the conspicuous similarities between the oratory of Douglass and that of Marnoo take on additional interest.

58 *horrified at the bare thought* ~ T 218-19.

58 *Samuel Otter has recently shown* ~ See "Losing Face in Typee," Chapter 1 in Otter, 1999. In addition to showing that tattooing is more of a threat to Tommo than cannibalism, Otter contrasts the cultural practices of tattooers in the South Seas with those of ethnologists and phrenologists in the United States.

60 *Duyckinck begins his review* ~ Leyda 434; Higgins and Parker 375-76. Douglass is likely to have seen Duyckinck's comparison of Moby Dick with the *Ann Alexander* whale either in the December 1851 reprint in the *Dollar Magazine* or the November 15 issue of the *Literary World*. Douglass referred to articles in the *Literary World* as editor of both the *North Star* and *Frederick Douglass' Paper*. References in the *North Star* discussed subjects ranging from George Bancroft ("Mr. Remington in the Den," January 26, 1849) to ethnology ("Squier's Discoveries in Central America," November 30, 1849). Two mentions in *Frederick Douglass' Paper* discussed the failure of the *Literary World* to adequately appreciate *Uncle Tom's Cabin* ("American and Foreign Anti-Slavery Society," May 27, 1852; and "Speech of Hon. Geo. W. Julian at the Free State Democratic State Convention," July 29, 1853). With the publication of *Pierre* in 1852, Melville had broken with Duyckinck, his former mentor, as decisively as Douglass had broken with Garrison the year before.

60 *Melville had made his own connection* ~ Leyda 431-32; C 208-10.

60 *Accessible Archives* ~ This electronic data base includes the *North Star*, *Frederick Douglass' Paper*, the *National Era*, the *Provincial Freeman*, the *Colored American*, and the *Christian Recorder* under the heading Nineteenth Century African American Newspapers.

60 *Melville's authorship* ~ IP, "Historical Note," 209-11.

61 *Post-Lauria* ~ Page 177.

61 *anonymous private* ~ Melville's phrase, in his dedication of *Israel Potter* "To His Highness the Bunker-Hill Monument" (IP viii).

61 *A Fourth of July Story* ~ Melville's use of this subtitle in July 1854 invites comparison with Douglass's 1852 address "What to the Slave is the Fourth of July?" Each undercuts the conventional patriotism of Independence Day by bringing forth Americans to whom the benefits of the day have been denied (enslaved Americans; soldiers who actually fought at Bunker Hill). The editors of the Northwestern-Newberry edition of *Israel Potter* too easily dismiss the meaning that the subtitle might have had for Melville, his readers, and his editors, including Charles Briggs, at *Putnam's* (IP 209).

61 *he himself like a beast* ~ IP 5.

61 *lordly eagle* ~ IP 6.

61 *emancipated himself* ~ IP 7.

63 *fire at his house* ~ L&T 709.

63 *Melville scholars since the 1950s* ~ See Higgins and Parker for contemporary reviews of Melville's works that had been discovered by 1995.

Chapter Five

65 *little or no money* ~ MD 3.

65 *Put money in thy purse* ~ Shakespeare, *Othello*, Act 1, scene 3.

65 *a purse is but a rag* ~ MD 5.

65 *Charms, conjuration—mighty magic* ~ NS, May 25, 1849.

65 *a different phrase* ~ Douglass cites the "head and front of my offending hath this extent—no more" in "At Home Again," NS, May 30, 1850.

65 *effortlessly quoted* ~ Blassingame 1.2.237n1.

65 *African and African-American culture* ~ Stuckey 1998, 51.

65 *the painter J. M. W. Turner* ~ Although Turner's name appears nowhere in *Moby-Dick*, his aesthetic pervades the novel beginning with the depiction of the painting in the Spouter-Inn in chapter 3 (see my *Melville and Turner*, especially chapters 7-9). ~ I discovered in the process of writing *Melville and Turner* that Melville saw paintings by Turner in London in 1849, met several of Turner's closest friends while he was in the city, and later collected more than twenty engravings after paintings by Turner. I have still not been able to determine whether Melville met Turner or visited his celebrated private studio while in London. Turner died in December 1851, two months before *Moby-Dick* was published, as *The Whale*, in London.

66 *ship's timbers of the Ann Alexander* ~ FDP, August 11, 1854.

Typee

66 *so vain had I become* ~ T 135-36.

67 *As soon as our palms* ~ T 139.

67 *tone and manner* ~ N 80, 83.

67 Melville in his Preface ~ T xiv.

67 *severely objected to the depiction* ~ Leyda 210-11, 221.

67 *to which Douglass replied* ~ Douglass's October 30 letter from Edinburgh was published in the *Liberator* on November 27, 1846. ~ See Foner, 1: 189-99.

67 *the fiend-like skill* ~ T 125.

67 *passages critical of colonial imperialism* ~ For a complete "List of Textual Expurgations" in the revised *Typee*, see Bryant 275-85.

68 *Mrs. Thomas Hamilton* ~ N 32-33.

68 *a missionary's spouse* ~ T 196-97.

69 *succeeded by intuitively alternating* ~ Wright xiv.

69 *pseudonym for James A. Houston* ~ Harrold 89-90.

69 *has been overlooked by Melville scholars* ~ Fortunately, the contents of the *National Era*, along with those of the *North Star* (complete) and *Frederick Douglass' Paper* (in part), are now more easily available through the Accessible Archives database.

69 *genteel tailors* ~ O 30-31.

Omoo

69 *poor old black cook* ~ O 41.

69 *New Zealand harpooner* ~ O 13.

70 *though not yet civilized* ~ O 70-71.

70 *onto a whale's back* ~ O 72.

70 *Life on the ocean wave* ~ One phrase in this part of the review, about the ship "rising and sinking with the quiet breathing of old ocean, like an infant upon the bosom of its mother," directly anticipates the language and spirit of Melville's depiction of the ocean in Chapter 13 of *Redburn*.

70 *the two men came together like magnets* ~ O 88.

70 *During the night watch* ~ O 89, 92-93.

71 *grab him and threaten to kill him* ~ O 91-93.

71 *Bembo has shipped on board* ~ O 71.

71 *Bembo's prospects* ~ O 94.

71 *When the British Colonial Barque Julia* ~ O 139, 148.

72 *the title of the work* ~ O xiv.

72 *intercourse with the Europeans* ~ O 187, 191, 192.

Mardi

73 *George Ripley's May 10 declaration* ~ Reprinted in Higgins and Parker 226.

73 *Gossip from Gotham* ~ Reprinted in Higgins and Parker 236.

73 *primitive valley of stark paganism* ~ Reprinted in Higgins and Parker 102.

73 *approach the national capitol of Vivenza* ~ M 512-13.

74 *If the lineal descendants of Ham* ~ N 15.

74 *a man with a collar round his neck* ~ M 515.

74 *hundreds of collared men . . . toiling in trenches* ~ M 532.

74 *When Babbalanja asks Nulli* ~ M 532-33.

74 *specifically about Calhoun* ~ In the January 14, March 10, May 19, July 7, August 25, and December 1 issues.

74 *One article on August 25* ~ "Disunion Threatened."

74 *Another reports* ~ "J. C. Calhoun on the Declaration of Independence."

75 *in a land where such scenes occur!* ~ A passionate letter from Cincinnati by Martin Delany in the June 9 issue of the *North Star* provided additional information about the final act of this "frantic and heroic mother" whose infanticide preceded by eight years the 1856 event in which Margaret Garner cut the throat of her infant daughter, after escaping through the same city of Covington, to spare her from being returned to their "happy" life in slavery.

75 *Yoomy cries out* ~ M 533.

76 *reprinted near the passage from Typee* ~ "Speech of Frederick Douglass."

76 *the next day in the Minerva Rooms* ~ "Editorial Correspondence," NS, May 26, 1848.

76 *Humanity cries out* ~ M 533-35.

76 *there is yet an under-current* ~ NS, June 2, 1848.

76 *Blassingame correctly identifies* ~ Blassingame 1.2.128n12.

76 *The musical setting of those words* ~ Cockrell 405.

76 *sweet singers of anti-slavery* ~ L&T 678.

76 *soul-stirring song* ~ As recounted by Douglass in "The Anniversary of New York," NS, May 19, 1848.

77 *the divinest gift that heaven has bestowed* ~ Hutchinson xvi.

77 *another meeting at which Douglass spoke* ~ This meeting was at New York's Convention Hall. Blassingame reprints Douglass's remarks under the title "Suppose You Yourselves Were Black" (1.2.128-29).

78 *more than his letters are worth* ~ Wallace 2004, 64-65.

78 *There are no mysteries out of ourselves* ~ WJ 398.

78 *It is a ridiculous and absurd notion* ~ Blassingame 1.2.170.

Redburn

79 *until I was twenty-five* ~ 1851 letter to Nathaniel Hawthorne, in Leyda 413.

79 *at first I was surprised* ~ R 202.

79 *unconsciously swayed in some degree* ~ R 202.

79 *most horribly cut and marred* ~ NS, May 25, 1849.

80 *our black cook* ~ R 82.

80 *warm love and affection* ~ R 82.

80 Two Reverend Thompsons ~ Both are listed *in Doggett's New York City Directory, 1848-49.* ~ Melville calls attention to the "City Directory" at the end of *Redburn* when Captain Riga, in the process of cheating Redburn and his friend Harry Bolton of their shipboard earnings, sarcastically asks, "Are your names down in the City Directory?" Comfortably ensconced in the City Hotel, smoking a "very fragrant cigar," he has been reading "the morning paper—I think it was the Herald" before asking "the Steward" to show them the door (R 305-6).

80 *St. Peter's in Rome* ~ R 203.

80 *warps into a berth* ~ R 301.

81 *who had taken no pay in advance* ~ R 305.

81 *popular oyster house restaurant* ~ Calarco 178.

82 *Thomas Downing chaired the meeting* ~ Blassingame 1.2.167.

82 *Mr. Chairman, I am in favor or running away* ~ "New York Vigilance Committee," NS, June 22, 1849.

82 *He had been a slave in the Mohawk Valley* ~ Blassingame 1.2.169n4.

82 *indispensable to the comfort* ~ Parker 1: 347.

82 *April 21 letter* ~ Published as "Editorial Correspondence," NS, April 27, 1849.

83 *all of whom had joined* ~ "Meeting in New York," NS, May 4, 1849.

83 *gorgeous turban* ~ R 83.

83 *sit together in the cook-house* R 83-84.

84 *of "The Steward," a mulatto* ~ FDP, December 24, 1852.

84 *He was a native of New York city* ~ R 56-57.

85 *a torrent of blood* ~ R 295-96.

White-Jacket

85 *about the extension of black slavery* ~ Otter 50.

85 *devout jubilations* ~ Leyda 396.

85 *one concession to the humane spirit* ~ "Congress," NS, October 31, 1850.

85 *Jumping Out of One's Skin* ~ Otter 50-100.

86 *dazzlingly white back* ~ WJ 138.

86 *Flogging not Lawful* ~ WJ 144-45.

86 *Flogging not Necessary* ~ WJ 150.

86 *the kind of legal reasoning* ~ See Cover 2-6.

86 *Douglass had praised Dana* ~ "Letter to his Readers" dated November 10, NS, November 17, 1848.

86 *Melville met Dana* ~ Leyda 249, 254.

86 *Their relationship appears to have blossomed* ~ Leyda 278; Lucid 1: 348.

86 *incomparable in dramatic story telling* ~ Leyda 293.

87 *the letter Melville wrote to Dana* ~ Leyda 374; C 160-62.

87 *fine negro* ~ WJ 66.

87 *Wooloo, a Polynesian* ~ WJ 117-18.

87 *Suppose you yourself were black* ~ As reported in the *National Anti-Slavery Standard*, May 18, 1848; talk reprinted as "Suppose You Yourself Were Black" in Blassingame, 1.2.129.

87 *a high and mighty functionary* ~ WJ 58.

87 *Head-bumping* ~ WJ 275.

88 *had been bumping one evening* ~ WJ 275-76.

88 *I now and then permit* ~ WJ 275-77.

88 *the boatswain's mate* ~ WJ 279-80.

89 *cartoon-like image* ~ WJ 301.

89 *Melville's argument against blaming the victim* ~ WJ 304.

89 *a sheet-anchor-man* ~ WJ 311.

89 *a very great disparity* ~ WJ 313.

89 *were the secret history of all sea-fights* ~ WJ 314-15.

89 *ineffaceable indentations* ~ WJ 315-16.

89 *blessings on war-makers* ~ Reported in *National Anti-Slavery Standard* on May 24, 1849; reprinted as "Too Much Religion, Too Little Humanity" in Blassingame, 1.2.188-91.

90 *Shaw, who decided the case in favor of Lucas* ~ See Huntress 639-41.

90 *Shaw was opposed to slavery in principle* ~ See Levy, chapter 5 ("The Law of Freedom") and Chapter 6 ("The Fugitive Slave Law").

90 *Never did I feel my condition* ~ WJ 379.

90 *treatment of Guinea under circumstances* ~ WJ 379.

91 *Landless always obeyed* ~ WJ 384.

91 *officers instinctively dislike* ~ WJ 384-85.

91 *the last resources of an insulted and unendurable existence* ~ WJ 280.

91 *sleeping-partner shipmate* ~ MD 16.

91 *our bulwarks might look* ~ WJ 69.

92 *roamed the city almost at will* ~ Richards 115-18.

92 *perversion of justice* ~ Tappan 206-7, 213-14.

92 *Gilje's recent reconstruction* ~ Gilje 162-68, map 5.

92 *In the May 16, 1850, issue* ~ "The Vigilance Committee Meeting."

93 *Writing two weeks later* ~ "At Home Again," NS, May 30, 1850.

93 *I have assumed to be a man* ~ "At Home Again."

93 *prompts even a worm* ~ WJ 280.

93 *There is a point beyond which* ~ Reprinted in MBMF 264.

Moby-Dick

94 *half way in his work* ~ C 160-62.

95 *Reporting on this heartening rally* ~ "Letter from the Editor," October 24, 1850.

97 *glancing bird's eye view* ~ MD xvii.

97 *One resistor is the sperm whale* ~ MD xxv-xxvi.

97 *three accounts of whalers* ~ MD xxvi-xxviii.

98 *Call me Ishmael* ~ MD 3.

98 *as reported in the New York Herald the next day* ~ Blassingame 1.2.170.

98 *as a simple sailor, right before the mast* ~ MD 5-6.

98 *the colored people do not appreciate sufficiently* ~ Blassingame 1.2.167-70.

98 *Who aint a slave?* ~ MD 6.

99 *hundred black faces turned around* ~ MD 9.

99 *A Jonah's Warning to America* ~ Karcher, chapter 3, 62-91.

99 *in the psalms and hymns of the Reformed Protestant Dutch Church* ~ Battenfeld 574.

100 *Where the psalmist had written* ~ Battenfeld 575.

100 *In black distress* ~ Battenfeld 575; MD 42.

100 *the preacher's text was about the blackness* ~ MD 9-10.

100 *how plainly he's a fugitive!* ~ MD 43.

100 *knows that Jonah is a fugitive* ~ MD 44-46.

100 *the more awful lesson* ~ MD 47-48.

100 *Woe to him who seeks* ~ MD 48.

101 *as Karcher pointed out* ~ Karcher 78.

101 *they pass the very wharves* ~ MD 60.

101 *how I spurned that turnpike earth!* ~ MD 60.

101 *widely reprinted Slumbering Volcano speech* ~ The "Slumbering Volcano" speech was reprinted in the *National Anti-Slavery Standard* on May 3, in the *Liberator* and the *Pennsylvania Freeman* on May 10, and in the *North Star* on May 11, 1849. See Blassingame 1.2.148.

101 *the slaveholders are sleeping* ~ Blassingame 1.2.151-55.

101 *In his oceanic conclusion* ~ Blassingame 1.2.158.

102 *Queequeg seemed to drink and reel* ~ MD 60-61.

102 *the racial discrimination on a packet boat* ~ Fred V. Bernard makes this connection in "The Question of Race in *Moby-Dick*," 385.

102 *in a very few minutes Madison Washington* ~ Blassingame 1.2.155.

102 *Queequeg is a composite non-white figure* ~ Karcher 63-65.

102 *Queequeg's dusky nostrils* ~ MD 60.

102 *the long retreating slope of Queequeg's forehead* ~ MD 50.

103 *anything more dignified than a whitewashed negro* ~ MD 60.

103 *According to the New York Globe* ~ As reprinted in the *Liberator* on May 17, 1850.

103 *a frosty-headed old darkie* ~ The *Globe*, as reprinted in the *Liberator*, May 17, 1850.

103 *The Herald and the Tribune* ~ As reprinted in the *Liberator* on May 17, 1850.

103 *According to the account from the New York Express* ~ As reprinted in the *Liberator*, May 17, 1850.

104 *tapering extremity of the whale* ~ MD 292.

104 *preach to the sharks* ~ MD 294.

104 *has something the matter with his knee-pans* ~ MD 294-97.

104 *operated a restaurant in New York City* ~ Blassingame 1.2.169.

104 *Willie Weathers, in a 1960 essay* ~ Weathers 483, 486.

105 *as soon as they reach port* ~ MD 257, 259.

105 *a new work by Mr. Melville* ~ Leyda 429.

106 *Douglass published a stirring account* ~ FDP, September 25, 1851.

106 *a certain wondrous, inverted visitation* ~ MD 242-43.

107 *Starbuck's tragic lack of valor* ~ MD 117.

107 *not in the dignity of kings and robes* ~ MD 117.

107 *all over, from centre to circumference* ~ Reported in the *National Anti-Slavery Standard* on May 20, 1847; reprinted in Blassingame 1.2.61.

107 *rocking this country from centre to circumference* ~ Reported in the *National Anti-Slavery Standard*, May 24, 1849; reprinted in Blassingame 1.2.177.

107 *only an Ishmael's hope of survival* ~ McFeely 173.

107 *gallant ship beating against a terrible storm* ~ MD 39, 106-7, 225.

108 *rescued Sandy Swan from the brig Florence* ~ Bearse 34-37.

108 *the boat had become too well known* ~ Petrulionis 69, 77n13.

108 *anathema to Chief Justice Shaw* ~ Kaplan 173-74.

Benito Cereno

109 *the well-known fugitive slave* ~ *Putnam's*, November 1855, 547; MBMF 416.

110 *slave I cannot call him* ~ BC 57.

110 *buy him for fifty doubloons* ~ BC 70.

110 *most negroes are natural valets and hairdressers* ~ BC 83-84.

110 *and saves Benito Cereno* ~ BC 116.

110 *Babo's decapitated head on a stake* ~ BC 116-17.

110 *might not the San Dominick* ~ BC 68.

110 *Maggie Sale, in her 1997 book* ~ Sale 146.

112 *exchange about cutting hair versus cutting throats* ~ By May 16, 1850, this exchange between Rynders and Douglass was already reprinted in the *North Star* from the New York *Evangelist*.

112 *inexhaustible sense of humor* ~ Higginson 574.

113 *his next operation was with comb, scissors and brush* ~ BC 87.

113 *acting out, both in word and deed* ~ BC 87.

114 *all reprinted in the Liberator on May 17* ~ For extensive coverage from these and other New York dailies, see the *Liberator*, May 17, 1850, 77-78.

114 *you do not object to the presence of the negro* ~ Blassingame 1.2.242.

114 *offended not by the presence of colored servants* ~ NS, May 25, 1849.

114 *one of the great moments in world literature* ~ Stuckey, "Follow Your Leader," 178.

114 *ground the prostrate negro into the bottom of the boat* ~ BC 99.

114 *dark satyr in a mask* ~ BC 49.

115 *there is something about the negro so buoyant* ~ Blassingame 1.2.242.

115 *recorded for posterity in a number of newspapers* ~ Blassingame 1.2.235.

115 *convicted by the courts of the Holy Crusade* ~ BC 103.

115 *dragged to the gibbet at the tail of a mule* ~ BC 116-17.

116 *I have a head to think* ~ Blassingame 1.2.243.

116 *two vessels, thanks to the pilot's skill* ~ BC 95.

116 *the white men from the American ship pursue the fugitives* ~ BC 100-1.

116 *the status of black slaves in America* ~ Karcher 141.

116 *ask the slave what is his condition* ~ MBMF 258.

117 *under whom the ship's cook in White-Jacket* ~ WJ 58.

117 *one of some 230 authors and editors* ~ C 278-79.

117 *not a single identifiable African American author or editor* ~ Greenspan 361-62.

117 *those who sent letters of regret* ~ C 281.

American Epilogue

119 *And where . . . is Herman Melville?* ~ Leyda 694.

119 *Death of a Once Popular Author* ~ Leyda 836-37.

119 *Thurlow Weed was no longer editor* ~ MBMF 316n17.

119 *a consular appointment for which letters of support* ~ Leyda 635-39.

121 *the first blood shed on Bunker's hill* ~ Blassingame 1.2.241.

122 *the success which has attended my labors in life* ~ L&T 900.

122 *who took me into their hearts and homes* ~ L&T 901-6.

122 *a similar list that Douglass had published* ~ MBMF 281.

123 *in Liverpool, now half a century ago* ~ BB 43.

123 *This sailor is so intensely black* ~ BB 43-44.

124 *In my clothing I was rigged out in sailor style* ~ L&T 644.

124 *a Representative American man* ~ MBMF 14.

125 *flowered like the aloe* ~ Leyda 364.

125 *What I feel most moved to write* ~ Leyda 412.

125 *bears upon his person and upon his soul* ~ MBMF 14.

125 *I who have endured the whip of the slaveholder* ~ Blassingame 2.1.238.

125 *No one can read the description* ~ "The American Sailor," *National Era*, May 2, 1850.

125 *substitutes the skeleton of a slaveholder* ~ BC 107.

128 *Rynders, not Douglass, injects* ~ Blassingame 1.2.238-39.

129 *a massive October 30 protest in Faneuil Hall* ~ My account of this event is drawn from the *Liberator*, November 4, 1842.

129 *Latimer's appearance caused an intense sensation* ~ Reported in the Salem *Observer* from the *Register*, as reprinted in the *Liberator*, December 9, 1842.

130 *When Toni Morrison explored this issue* ~ Morrison 51-52.

131 *the story of an enslaved husband and wife* ~ MBMF 239-40.

131 *caused much sensation* ~ Blassingame 1.1.128.

131 *tranquilly spouting his vapory jet* ~ MD 283, 286.

131 *whale's optical ability to see* ~ MD 331.

132 *would have been mobbed in three minutes* ~ R 202.

132 *grand parliament of masts* ~ R 165.

132 *there is no necessity for any extended notice* ~ MBMF 193.

132 *Old as the everlasting hills* ~ MBMF 284.

132 *that democratic dignity* ~ MD 117.

WORKS CITED

WORKS BY DOUGLASS

Cited by abbreviations or editor's name in Notes:

Blassingame ~ Blassingame, John W., et. al. *The Frederick Douglass Papers, Series 1: Speeches, Debates and Interviews.* 5 vol. New Haven: Yale University Press, 1979-1992.

FDP ~ *Frederick Douglass' Paper.* Weekly newspaper. Rochester, New York, 1851-59.

Foner ~ Foner, Philip S, ed. *The Life and Writings of Frederick Douglass.* 5 vol. New York: International Publishers, 1950-55, 1975.

L&T ~ *Life and Times of Frederick Douglass.* In Frederick Douglass, *Autobiographies.* Ed. Henry Louis Gates, Jr. New York: Library of America, 1994. 453-1045.

MBMF ~ *My Bondage and My Freedom.* Vol. 2 in Series 2, *The Frederick Douglass Papers.* Ed. John W. Blassingame, et. al. New Haven: Yale University Press, 2003.

N ~ *Narrative of the Life of Frederick Douglass, An American Slave, Written by Himself.* Vol. 1 in Series 2, *The Frederick Douglass Papers.* Ed. John W. Blassingame, et. al. New Haven: Yale University Press, 1999.

NS ~ *The North Star.* Weekly newspaper. Rochester, New York, 1847-51.

WORKS BY MELVILLE

Cited by abbreviations in Notes *(the abbreviation NN in the list below refers to the Northwestern-Newberry edition of* The Writings of Herman Melville, *Evanston and Chicago: Northwestern University Press and the Newberry Library, 1968–):*

BB *Billy Budd, Sailor (An Inside Narrative).* Ed. Harrison Hayford and Merton M. Sealts, Jr. Chicago: University of Chicago Press, 1962.

BC *Benito Cereno.* In *The Piazza Tales and Other Prose Pieces: 1839-1860.* NN, 1987. Historical note by Merton M. Sealts, Jr. 46-117.

C *Correspondence.* NN, 1993. Historical note by Lynn Horth.

IP *Israel Potter: His Fifty Years of Exile.* NN, 1982. Historical note by Walter E. Bezanson.

M *Mardi; and A Voyage Thither.* NN, 1970. Historical note by Elizabeth S. Foster.

MD *Moby-Dick; or, The Whale.* NN, 1988. Historical note by Harrison Hayford, Hershel Parker, and G. Thomas Tanselle.

P *Pierre; or, The Ambiguities.* NN, 1971. Historical note by Leon Howard and Hershel Parker.

O *Omoo: A Narrative of Adventures in the South Seas.* NN, 1968. Historical note by Gordon Roper.

R *Redburn; His First Voyage.* NN, 1969. Historical note by Hershel Parker.

T *Typee: A Peep at Polynesian Life.* NN, 1968. Historical note by Leon Howard.

WJ *White-Jacket; or, The World in a Man-of-War.* NN, 1970. Historical note by Willard Thorp.

OTHER WORKS CITED:

Andrews, William L. "Frederick Douglass, Preacher." *American Literature* 53 (December 1982): 592-97.

--------. "Introduction" to Frederick Douglass, *My Bondage and My Freedom.* Urbana: University of Illinois Press, 1987. xi-xxviii.

Battenfeld, David H. "The Source for the Hymn in *Moby-Dick.*" In Parker and Hayford 2002: 574-5. Reprinted from *American Literature* 27 (November 1955): 393-96.

Bearse, Austin. *Reminiscences of Fugitive-Slave Law Days in Boston.* Boston: Warren Richardson, 1880.

Bernard, Fred V. "The Question of Race in *Moby-Dick.*" *The Massachusetts Review* 43 (Autumn 2002): 384-404.

Berthold, Dennis. "Class Acts: The Astor Place Riots and Melville's 'The Two Temples.'" *American Literature* 71 (September 1999): 429-61.

Bryant, John, ed. Herman Melville. *Typee.* New York: Penguin, 1996.

Calarco, Tom. *The Underground Railroad in the Adirondack Region.* Jefferson, NC: McFarland, 2004.

Cockrell, Dale, ed. *Excelsior: Journals of the Hutchinson Family Singers, 1842-1846.* Stuyvesant, NY: Pendragon Press, 1989.

Cover, Robert. *Justice Accused: Antislavery and the Judicial Process.* New Haven: Yale University Press, 1975.

Crapo, Henry H. *The New-Bedford Directory.* New Bedford, MA: Benjamin Lindsey. 1839 and 1841 eds.

Delano, Amasa. *A Narrative of Voyages and Travels, in the Northern and Southern Hemispheres: Comprising Three Voyages Round the World.* Boston: E. G. House, 1817.

Doggett's New York City Directory for 1849-50. 8th ed. New York: John Doggett.

Ellison, Ralph. *Invisible Man.* New York: Random House, 1952.

Gansevoort Melville's 1846 London Journal and Letters from England, 1845. Ed. Hershel Parker. New York: New York Public Library, 1966.

Gilje, Paul. *The Road to Mobocracy: Popular Disorder in New York City, 1763-1834.* Chapel Hill: University of North Carolina Press, 1987.

Greenspan, Ezra. *George Palmer Putnam: Representative American Publisher.* University Park: Pennsylvania State University Press, 2000.

Grover, Kathryn. *The Fugitive's Gibraltar: Escaping Slaves and Abolitionism in New Bedford, Massachusetts.* Amherst: University of Massachusetts Press, 2001.

Harrold, Stanley. *Gamaliel Bailey and Anti-Slavery Union.* Kent: Kent State University Press, 1986.

Higgins, Brian, and Hershel Parker, ed. *Herman Melville: The Contemporary Reviews.* Cambridge: Cambridge University Press, 1995.

Higginson, Thomas Wentworth. "The Sunny Side of the Transcendental Period" (*Atlantic Monthly*, January 1904). In *Magnificent Activist: The Writings of Thomas Wentworth Higginson (1823-1911).* Ed. Howard N. Meyer. New York: Da Capo Press, 2000. 565-76.

Huntress, Keith. "'Guinea' of *White Jacket* and Chief Justice Shaw." *American Literature* 43 (January 1972): 639-41.

Hutchinson, John Wallace. *Story of the Hutchinsons (Tribe of Jesse).* 2 v. Ed. Charles E. Mann, with an Introduction by Frederick Douglass. Boston: Lee and Shepherd, 1896.

James, C. L. R. *Mariners, Renegades, and Castaways: The Story of Herman Melville and the World We Live In.* Ed. Donald E. Pease. 1953: rpr. Hanover NH: Dartmouth / University Press of New England, 2001.

James, Thomas. *The Life of Rev. Thomas James, by Himself.* Rochester: Post Express Printing Company, 1886.

Kaplan, Sidney. "The *Moby Dick* in the Service of the Underground Railroad." *Phylon* 12 (1951): 173-76.

Karcher, Carolyn. *Shadow over the Promised Land: Slavery, Race, and Violence in Melville's America.* Baton Rouge: Louisiana State University Press, 1980.

Keep, Austin Baxter. *History of the New York Society Library.* New York: De Vinne Press, 1908.

Kenney, Alice P. *The Gansevoorts of Albany: Dutch Patricians in the Upper Hudson Valley.* Syracuse: Syracuse University Press, 1969.

Levy, Leonard W. *The Law of the Commonwealth and Chief Justice Shaw.* New York: Harper and Row, 1957.

Leyda, Jay. *The Melville Log: A Documentary Life of Herman Melville, 1819-1891.* New York: Gordian Press, 1969. 2 v. (with continuous paging).

Lucid, Robert F., ed. *The Journal of Richard Henry Dana, Jr.* 2 v. Cambridge: Harvard University Press, 1968.

McFeely, William S. *Frederick Douglass.* New York: Norton, 1991.

Morrison, Toni. *Playing in the Dark: Whiteness and the Literary Imagination.* Cambridge: Harvard University Press, 1992.

Munsell, J. *Collections of the History of Albany, from its Discovery to the Present Time.* 4 vol. Albany: J. Munsell, 1867.

Otter, Samuel. *Melville's Anatomies.* Berkeley: University of California Press, 1999.

Parker, Hershel. *Herman Melville, A Biography, Volume 1, 1819-1851.* Baltimore: Johns Hopkins University Press, 1996. *Volume 2, 1851-1891,* 2002.

Parker, Hershel, and Harrison Hayford. *Moby-Dick as Doubloon: Essays and Extracts (1851-1970).* New York: Norton, 1970.

--------, eds. *Norton Critical Edition of Herman Melville's* Moby-Dick. 2nd Ed. New York: W. W. Norton, 2002.

Petrie, William L., and Douglass E. Stover. *Bibliography of the Frederick Douglass Library at Cedar Hill.* Fort Washington, MD: Silesia Companies, 1995. 337-374.

Petrulionis, Sandra Harbert. "Fugitive Slave-Running on the *Moby-Dick*: Captain Austin Bearse and the Abolitionist Crusade." *Resources for American Literary Study* 28 (2003): 53-81.

Post-Lauria, Shiela. *Correspondent Colorings: Melville in the Marketplace.* Amherst: University of Massachusetts Press, 1996.

Richards, Leonard L. *"Gentlemen of Property and Standing": Anti-Abolition Mobs in Jacksonian America.* New York: Oxford University Press, 1970.

Robertson-Lorant, Laurie. *Melville: A Biography.* New York: Clarkson Potter, 1996.

Rodman, Samuel. *The Diary of Samuel Rodman: A New Bedford Chronicle of Thirty-Seven Years: 1821-1859.* Ed. Zephaniah W. Pease. New Bedford: Reynolds Printing, 1927.

Sale, Maggie Montesinos. *The Slumbering Volcano: American Slave Revolts and the Production of Rebellious Masculinity.* Durham: Duke University Press, 1997.

Schultz, Elizabeth. *Unpainted to the Last:* Moby-Dick *and Twentieth-Century American Art.* Lawrence: University Press of Kansas, 1995.

Sealts, Merton M., Jr. *Melville's Reading: Revised and Enlarged Edition.* Columbia: University of South Carolina Press, 1988.

Shakespeare, William. *The Complete Works of William Shakespeare.* New York: Garden City Books, 1936.

Stauffer, John. *The Black Hearts of Men: Radical Abolitionists and the Transformation of Race.* Cambridge: Harvard University Press, 2002.

--------, ed. "A Note on the Text." Frederick Douglass. *My Bondage and My Freedom.* New York: Modern Library, 2003. xxix-xxx.

Stuckey, Sterling (with Joshua Leslie). "Avoiding the Tragedy of Benito Cereno: The Official Response to Babo's Revolt." *Criminal Justice History* 3 (1982): 128-31.

--------. "The Death of Benito Cereno." *Journal of Negro History* (Winter 1982): 297-301.

--------. "'Follow Your Leader': The Theme of Cannibalism in Melville's *Benito Cereno.*" In *Going through the Storm: The Influence of African American Art in History.* New York: Oxford University Press, 1994. 171-184.

--------. "The Tambourine in Glory: African Culture and Melville's Art." In *The Cambridge Companion to Herman Melville.* Ed. Robert S. Levine. Cambridge: Cambridge University Press, 1998. 37-64.

Sundquist, Eric J. *To Wake the Nations: Race in the Making of American Literature.* Cambridge: Harvard University Press, 1993.

Tappan, Lewis. *The Life of Arthur Tappan.* New York: Hurd and Houghton, 1871.

Wallace, Robert K. "Douglass, Melville, Quincy, Shaw: Epistolary Convergences." *Leviathan* 6 (October 2004): 63-71.

--------. *Melville and Turner: Spheres of Love and Fright.* Athens: University of Georgia Press, 1992.

Weathers, Willie T. "*Moby-Dick* and the Nineteenth-Century Scene." *Texas Studies in Literature* 1 (Winter 1960): 477-501.

Weed, Thurlow. *Life of Thurlow Weed including his Autobiography and a Memoir.* 2 v. Boston: Houghton Mifflin, 1883-1884.

Wilson's Illustrated Guide to the Hudson River. 4th ed. New York: H. Wilson, 1849.

Wright, John S. "Introduction" to Frederick Douglass, *My Bondage and My Freedom.* New York: Washington Square Press, 2003.

Aknowledgments

First I want to thank my colleagues in the Melville Society Cultural Project in New Bedford—Beth Schultz, Chris Sten, Wyn Kelley, Mary K. Bercaw Edwards, Doug Robillard, and Jill Barnum. Without the teamwork that led to our affiliation with the New Bedford Whaling Museum in 2001 and our plans for the Douglass and Melville Conference in 2005, this book would not exist.

Among our many community partners in the work of the Cultural Project, I am particularly grateful to Anne Brengle and her colleagues at the New Bedford Whaling Museum for offering to host the Douglass and Melville Conference (and Exhibition) in June 2005; to Joan Beaubian and Carl Cruz of the New Bedford Historical Society for embracing the Douglass and Melville pairing so warmly; and to Laurie Robertson-Lorant for directing the NEH Summer Seminar on "Melville and Multiculturalism" in the summer of 2001.

Many individuals and institutions have provided essential assistance for my research on this book. In Pittsfield, Massachusetts, I am especially grateful to Catherine Reynolds at the Berkshire Historical Society at Arrowhead and Kathy Reilly at the Melville Memorial Room of the Berkshire Athenaeum. In Boston, I am similarly grateful to Roberta Zonghi and Eric Frazier in the Department of Rare Books and Manuscripts of the Boston Public Library; to Jane Winton in the Print Department of the Boston Public Library; to Kim Nusco at the Massachusetts Historical Society; and to June Strojny at the Social Law Library. In Cambridge, I am grateful to Dennis Marnon of the Houghton Library of Harvard University and to Wyn Kelley for all of the ways in which she furthered my research. My research in New Bedford has been assisted by Carl Cruz and Kathryn Grover of the New Bedford Historical Society; Laura Pereira, Michael Dyer, and Stuart Frank of the Kendall Institute Library; Jen Gonsalves of the New Bedford Whaling National Historical Park; and Paul Cyr of the New Bedford Free Public Library.

My research in the State of New York has been greatly assisted by the Newspaper and Manuscripts divisions of the New York State Library in Albany; Rebecca Rich-Wulfmeyer of the Albany Institute of History and Art; Stefan Bielinski of the Colonial Albany Project; Tom Calarco and Paul and Mary Liz Stewart of the Underground Railroad History Project in Albany; Shelly Stocking of the New York Historical Association; Jenny Gotwald of the New-York Historical Society; and Sara Holliday of the New York Society Library. In the District of Columbia, Catherine Ingram at the Frederick Douglass Historical Site at Cedar Hill and Donna Wells at the Moorland-Springarn Research Center of Howard University have been similarly helpful. I am also grateful for assistance from James Greene of the Library Company of Philadelphia and Leigh Fought of the Frederick Douglass Papers Project at Indiana University-Purdue University in Indianapolis.

For research on this project closer to my home in Northern Kentucky, I am extremely grateful to the History, Literature, Newspaper, Education, Government, Art, and Rare Book divisions of the Public Library of Cincinnati and Hamilton County as well as to the University of Cincinnati Libraries, the Cincinnati Historical Society, and the W. Frank Steely and Chase Law Libraries of Northern Kentucky University. At the Steely Library I am especially grateful to the interlibrary loan department and to Jennifer Gregory of the Schlachter Family Archives. In Cincinnati I am equally grateful to Lee Person and Theresa Leininger-Miller at the University of Cincinnati and to Rita Organ at the National Undergound Railroad Freedom Center.

For opportunities to present the results of my research as the project has evolved, I am grateful to Joan Beaubian of the New Bedford Historical Society; Larry Hudson of the University of Rochester; the Melville Lyceum at the New Bedford Whaling Museum; the Kentucky Philological Association; Roxanne Kent-Drury, Allen Ellis, and John Valauri at Northern Kentucky University; and Books and Beliefs at Trinity Episcopal Church in Covington.

During the process of writing this book I have received essential encouragement and advice from Sam Otter and John Stauffer. They have followed the entire process by which the book has emerged from the communal research we have all been doing in preparation for the Douglass and Melville Conference in June 2005. They have each read the manuscript as it has evolved, made excellent suggestions for revisions, and generously shared the results of their own research. I am also grateful to Beth Schultz and Chris Sten for their responses to portions of the text in various stages, and to Hershel Parker, Steven Olsen-Smith, and Robert Levine for specific help in matters pertaining to Melville.

During the entire period in which I have been working to bring Douglass and Melville together in a variety of ways, I have blessed with gratifying support from administrators, faculty, and students at Northern Kentucky University. My appointment as Regents Professor has provided the time necessary for researching and writing this book in a relatively short period of time. Additional assistance for research or travel has generously been provided by Danny Miller, Chair of Literature and Language; Phil Schmidt, Interim Dean of Arts and Sciences; Gail Wells, Provost; and Prince Brown, Director of the Institute for Freedom Studies. Among colleagues who have encouraged and advised me in the writing of this book I am particularly grateful to John Alberti, Kris Yohe, Prince Brown, Delores Walters, and Tom Zaniello. Among students, I am especially grateful to those who enrolled in my first Douglass-Melville class in the Fall 2003. Throughout the semester and in their own creative projects they confirmed my hunch that Douglass and Melville relate to each other in powerful and unexpected ways. Subsequent students have continued to expand my own understanding of ways in which the two men's lives and works relate to each other.

As I began to assemble materials for the actual production of this book, I was fortunate to be able to recruit my Melville student Kathleen Piercefield to draw the maps I wished to create of New Bedford, Albany, and New York City. For assistance in providing all of the other illustrations in this book, and for permission to reproduce them, I am grateful to all of the sources listed in the captions as well as to Spinner Publications and its extensive photo archive. I am grateful to Jay Avila of Spinner Publications for his expert attention to all visual elements of the book, beginning with the cover design.

At Spinner Publications I am enormously grateful to publisher Joe Thomas for his interest in this book, for the editorial team of Marsha McCabe, Kathryn Grover, Andrea Tavares, and Dianne Wood, whose efforts he coordinated, and for the bookmaking skill with which he enhaced my text. Having written most of my previous books for somewhat specialized academic audiences, it has been a welcome challenge to try to write this one for a more general audience, and Joe's encouragement and admonitions have helped me to make some of the necessary adjustments.

Finally, and above all, I am grateful to my wife Joan Ferrante. She has been very understanding about the extensive travel that this project has required. She has encouraged my exploration of the Douglass-Melville subject from the very beginning, and has deepened my own understanding of it through her own work on the social construction of race and ethnicity. Most of all, she has provided the love and support that a sometimes obsessive researcher and writer needs.

INDEX

Symbols

54th Massachusetts Regiment 8

A

Abyssinian Baptist Church, New
    York 44-45, 78, 80, 82-84, 92,
    98, 126
Accessible Archives 60
Acorn, brig 96
Acushnet, whaleship 6, 15, 21, 129
Adams, Charles Francis 95
Albany Academy 26-27
Albany City Hall 24-26, 116
Albany *Evening Atlas* 24
Albany *Evening Journal* ix, 24-26,
    28, 30-33, 39, 63, 67, 71, 73,
    79, 119, 130
Albany, New York ix, 4, 6, 11, 13, 22,
    23-33, 35, 36, 39, 51, 53, 63,
    66-68, 71, 82, 84, 98-99, 101,
    116, 119, 122, 125-27, 134-35
Albany *Patriot* 134
American Anti-Slavery Society 6, 35,
    41, 44, 51, 76, 103
Ann Alexander, whaleship 58-60, 66
Anthony, Susan B. 120
Arrowhead, Melville's home 51,
    120, 123
Astor House, New York 48, 87, 117
Astor Place Opera House 45-47, 78, 92
Astor Place riots, 1849 45-47, 51,
    77-78, 84-85
Atlantic Monthly 112, 120
Auld, Hugh 4, 68

B

Babo 8, 109-116, 123, 125-27, 132
Bailey, Harriet 4
Baltimore, character in Omoo 69-70,
    80, 105
Baltimore, Maryland 4, 5, 23, 68-
    69, 124
Battenfeld, David 99-100
Battery, the (New York City) 48, 50,
    65, 93, 128, 132
Battle of Bunker Hill 61, 120-21, 135
Bay of Islands, New Zealand 71
Beale, Thomas 97
Bearse, Austin 107-08
Bembo 69-72, 105, 126, 136
Bennett, Frederick 97
Berkshire Athenaeum 24, 31, 52,
    64, 118
Berthold, Dennis 46, 134

Bet, enslaved to the Van Rensselaers
    of Albany 27, 82, 98, 134
Black Bet, gun in *White-Jacket* 87, 91
Black Handsome Sailor 122-24,
    126, 139
Blassingame, John W. 10, 29, 76
Boston *Chronotype* 63, 73, 78-79, 130
Boston Committee on Vigilance 107
Boston Court House 95
Boston *Daily Mail* 129
Boston *Post* 45, 61, 90
Boston Public Library 39, 57, 108, 134
Boston Tea Party 4
Briggs, Charles F. 38-39, 60-61, 109,
    119, 126, 136
    as "B" 37-38, 57, 60, 69, 109, 126
Broadway, New York City 39-41, 44-
    50, 63, 79-84, 89-92, 127-28
Broadway Tabernacle 6, 35-38, 40-
    44, 48-50, 73, 76-83, 85, 92,
    105, 107, 111-16, 126-29, 132
Broadway Theater 46
Brown, John 119, 121-22
Bryant, William Cullen 122, 136
Buffalo *Commercial Advertiser* 31
Bulkington 91
Burleigh, C. C. 113-14
Burns, Anthony 56, 59, 61
Burns, Robert 32-33, 42

C

Calhoun, John C. 42, 73-76, 136
Cambria, Cunard Line steamship 31-
    32, 35, 37-38, 41, 71, 73, 76
Cedar Hill, Douglass's home 8, 120-22
Charles, whaleship 16
Chase, Owen 72, 97
Chatham Street Chapel 91
Chesapeake Bay, Maryland 4
Child, Lydia Maria 122
Christiana, Pennsylvania 106
Civil Rights Movement 10, 61, 128
Civil War, The 8, 119-20, 130, 139
Claret, Captain 87-89
Clay, Henry 42, 95
Coffin, William C. 21
Coleman and Stetson, Astor House
    cooks 87
Columbia University 9
Columbus, Christopher 125
Conference on Douglass and Melville
    vi-vii, 3
Constable Edition of Melville's
    works 9
Covey, Edward 4, 88, 91

Covington, Kentucky 75, 136
Cox, Rev. Samuel Hanson 67
Creole, slave ship 101-02

D

Dana, Richard Henry, Jr. 50, 86-87,
    94-96, 99, 119
Delano, Captain Amasa
    author of narrative 8, 110-11,
    114, 127
    fictional character 8, 110-11,
    113-17, 125, 127, 132
Del, E. C., *Practical Illustration of the
    Fugitive Slave Law* 96-97
Dinah, enslaved to Volkert Douw of
    Albany 27
Dix and Edwards, New York
    publishers 109
Doggett's New York City Directory 82
Douglass, Anna Murray 2, 4, 12, 44, 120
Douglass, Frederick, and Astor Place
    Riots 45-48; and Christianity
    67, 74, 78; and Lemuel Shaw
    23-24, 48, 120-21, 127; at Zion
    Church, New Bedford 19-21,
    99; comments on *Punch* in 1848
    42-44, 89; confrontation with
    Rynders in 1850 48-50, 111-16,
    121, 125, 128-30; homecoming
    speech in 1847 35-36, 41, 44,
    107, 127, 134; prints "Moby Dick
    Captured" 58-59, 66, 106, 108;
    prints "Tattooing" from *Typee*
    42, 48, 56-58, 63, 69, 74-75
articles, essays, speeches, and
    debates
    "Claims of the Negro Ethno-
        logically Considered, The" 6
    "Colorphobia in New York!" 47-48,
        63-65, 79, 93, 114, 131-32
    "Constitutionality of American
        Slavery," 44, 47, 82, 83, 86
    "Flogging in the Navy" 85
    "Freedom's Battle at Chris-
        tiana" 106
    "Lecture(s) on Slavery" 93,
        107, 116
    "Self-Help" 78, 80-84, 92, 98
    "Slaves are Happy and
        Contented!" 74-75

Herman Melville, carte-de-visite, 1861. Berkshire Athenaeum.

"Slumbering Volcano, The"
44-45, 53, 101-2, 110-11,
115, 121, 138
"What to the Slave is the
Fourth of July?" 6, 107,
121, 136
autobiographies and novellas
Heroic Slave, The 6, 71, 101,
115
*Life and Times of Frederick
Douglass* 9, 76, 120, 122,
124, 127
My Bondage and My Freedom
6-10, 15, 21, 55, 109-10,
114, 116-17, 119, 122,
124-26, 130-32
Narrative of Frederick Douglass
5, 23-26, 30-32, 67-69
Douglass, Rosetta (Frederick's
daughter) 15, 32
Downing, George T. 82-83, 127
Downing, Thomas 81-82, 92, 98,
122, 127
Duyckinck, Evert 39-40, 46, 60, 85,
134, 136

E

Ellison, Ralph, *Invisible Man* 88
Emancipation Proclamation 8
Empire Club, New York City 51
Essex, whaleship 97

F

Fairhaven, Massachusetts 15-16
Faneuil Hall, Boston 86, 95, 129
Finsbury Chapel, Moorfields,
England 130
Fitzgerald, Edward 89-90
Fleece 103-05, 127
Florence, brig 108
Foner, Philip S. 9
Forrest, Edwin 46
Fort Stanwix, New York 4
Franklin House, New York City 47-48
Frederick Douglass' Paper viii, 5-6,
51, 53-56, 58-63, 84, 106,
108, 121, 125-26, 130-31,
136, 137
Frederick Douglass Papers, The
viii, 10
Fugitive Slave Law of 1793 23,
94, 127
Fugitive Slave Law of 1850 56, 59,
61, 93-96, 105-6, 108, 116,
131, 138

G

Gansevoort, General Peter (Herman's
grandfather) 4, 27
Gansevoort, General Peter (Herman's
uncle) 26-27, 33, 119
Gansevoort, Leonard (Herman's
great uncle) 27-28, 98

Gansevoort, Maria (Herman's
mother) 4, 26
Garfield, President James 8, 120
Garrison, William Lloyd 4-6, 23,
31, 32, 35-37, 48-51, 96, 103,
113-14, 122, 134
George Howland's Wharf 15, 17
Gilje, Paul, *The Road to Mobocracy* 92
Globe Mutiny 97
Golconda, whaleship 15
Gorsuch, William 106
Grant, President Ulysses S. 8, 120
Greeley, Horace 26, 45, 55-56
Greene, Richard Tobias "Toby" 30
Greenspan, Ezra 117
Griffiths, Elizabeth 48
Griffiths, Julia 48, 63, 106
Guinea 89-90, 99, 124, 127

H

Ham, Biblical curse upon 74, 123, 136
Hamilton, Mrs. Thomas 25-27, 38,
43, 68, 112, 136
Harlan, Chief Justice John Marshall 120
Harper and Brothers, New York
publisher 33, 45, 72, 105
Harper's Ferry 119
Harper's Monthly Magazine 7, 60-61,
63, 105-6
Harrison, President Benjamin 8, 120
Hayes, President Rutherford B. 8, 120
Hendrick Hudson, steamboat 33
Higginson, Thomas Wentworth 49,
59, 112-13, 115
Highlander, merchant ship in
Redburn 81
Hobomock, whaleship 97
Holden's Dollar Magazine 7, 38, 60,
63, 106
Honolulu, Hawaii 58, 68
Hope Chapel, 718 Broadway 44-45,
47, 79, 89, 107, 135
Hudson River 23-24, 27-28, 33, 51, 98
Hutchinson Family Singers 32, 41-
42, 49, 76-77, 87, 122, 135
Hutchinson, Jesse 41, 77
Hutchinson, John 41, 49

I

Irving, Washington 46

J

Jackson, character in *Redburn* 84-85
James, C. L. R. 56, 136
James, Rev. Thomas 20
Java, whaleship 15
Jefferson, Thomas 101
Jermin 70-72
Johnson, Nathan and Polly 4, 12,
15, 122

Jonah, in *Moby-Dick*, 99-100, 138
Judkins, Captain of the *Cambria* 32,
37, 38, 71
Julia, whaleship in *Omoo* 69, 71-72

K

Karcher, Carolyn 10, 99, 101-02, 116
Karky 58
Kent, Rockwell 9

L

Landless 90-91
Lansingburgh, New York 6, 23-25,
32, 38-40, 51
Latimer, George 23-24, 30, 39, 56,
86, 121, 127, 129
Lavender 48, 53, 79, 83-84, 92, 99,
123-27, 132
Leyda, Jay viii
Liberator, The 4, 23, 25, 28, 31-32,
63, 67, 90, 107-08, 114-15
*Life and Remarkable Adventures of
Israel R. Potter* 61
Lincoln, President Abraham 8, 119
Liverpool, England 4, 31-32, 38, 41,
48, 79-80, 83- 84, 123-27, 132
Livingston *Whig* 26
London Athenaeum 45
London *Examiner* 45
London *Literary Gazette* 45
Lowell, James Russell 63, 122, 131
Lucas, Robert 89-90
Lynn, Massachusetts 5, 23, 32-33
Lynn *Pioneer* 32

M

Macbeth (Shakespeare) 45-46
Macedonia, British frigate 89
Mackay, Charles 76
Macready, William 45-48
Mansion House, Albany 26, 98
Mansion House, New Bedford 20
Mapple, Father 21, 99-101, 107
Marnoo 28-30, 39, 53, 57, 66-67, 72,
90, 123-27, 134, 136
Matthiessen, F. O. 9
May-Day 87-88
McFeely, William 16, 107
Melvill, Allan (Herman's father) 4
Melvill, Major Thomas (Herman's
grandfather) 4
Melville, Allan (Herman's brother)
82, 127
Melville, Augusta (Herman's sister)
82, 98
Melville, Elizabeth Shaw (Herman's
wife) viii, 6, 39, 86
Melville, Gansevoort (Herman's
brother) 24, 26, 29, 33, 41-42,
51, 135

Frederick Douglass, engraving, circa 1853. National Archives.

Melville, Herman, and Astor Place
  riots 45-47, 51, 84-85; and
  Christianity 67, 72, 78; and
  Lemuel Shaw 23, 39-40,
  45, 48, 86, 96, 121, 131; and
  Thurlow Weed 30-31, 33, 39,
  119, 125-26; member of New
  York Society Library 40-41, 51,
  94, 105, 113-14, 129-30;
  novels and novellas
  Benito Cereno 6-11, 51, 53, 61,
    65-66, 71, 84, 105, 109-17,
    119, 122-32; shaving scene,
    110-14, 126. *See also* Babo;
    Delano, Captain Amasa
  Billy Budd 8-9, 86, 119,
    122-24, 126. *See also* Black
    Handsome Sailor
  Confidence Man, The 119
  Israel Potter 60-63, 106, 109,
    121, 136
  Mardi 6, 40, 45, 48, 73-78,
    87, 125-26. *See also* Nulli;
    Yoomy
  Moby-Dick 4-6, 9-10, 13, 15-
    16, 18, 21, 40, 50-56, 58-
    63, 65-66, 78, 80, 86, 91,
    94-108, 110-11, 114, 121,
    125-26, 128, 130-32; negro
    church, 19-21, 80, 99-100,
    124, 126-27; whitewashed
    negro, 102-03, 130. *See
    also* Bulkington; Fleece;
    Jonah; Mapple, Father;
    Moby Dick; Queequeg;
    Starbuck; Steelkilt
    "Carpet-Bag, The" 5, 99
    "Extracts" 96
    "Fast-Fish and Loose-Fish" 13
    "Knights and Squires" 106
    "Lee Shore, The" 107, 121
    "Loomings" 96, 98-99
    "Sperm Whale's Head, The" 131
    "Stubb Kills a Whale" 56, 131, 135
    "Stubb's Supper" 104
    "Town-Ho's Story, The" 105-
    06, 138
    "Wheelbarrow" 5, 18, 101-02
  Omoo 6, 32-33, 37-39, 45, 63,
    69-73, 78, 80, 87, 105, 125.
    See also Baltimore; Bembo;
    Jermin
    "Tattooers of La Dominica,
    The" 63, 69
  Pierre 6, 27, 60
  Redburn 6, 40, 45, 48, 79-86;
    grand parliament of masts,
    132; negro churches, 80,
    99, 126; underground
    oyster-cellars, 83, 126-27.

  See also Jackson; Lavender;
    Thompson, Mr.
  Typee ix, 6, 23-24, 28-33, 37-
    39, 42, 45, 53, 56-58, 61,
    63, 66-69, 72-79, 87, 90,
    101, 119, 121, 125, 128,
    131, 136. *See also* Karky;
    Marnoo; Toby
  White-Jacket 6, 40, 45, 78, 85-
    94, 99, 103, 107, 111, 117,
    121, 124-27, 130; Negro
    Mob, 91-92, 103; unendur-
    able, 91, 93, 127; worm
    that turns, 88, 93, 107, 115.
    See also Black Bet; Claret,
    Captain; Guinea; Landless;
    May-Day; Rose-Water;
    Sunshine; Tawney; Wooloo
  other writings
    "Authentic Anecdotes of 'Old
    Zack'" 44
    "Bartleby, the Scrivener"
    7, 109
    Battle-Pieces 8, 119, 121
    Clarel 119
    Correspondence viii, 134
    "Encantadas, The" 109
    Piazza Tales, The 8
    "Tartarus of Maids, The" 7
Melville, Malcolm (Herman's son) 45
Melville, Maria Gansevoort (Herman's
  mother) 4, 26, 122, 127
Metropolitan A. M. E. Church,
  Washington, D.C.. 120
Mexican War 44
Minerva Rooms, 460 Broadway 42,
  44-45, 76, 79, 83
Minkins, Shadrach 95
Moby Dick, character in *Moby-Dick*
  58-60, 66, 105-06
Moby Dick, yacht 107-08
Moorland-Springarn Research
  Center, Howard University 54
Morrison, Toni, *Playing in the Dark* 130
Mott, Abigail 28, 32-33
Mott, Lucretia 41, 122
Mott, Lydia 28, 32-33
Mount Hope Cemetery, Rochester
  8, 120
Mumford, Howard 9
Murray, Anna. *See* Douglass, Anna
  Murray
Murray, John, London publisher 24, 30

N

Nantucket, Massachusetts 5, 18-19,
  21, 23, 101-02
National Era, The 63, 125, 126, 130
  reviews *Typee* 69
  reviews *Omoo* 69-71

  reviews *Mardi* 73
  reviews *White-Jacket* 85, 130
Nell, W. C. 47, 134
Neversink, man-of-war in *White-
  Jacket* 87-92, 125
New Bedford, Massachusetts vi, vii,
  2-6, 11-21, 23, 39, 44, 51, 58,
  64, 72, 80, 84, 86, 90, 99-102,
  122, 124-27, 129
New Bedford *Standard* 58
New York City ix, 4, 6, 8, 11, 13, 31-
  34, 35-51, 55, 63, 65, 67, 71-73,
  76-85, 87, 91-99, 101, 103-119,
  125-32, 134-38
New York *Courier and Enquirer* 36,
  38, 92
New York *Daily Mirror* 38
New York *Daily Tribune* 119
New York *Evangelist* 36, 49-50, 67
New York *Express* 103, 113, 134, 138
New York *Globe* 93, 103-04, 113-14
New York *Herald* 46, 48-49, 93, 98,
  103-04, 113, 115, 135, 137
New York *Inquirer* 36
New York *Journal of Commerce* 93
New York *Observer* 36
New York *Press* 119
New York Society Library 40-41, 44-
  45, 48-51, 81-83, 92, 127-29, 132
  site of 1850 riots 51, 94, 103-5,
  113-14, 128-30
New York State Bank, Albany 26, 28

New York State Vigilance Committee
  47, 49, 82, 135, 137
New York *Tribune* 26, 36, 45, 47, 50,
  73, 78, 103-04, 115
North American Review 120
North Star, The viii, 5-6, 39, 41-44,
  56-63, 69, 73-79, 83, 85-88,
  92-93, 95, 116, 121, 126-28,
  130, 132, 136-37
Northern Kentucky University 8
Northwestern-Newberry edition of
  Melville's works viii
Nukuheva, Marquesas Islands 6,
  28, 30, 69
Nulli 73-75, 136

O

Old South Wharf, Fairhaven 15-16
Othello (Shakespeare) 65, 93
Otter, Samuel 58, 85, 136

P

Parker, Rev. Theodore 41, 59, 95, 122
Pearl, schooner 42, 76
Pennington, Rev. James W. C. 44,
  80, 83, 92
Pequod, whaleship in *Moby-Dick* 59,
  104-06, 123
Petrie, William L., and Douglass E.
  Stover viii
Phillips, Wendell 23, 41, 47, 50, 95,
  103, 113-14, 122, 129-30

Pierpont, John 122
Pinsker Hill, Albany 27, 82, 98, 116, 135
Polk, President James 25, 51
Pollock, Jackson 9
Pomp, enslaved in Albany 27
Prince Albert, packet ship 33
Punch (London) 42-44, 89
Putnam, George P. 67, 72, 101, 109, 134
Putnam's Monthly magazine 7, 11, 38, 60-63, 109-17, 119, 125-26, 136

Q

Queequeg 18-19, 99-104, 107, 127, 130
Quincy, Edmund 27, 38, 39, 47, 78, 122, 135

R

Race riots, New York City, 1834 91-92, 103, 126
Ram's Horn 82, 104
Rebecca Sims, whaleship 58
Remond, Charles Lenox 129
Richmond's Brass Foundry 15
Ricketson's Candleworks 15
Ripley, George 45, 73, 78
Robertson-Lorant, Laurie 134
Rochester, New York 5, 8, 18, 23, 41, 48, 50, 54, 63, 93, 106-07, 116, 120
Rodman, Samuel 17
Rodman's Wharf, 17
Rose-Water 87-88
Rynders, "Captain" Isaiah 45-46, 48-51, 53, 65, 77-78, 84-85, 92, 103, 111-16, 121, 125-30, 139

S

Saco Valley, New Hampshire 40
St. Paul's, London 80
St. Peter's, Rome 80, 137
Sale, Maggie 110, 138,
Salem, Massachusetts 29, 129
Sally Ann, schooner 108
Sealts, Merton, Jr. viii
Seaman's Bethel, New Bedford 21, 99-100
Second Street, New Bedford 19-21, 99
Seward, William 55
Shakespeare, William 65, 112. *See also* Macbeth, Othello.
Shaw, Chief Justice Lemuel 24, 39-40, 45, 48, 86, 95-96, 121, 131; and the Fugitive Slave Law, 23-24, 39, 56, 90, 101, 106, 116, 121, 127-28, 138
Shaw, Elizabeth. *See* Melville, Elizabeth Shaw

Shiloh Presbyterian Church 44-45, 47-50, 79-83, 85, 92, 101-02, 126
Sims, Thomas 56, 58-59, 95-96, 106
Smith, James McCune 47, 55-56, 60, 63, 83-84, 92, 98, 104, 106, 122, 124-26, 131
Smith, J. B. 107
Smith, John, the Younger (James A. Houston) 69
Stanwix Hall, Albany 27-28
Starbuck 105-07
Stauffer, John 52, 55, 63
Steelkilt 105-06
Stetson, Charles 87, 117. *See also* Coleman and Stetson
Stover, Douglass E., and William L. Petrie viii,
Stowe, Harriet Beecher 122, 131; *Uncle Tom's Cabin*, 63, 136
Stubb 55-56, 104, 127, 131
Stuckey, Sterling 10, 65, 114, 135
Sumner, Charles 119
Sundquist, Eric J. 10
Sunshine 87
Swan, Sandy 108
Syracuse, New York 51

T

Tammany Hall, New York City 51
Tappan, Lewis 92
Tawney 89, 92
Taylor, President Zachary 89
Thompson, A. C. C. 32
Thompson, John P. 80
Thompson, Joseph P. 80
Thompson, Mr., cook in *Redburn* 80-81, 83-84
Toby 31. *See also* Greene, Richard Tobias
Troy, New York 6, 23-25, 30, 33, 51, 66-68
Trumbull, Henry 61
Trumbull, John 120
Turner, J. M. W. 65, 136
Turner, Nat 110
Twitchell, Asa W. 31, 33

U

United States, U.S. frigate 6
Utica *Daily Gazette* 32

V

Van Rensselaer Family, Albany 27, 82
Van Rensselaer, Harriet 82
Van Rensselaer, Stephen 82
Van Rensselaer, Thomas 82-84, 98, 103-4, 114, 122
Vere, Captain 86

W

Wall Street, New York City 81-82
Ward, Samuel Ringgold 44, 47, 49-50, 82-83, 86, 116
Washington, George 102
Waterford, New York 51
Weathers, Willie 104
Webster, Daniel 93-96, 101
Weed, Thurlow ix, 25-26, 28, 30-33, 39, 63, 68, 71-72, 119, 125-26, 134-35
West Broadway, New York 48, 55, 83-84, 91-92, 103, 126
Weston, Caroline 39, 78
Whittier, John Greenleaf 63, 122, 131
Wiley and Putnam, New York publisher 30-31, 39, 67, 72, 101

Wilson's Illustrated Guide 27
Woodlawn Cemetery, New York 8
Worcester, Massachusetts 23
Wright, Elizur 63, 73, 95
Wright, John S. 69

Y

Yankee Doodle, New York 44
Yoomy 73-77, 125

Z

Zion Church, New Bedford 19-21, 99-100
Zion Church, New York 36-37, 44, 80, 82-83, 92

The Morning Journal.

ALBERT PULITZER,
Founder and Editor.

TUESDAY, SEPTEMBER 29, 1891.

162 NASSAU STREET, NEW YORK.

AUTHOR MELVILLE GONE.

He Was Held by Cannibals, but He Made It Lucrative.

Herman Melville, author of some fifteen novels published about forty years ago, died on Sunday night at his home, No. 104 East Twenty-sixth street, aged seventy-three years.

He was born in this city on August 1, 1819. In 1837 he went to sea in a sailing vessel before the mast, but on account of harsh treatment he and a shipmate deserted and made their way to an island in the Marquesas group, where he was held in captivity by a tribe of cannibals called Typees. He remained in captivity for several years, but when he escaped and returned to this country he made the Typees the subject of his first novel, published in 1847. The book had a wide circulation, as did also fourteen others.

Mr. Melville married a daughter of the late Chief Justice Shaw, of Boston. Two of his children are living. He has been a recluse for the past fifteen years, preferring his books and pictures to society.

The funeral services will be held at his late residence on Wednesday afternoon at 2 o'clock. The interment will be at Woodlawn Cemetery.

ABOUT THE AUTHOR

Robert K. Wallace is Regents Professor of Literature and Language at Northern Kentucky University (NKU), where he has taught for more than 30 years. He earned his PhD in English from Columbia University and has since received several fellowships, including a Fulbright. Dr. Wallace's research has brought him to Spain, Japan, England, Germany, and Greece, where he attended the first International Melville Conference in 1997.

Born and raised in Washington, the author worked on tugboats and in lumber mills on Puget Sound in high school and college. It was these experiences that first sparked his interest in all things maritime, in social justice, and in racial equality. It is only natural, then, that he would someday come to write *Douglass & Melville: Anchored Together in Neighborly Style*.

Dr. Wallace's previous books include *Frank Stella's Moby-Dick, Melville and Turner* (*Choice* Outstanding Book Award, 1994), *Jane Austen and Mozart* (SAMLA Book Award, 1982), *Emily Brontë and Beethoven* (Post-Corbett Award, Cincinnati, 1987), and *A Century of Music-Making*, which received a Midwest Book Awards Honorable Mention in 1976.

A former president of the Melville Society, Dr. Wallace initiated and helped to organize the international conference on Douglass and Melville in New Bedford, Massachusetts, in June 2005. He was a guest curator for the 2005 exhibition at the New Bedford Whaling Museum entitled *Our Bondage/Our Freedom: Frederick Douglass and Herman Melville*. As senior faculty advisor for NKU's Institute for Freedom Studies, he also helped conceive and coordinate the Inaugural Biennial Juried Underground Railroad Art Exhibition to celebrate the August 2004 opening of the National Underground Railroad Freedom Center in Cincinnati. Other exhibits he has curated have featured Herman Melville's print collection and Frank Stella's artwork.

He and his wife Joan live in a Kentucky suburb of Cincinnati.

SPINNER PUBLICATIONS, INC.

As a nonprofit cultural organization, Spinner Publications is committed to the publication of books that promote the history and culture of people in southeastern New England and foster the understanding of the diverse groups that live in the region. We are grateful to the people whose generous support will help us achieve these goals.

Douglass and Melville: Anchored Together in Neighborly Style received financial support from the Massachusetts Cultural Council and the Henry Crapo Charitable Foundation.

164 William Street • New Bedford, MA 02740 • 508-994-4564
www.spinnerpub.com • spinner@spinnerpub.com